A Different God?

To Suzanne, Robert, Shannon, and Senia

A Different God?

Mitt Romney,
the Religious Right,
and the Mormon Question

Craig L. Foster

GREG KOFFORD BOOKS
SALT LAKE CITY, 2008

2012 11 10 09 08   5 4 3 2 1
Greg Kofford Books, Inc.
P.O. Box 1362
Draper, UT 84020
www.koffordbooks.com

Paperback, ISBN 978-1-58958-117-3
Library edition hardcover, ISBN 978-1-58958-118-0

Illustrations on pages 158 & 214 are courtesy of Pat Bagley, Salt Lake Tribune
Illustrations on pages 156 & 184 are courtesy of Brian Fairrington

Library of Congress Cataloging-in-Publication Data

Foster, Craig L.
   A different god? : Mitt Romney, the religious right, and the Mormon question / Craig L. Foster.
      p. cm.
   ISBN 978-1-58958-117-3 — ISBN 978-1-58958-118-0 1. Romney, Mitt—Religion. 2.   Romney, Mitt—Political and social views. 3. Mormons—United States—Biography. 4.   Mormons—United States—Political activity—History. 5.   Mormonism—Political aspects—United States. 6.   Christianity and politics—United States. 7.   Religious right—United States. 8.   Presidents—United States—Election—2008. I. Title.
   E840.8.R598F67 2008
   974.4'044092--dc22
                                          2008023281

Contents

Introduction

The world of politics is rough. At its best, it is adversarial in nature, and at its worst, it can be vicious, even violent. Politicians and pundits alike emphasize the art of the compromise—the give-and-take of politics. Rarely do they mention that the giving is usually done grudgingly and the taking is done with self-satisfied gloating. Even while basking in the diplomatic cooperation of a newly attained compromise, the parties involved are usually already plotting how the next time around they can be the taker rather than the giver, the winner rather than the loser.

While this unpleasant truth may be disconcerting, even shocking for some people to accept, the reality is that it's simple human nature. Politics is more than a game of strategy and one-upmanship or even the lubricant in the ever-running-but-not-always-efficient machinery of government. Politics, at its very core, represents identity. It is the raison d'être of the individual, group, community, tribe, and nation.

The political process is expressed by the usually hard-edged negotiations required to define gender, race, ethnicity, social class, economics, and religion. It encompasses all aspects of life. In a very real way, it is life itself. Political expression can be so passionate and emotional because it reinforces and justifies people's purpose, identity, even their very existence.

In other words, politics is the outward expression of the individual. Because human beings are social animals, individuals inevitably form groups with other individuals of common backgrounds and worldviews. How comfortable an individual, group, community, tribe, or nation is with itself determines how they view others. Their level of social maturity is reflected in their level of acceptance, tolerance, and willingness to work with others not of their own ethnic, racial, cultural, social, religious, or political background.

Some parts of the world and some groups of people have been more successful than others in achieving a level of sufficient social maturity to understand and accept others who are not like them. The United States has, without question, been at the vanguard. This great experiment has welcomed people from around the world and has become, as religious scholar Milton V. Backman explained, "a cosmopolitan nation whose inhabitants represent various cultures, races, and religions. . . . The result of this transplanting, blending, and innovation has been an astounding increase in religious pluralism. . . . America's religious mosaic is so complex that no one has succeeded in enumerating all of the faiths worshiping in the land."[1]

At the dawn of the twenty-first century, religious pluralism in the United States reflects, for the most part, a significant trend toward social cooperation and ecumenicalism. Churches and religious groups have expressed a deep interest in working together on humanitarian and social programs, rising above theological differences to see the importance of cooperating to alleviate the deeper problem of human suffering. In many ways, religion and politics have worked together well to further the basic needs of American society. Nevertheless, despite significant strides, the interaction of religion and politics in today's society is far from perfect.

America's religious and political history is even more turbulent. While the United States has, since its beginning, been considered a land of liberty, a land of refuge, it has not always welcomed refugees with outstretched arms. For that matter, it has not always tolerated the religious idiosyncrasies of its own citizens. As Chapter 1 describes, the history of the United States is mainly of a Protestant Christian nation, and those who did not fit into the mainstream religious milieu often felt its ostracism, even violence.

Yet even Protestant denominations faced off in a history of intolerance and conflict. During the last half of the seventeenth-century, hostility toward the Society of Friends (Quakers) was evident in parts of the American colonies. Virginia, for example enacted laws forbidding Quakers from "settling, preaching, and worshiping in that colony" while Quaker missionaries in New York were arrested, imprisoned, and expelled. Persecution and punishment in New England was even more painful. "The earliest followers of [George] Fox in the Bay colony were not only fined, whipped, imprisoned, and banished, but their bodies were mutilated by branding and by the clipping of their ears and tongues."[2]

Quakers were not alone in being mistreated by other, more dominant Protestant congregations. Evangelical Baptists of Virginia, for example, suffered from a wave of persecution in the 1780s.[3] Among the hardships experienced by frontier Methodist circuit riders was ridicule from the unchurched. Worse yet, according to Christian writer Michael Edds, some circuit riders were "jailed, tarred and feathered, beaten, abused and martyred for the message of God."[4]

While the treatment of some of the upstart Protestant denominations was certainly cruel, these experiences were sporadic and limited; malicious treatment of some non-Protestants was harsher, more sustained, and widespread throughout the United States. One of the prime examples of such treatment was the Catholics. Many Protestant emigrants brought with them antipathy for Roman Catholicism and its adherents. Early English Protestants feared the possibility of Vatican-encouraged invasion by Spain, France, and other Catholic countries. These fears of papal "treachery" were also imported to America and fed by such salacious pseudo-exposés as Maria Monk's sensational novel *Awful Disclosures of the Hotel Dieu Nunnery*.[5] Monk's tale was perhaps the most influential of the flourishing genre, detailing the purported immorality of Catholic priests and nuns. Politically, such fictions reinforced the supposed evil nature of Roman Catholicism and encouraged religious and political attack.[6]

At various times and places in America's history Catholics were excluded from the political process. In Maryland, for example, a colony founded by and for Catholics and ruled for the first half-century by "benevolent Catholic rulers" and where America's first toleration act was passed in 1649, Catholics eventually lost political control and paid the price. Not only were they neither allowed to vote nor hold public office, they were not even allowed to openly practice their religion, proselyte, or establish parochial schools. Other colonies had equally stringent laws.[7]

By the middle of the nineteenth century the Catholic population had grown significantly. This was, in part, because of the arrival of a multitude of Irish Catholics fleeing the devastation caused by the Irish potato famine. In the early part of the century a group of Americans opposed to the immigration of German and Irish Catholics had formed a secret society known informally as the "Know-Nothings" because they would claim to "know nothing" about the anti-immigration organization. "They accepted into their group only native-born Protestants who were unrelated to Catholic either by blood or marriage."[8]

Partly as a reaction to the large amount of Irish immigrants, the Know-Nothings and other nativists became politically powerful. Irish and Roman Catholics, whether foreign born or not, were always derisively called foreigners. Nineteenth-century social commentator Orestes A. Brownson wrote that the Native American Party or Know-Nothings "is not a party against admitting foreigners to the rights of citizenship, but simply a party against admitting a certain class of foreigners. It does not oppose Protestant Germans, Protestant Englishmen, Protestant Scotchmen, not even Protestant Irishmen. It is really opposed to Catholic foreigners. The party is truly an anti-Catholic party, and is opposed chiefly to the Irish, because a majority of the emigrants to this country are probably from Ireland, and the greater part of these are Catholics."[9]

While both the religious and political atmosphere had improved for the Catholics by 1928, it had not improved to the point that a Catholic could be elected president of the United States. That year New York Governor Alfred E. Smith's Democratic nomination as presidential candidate "invoked a vehement anti-Catholic reaction among some factions of the populace." There were numerous anti-Catholic newspaper articles and publications warning of the menace of Rome and proclaiming the horrors of popery as a result of his campaign.[10]

The main concern, sometimes openly expressed but often covert, was whether a Catholic president could be trusted to make the interests of the United States his top priority or whether his first loyalty would be to the Vatican, making him vulnerable to influence from abroad. That question and concern were not adequately put to rest for a majority of Americans until 1960 when John F. Kennedy, Massachusetts Senator and Democratic candidate for U.S. president, faced the anti-Catholic prejudice head-on in a landmark speech given to the Greater Houston Ministerial Association. He proclaimed:

> I believe in an America where the separation of church and state is absolute—where no Catholic prelate would tell the President (should he be Catholic) how to act, and no Protestant minister would tell his parishioners for whom to vote—where no church or church school is granted any public funds or political preference—and where no man is denied public office merely because his religion differs from the President who might appoint him or the people who might elect him.[11]

Near the end of his speech and to reinforce his promise not to put his religion above his public duty, Kennedy assured his listeners and all Americans that he was not "the Catholic candidate for President." Instead, he was "the Democratic Party's candidate for President who happens also to be a Catholic."[12]

Kennedy's speech and subsequent election victory was a turning point for Catholics and American politics. While there are still anti-Catholics who would not vote for an otherwise qualified Catholic, they are few compared to the rest of the American populace. Furthermore, Catholics have continued to play a prominent role in American politics, not only on local and state levels but also on the national political stage.

Members of the Church of Jesus Christ of Latter-day Saints (Mormons) have not achieved the same status. Like Catholics, Mormons have been feared and distrusted by a large segment of the American population. Also like Catholics, Mormons were the victims of vicious literature attacking their beliefs and perpetuating sneers and stereotypes. They, too, were the victims of violent physical assault. Also like Catholics, Mormons were the targets of legislation and government actions that deprived them of such basic civil rights as voting.

The social and political history of Latter-day Saints is troubled and painful because of the intense and prolonged persecution they suffered, some of which they brought on themselves as a result of their beliefs and actions. Members of the LDS Church spent their first seventy years on the fringes of society and the subsequent century trying to move more into the mainstream. Their move to the center and respectability has met with varying degrees of success.

Mormons are respected, even admired, for many things, including their dedication to hard work and orderly living, their emphasis on the family, and their worldwide humanitarian service. Members of the LDS Church have also made strides in science, business, literature, and even—perhaps ironically, given the strict LDS code of dress and ethics—in pop culture. They have also achieved notable political success, including in their number governors, members of Congress (Senate Majority Leader Harry Reid, D-NV, for example), and U.S. Cabinet members.

The office of U.S. president, however, has eluded Mormons. Once each in the nineteenth and twenty-first centuries, and eight times in the twentieth century, a Mormon has aspired to that office, but none has yet achieved it. (See Appendix B.) Like the Catholic Church and John F. Kennedy almost half a century ago, Latter-day Saints are still waiting for the first Mormon to be elected president of the United States of America.

As detailed in the recent publication, *The Mormon Quest for the Presidency*,[13] Joseph Smith, the founder of Mormonism, led the way with his fateful 1844 presidential campaign, gaining the distinction of becoming the first presidential candidate to be assassinated. Of the nine candidates with Mormon connections who followed him, W. Mitt Romney, who launched a well-organized and well-funded campaign in 2007, had the best chance of winning the nomination and certainly went the furthest toward that goal. (See Chapter 4.)

Romney's near-success can be chalked up to four reasons. First, he was running for the nomination of one of the two major U.S. parties, not as a third-party or no-party candidate, a status shared by only three other candidates. Second, he entered the race earlier and stayed in longer. Third, he won some state primaries. Fourth, he had more money than the previous Mormon candidates and spent it prudently on campaign advertisements, staffing, travel, and other necessary expenditures. Although Romney is a self-made multimillionaire, he is, more importantly, a prodigious fund-raiser, able to capitalize not only on Mormon enthusiasm about his candidacy but the enthusiasm of many other supporters for whom his message resonated. Fifth, Romney's background as a businessman, management consultant, investment strategist, and turnaround CEO of the 2002 Salt Lake Olympics gave him great organizational experience, which he used to build a nationwide campaign. And sixth, Romney's campaign was able to go down the trail farther than previous Mormons for the same reason that also forced it to the sidelines: the increasing public presence, power, and influence of the Latter-day Saints.

Contrary to some claims and many fears, the Church of Jesus Christ of Latter-day Saints as a religious organization did not do anything for or against Romney and his presidential ambitions. The Church remained neutral. The power and influence came from the members themselves. The Church is no longer just a mountain-states-based religion with a few modestly sized congregations scattered about the United States and few foreign countries. The LDS Church has experienced phenomenal growth since World War II and now has strong membership in other regions of the country, particularly the Pacific Coast and the South.

Much like the fear and resentment expressed against the increasing Catholic population in the middle of the nineteenth-century, fear and resentment against the LDS Church and its members surfaced during Mitt Romney's presidential campaign. Although prejudice, even antipathy, were openly displayed from both the left and the right, from both liberals and conservatives, it was the religious right that had a greater impact. The right has this power because of its significant influence during the Republican Party's primary process. If Mitt Romney had actually won the Republican Party's presidential nomination, he would likely have seen even more negative reactions flaring up from the far left than what he endured from the right before and during the primaries. The religious right's flamboyant public positioning against Romney came, in part, because it had more to lose in terms of political power, prestige, and influence but also, more importantly, in terms of what many members of the religious right see as the never-ending battle between Latter-day Saints and evangelicals over souls. (See esp. Chapters 2 and 6.)

In many ways, the religious divide between Latter-day Saints and evangelicals is wide and deep. Evangelicals regard Mormonism with enmity and suspicion because of the theological differences between them. Latter-day Saints not only have a different set of scriptures beyond the traditional Bible, they even have a different interpretation of some biblical verses. Furthermore, they have a different understanding about Jesus Christ and what is considered traditional Christian theology. Because of these compelling differences, many evangelicals believe Mormons don't even worship the true Jesus. Instead, they insist that Latter-day Saints worship a different god—an accusation that is naturally offensive to members of the LDS Church.

Thus, while Mitt Romney's campaign failed for a number of reasons, one of the major reasons was because of the evangelical-dominated religious right and what can be called the Mormon Question. It closely parallels historic Protestant suspicions and fears regarding perceptions that Catholicism was a false religion and that Catholics would give their first allegiance to Rome. This was the "Catholic question" that haunted Catholic candidates up to and including John F. Kennedy. Mormonism's comparatively short history—less than two centuries—has seen many variations of its own Mormon Question. This book focuses on the permutations and manifestations of the Mormon Question during Mitt Romney's 2008 presidential campaign. In essence, the Mormon Question during Romney's campaign took this form: Because Mormons believe in what most Americans see as alien, even non-Christian, doctrines and strange practices, can a Mormon be trusted to preserve, protect, and promote the common good of the United States as president?

This book analyzes the 2008 campaign against the historical context of both Mormonism's frequently troubled history (Chapter 3), which is one element of the hostility and suspicion with which Americans from colonial days have frequently regarded any religion deemed to be non-mainstream. For much of American history, that mainstream was evangelical Protestantism. (See Chapter 1.) Yet it was forced into a self-imposed exile as a result of landmark contests like the 1925 Scopes trial, only to resurge with a determination to take back the nation from godless secularists. (See Chapter 2.)

Although its power waned from the high point of influence during the Ronald Reagan presidency in the 1980s, the religious right still remains alert, politically active, and susceptible to thinking in stereotypes. Mormonism's open contestation of evangelicalism with its uncompromising truth claims and assertive proselytizing made conflict with American evangelism inevitable (Chapter 1), and the political rough-and-tumble campaign resulted in an abandonment of even the low standards of political decorum. The 2008 campaign may have been the most colorful yet, with an African American, a woman, and a Mormon all mounting serious and effective campaigns on both sides of the political trail.

Mitt Romney, unlike most candidates, had virtually no scandalous baggage. Unable to focus on personal, financial, or sexual wrongdoing, both the press and his opposition focused on his religion. The rhetoric rapidly surpassed the usual political slurs and name-calling to ask invasive questions about his underwear and resurrect folk beliefs from the nineteenth century as examples of Mormon weirdness. Such attacks came from both the religious right and the liberal left (Chapters 5, 6, 7) and, at their most vicious, engaged in the kinds of tactics that would have tarred the speaker with opprobrium if "Mormon" had been replaced by "black" or "Jewish."

At this writing (July 2008), Romney, though no longer a presidential candidate, has become a loyal supporter of John McCain, who will unquestionably become the Republican Party's standard bearer and perhaps the U.S. president in November. Furthermore, Romney has emerged as the front-runner in discussions concerning McCain's vice-presidential prospects. Although Mitt has taken himself out of this race, he has obviously not taken himself out of politics. The American nation has not seen the last Romney campaign.

Notes

1. Milton V. Backman Jr., *Christian Churches of America: Origins and Beliefs*, rev. ed. (New York: Charles Scribner's Sons, 1983), 1.

2. Ibid., 140–41. George Fox (1624–91) was the founder of the Society of Friends.

3. Steven Waldman, "The Evangelical Founding Fathers," *Christianity Today*, March 25, 2008, http://www.christianitytoday.com/ct/2008/marchweb-only/113-22.0.html (accessed April 26, 2008).

4. Michael Edds, "Old Wells, Fallen Mantles, and New Fountains," *Ministry of Helps*, September 5, 2005, http://216.147.107.158/destinyquests/destinyquest_010.htm (accessed June 4, 2008). According to Roger Finke and Rodney Stark, *The Churching of America, 1776–1990: Winners and Losers in Our Religious Economy* (New Brunswick, N.J.: Rutgers University Press, 1992), 16, contrary to the popular perception that America was more religious historically than today, the percentage of religious adherents increased from a mere 17% in 1776 to 34% by 1850 and to 62% in 1980. According to B. A. Robinson, "Religious Identification in the U.S.: How American Adults View Themselves," ReligiousTolerance.Org (2001, 2007) http://www.religioustolerance.org/chr_prac2.htm (accessed June 4, 2008), 81% of American adults identified themselves with a specific religion. That percentage was estimated to drop below 70% in 2008.

5. Maria Monk, *Awful Disclosures of the Hotel Dieu Nunnery* (New York: American Society for Promoting the Principles of the Protestant Reformation, 1836).

6. For a discussion of anti-Catholic, anti-Mason, and anti-Mormon themes and stereotyping, see David Brion Davis, "Some Themes of Counter-Subversion: An Analysis of anti-Masonic, Anti-Catholic, and Anti-Mormon Literature," *Mississippi Valley Historical Review* 47 (September 1960): 205–24; Mark W. Cannon, "The Crusades against the Masons, Catholics, and Mormons: Separate Waves of a Common Current," *BYU Studies* 2, no. 2 (1961): 23–40; and Craig L. Foster, *Penny Tracts and Polemics: A Critical Analysis of Anti-Mormon Pamphleteering in Great Britain, 1837–1860* (Salt Lake City: Greg Kofford Books, 2002).

7. Backman, *Christian Churches of America*, 21–22.

8. "I Know Nothing!" St. Joseph Messenger Online, http://www.aquinas-multimedia.com/stjoseph/knownothings.html (accessed May 31, 2008).

9. Orestes A. Brownson, *Essays and Reviews, Chiefly on Theology, Politics, and Socialism* (New York: D & J Sadler & Co., 1880), 428.

10. "Anti-Catholic Literature Collection: An Inventory of the Anti-Catholic Literature Collection at the American Catholic History Research Center and University Archives" (Washington, D.C.: Catholic University of America, 2004–8) http://libraries.cua.edu/achrcua/anticath.html (accessed June 4, 2008).

11. John F. Kennedy, "I Believe in an America Where Separation of Church and State is Absolute," beliefnet.com, http://www.beliefnet.com/story/40/story_4080 _3.html (accessed June 4, 2008).

12. Ibid.

13. Newell G. Bringhurst and Craig L. Foster, *The Mormon Quest for the Presidency* (Independence, Mo.: John Whitmer Books, 2008).

Acknowledgments

In the spirit of full disclosure, I must confess that I am (and have been since my teens) a political junkie. I have read innumerable political works, followed national and local contests with interest, and still dream of someday being a delegate to a national nominating convention. (I gave up, a number of years ago, the hope of traveling on Air Force One.)

I am a lifelong active member of the Church of Jesus Christ of Latter-day Saints but can count among my ancestors Baptists, Catholics, Lutherans, Methodists, Presbyterians, and not a few "unchurched." Nevertheless, my immediate family, upbringing, and worldview have all been influenced by a rich Mormon heritage for which I have great pride and appreciation. I am a Latter-day Saint not only because I was born and raised in it but because I want to be.

I am also a conservative Republican. In fact, I was the first Republican in my family, having come from Democrats on both sides. My parents and brother eventually registered as Republicans. Over the years, I have been actively involved in the Republican Party, assisting with campaigns and holding positions on both the state and local level—which brings me to Mitt Romney and his presidential campaign. I supported Romney's presidential race, both financially and as a volunteer worker. To be honest, he was not my choice at first because I was troubled about his stand on abortion and other social issues. After a lot of reading and visiting with friends and family, I finally decided to support him. I do not regret that decision.

Because I am a conservative Republican Mormon who actively supported Mitt Romney, I will be the first to admit to my biases. To the best of my ability, I have recognized those biases and tried to make this work as unbiased as possible. As my good friend and mentor, Newell G. Bringhurst, a liberal Democrat and lapsed Mormon, and I worked on our recently completed book, *The Mormon Quest for the Presidency* (Independence, Mo.: John Whitmer Books, 2008), we joked that we were keeping each other honest by approaching the subject from polar opposite political and religious views.

While Newell Bringhurst was not my co-author for this book, he did, nonetheless, read earlier drafts and provide invaluable advice as well as encouragement for which I am very grateful. There were also a number of individuals who provided information, advice, and assistance, among whom are Thomas G. Alexander, Philip L. Barlow, Senator Robert F. Bennett, Congressman Rob Bishop, Kim Farah, John Hamer, Elaine E. Hasleton, Senator Orrin G. Hatch, Steven L. Mayfield, Louis C. Midgley, Daniel C. Peterson, William D. Russell, and Biloine Whiting Young.

The institutions and organizations that have provided advice, information, and research materials are the L. Tom Perry Special Collections, Harold B. Lee Library, Brigham Young University, Provo, Utah; Church Public Affairs, Church of Jesus Christ of Latter-day Saints, Salt Lake City; LDS Church Historical Department, Salt Lake City; LDS Family History Library, Salt Lake City; the Foundation for Apologetic Information and Research (FAIR); the John Whitmer Historical Association; Manuscripts and Special Collections, J. Willard Marriott Library, University of Utah, Salt Lake City; and members of the Utah State Republican Central Committee.

I would especially like to thank Lavina Fielding Anderson for her very helpful editorial advice and Greg Kofford for pushing me along and keeping me to an exacting schedule on this project.

Finally, I would like to give my most appreciative thanks to my wife, Suzanne Long Foster, and my children, Robert, Shannon, and Senia, for their patience and long suffering. This project has consumed a significant part of my life for the past ten plus months and literally taken over our living room, forcing Suzanne and the children to tiptoe around deep stacks of files scattered thickly about the room. I will try to make it up to them but am not sure how I can repay them for almost a year of well-meaning but still disruptive turmoil.

Chapter 1
Rise of the Religious Right

The stereotypical image many Americans have of the religious right is of a well-organized, socially and religiously homogeneous, ultra-conservative organization of radical right-wing people who want to force their concept of religion on America. In reality, this alliance and their story is much more complex. The rise of the religious right in the 1970s could better be described as a reemergence. Furthermore, the religious right was more an awkward coalition of different groups than a unified monolith.

What is now known as the religious or Christian right was not only present but very powerful politically during the nineteenth century, although there is considerable disagreement and debate over its beginnings. While some historians trace its roots to the Puritans, others locate its origins in the early Republic period when American society was in great turmoil.[1] Historian Janet Moore Lindman, who focused on its success in eighteenth-century Virginia, documents the accompanying backlash as "a complicated mix of defensiveness and attraction, admiration and fear, criticism and violence on the part of nonbelievers." Much like the reaction that greeted Latter-day Saints a half-century later, evangelical Baptists of Virginia suffered from a wave of persecution in the 1770s and 1780s that included whippings and the imprisonment of its preachers and adherents.[2]

As a result of this persecution, evangelicals were strongly in favor of religious freedom for all Christian religious persuasions. In fact, in 1784, Patrick Henry proposed taxing Virginia citizens "to sustain and support churches." While even the Baptists would have received a share of the tax money, they opposed the proposed tax for both political and theological reasons. Baptists believed that "Christians were to render unto Caesar what was his—the religious and political spheres were meant, by Jesus, to be separate."[3]

Evangelical Baptists were aided by political luminaries like James Madison, whom they prodded into proposing the Bill of Rights "that guaranteed religious freedom and limited the government role with religion." Thomas Jefferson was another Virginia politician who supported the separation of church and state. Because of their common belief about the role of government in religion, Baptists supported Madison and Jefferson in their political careers, an alliance that proved beneficial for all involved.[4]

The growing influence and prestige of the Christian right was undeniable. And why wouldn't it be? In many ways, the Christian right was, at that time, the mainstream of American politics and religious thought. By 1850 Methodists and Baptists ranked first and second respectively in national membership numbers. The old "colonial elite" denominations—Congregationalists, Anglicans, and Quakers—had long since lost their predominance while the revival-minded congregations had continued to grow.

Before the Civil War, members of the religious right fought against but also defended slavery, depending on which state they called home. The Southern Baptist Convention was created in 1845 because of the growing enmity between northern, anti-slavery Baptists and their southern, pro-slavery co-religionists. The split was rancorous and permanent.

Following the Civil War, summarizes Bryan F. Le Beau, "the Christian Right launched a conservative cultural crusade to defend its values against the forces of liberalism and modernism." Rather than being just a reactionary movement, the Christian or religious right was quite progressive in its approach to better the common people's condition, both spiritually and physically. Among the issues they addressed were "currency reform, regulation of corporate abuses, and adoption of direct democracy through initiative, referendum, and recall."[5]

Within the modern religious right movement are several groups that, for the most part, have similar origins and even appear to have overlapping adherents. Still, they have different demographics and dynamics that keep them separate—although, depending on the time and situation, the same characteristics act for inclusiveness.

Evangelicalism

Regardless of the date of its origins, the American evangelical movement emerged as one of the more significant religious movements of the First Great Awakening in the mid-eighteenth century. As religious historian D. G. Hart explained, evangelicalism became "virtually a new form of Protestantism."[6]

Evangelicalism was reinforced by the exuberance of the Second Great Awakening of the early nineteenth century, which was expressed in revivals, camp meetings, and activist energy. "Nineteenth-century evangelicals like [Charles G.] Finney, or Lyman Beecher, or Francis Asbury . . . focused on sin as human action. For all they preached hellfire and damnation, they nonetheless harbored an unshakable practical belief in the capacity of humans for moral action, in the ability of humans to turn away from sinful behavior and embrace moral action."[7]

Evangelicals, for the most part, rejected the Calvinistic doctrine of predestination, or the belief that, even before creation, God had determined the fate of the universe, including who would and would not be saved by His grace. Instead, they emphasized conversion, spiritual rebirth, and a more universal salvation.

This new revivalism and emphasis on a personal relationship with God was a radical departure from the more traditional denominations, and the popularity of this new approach to religion increased the erosion of Anglicans and Congregationalists as dominant American churches. Christianity in the United States, according to Kevin Phillips, "has always had an evangelical . . . and frequently a radical or combative streak." This outcome was almost predictable, given that the original colonies were populated, in large part, by "Scripture-reading religious dissenters."[8]

Throughout the nineteenth century, evangelicalism was important in American culture and was expressed in a number of different Christian denominations. "In 1892, when the Supreme Court de-

scribed the U.S. as 'a Christian nation,' it might as well have said an
'evangelical nation.'" This might certainly have been so, but within
the evangelical movement were various factions.[9]

Pentecostal and Charismatic Movements

Early Methodist preachers in America popularized "a pentecostal
type of religious enthusiasm." Participants at these camp meetings
experienced a number of outward manifestations of this enthusiasm,
including weeping, wailing, glossolalia ("speaking in tongues" in an
unknown language), jerking, and fainting. Eventually, Methodism,
then America's largest Protestant denomination, developed divisions
in reaction to what many saw as infiltrations of secularization and
worldliness. Some members wanted a return to Methodism's simpler
and humbler origins. This division produced the Holiness movement, which in turn gave rise to Pentecostalism between 1901 and
1906. According to historian Martin Marty, the Pentecostal movement could be called "the religious phenomenon of the twentieth
century."[10] Among the doctrines it popularized were sanctification,
premillennialism, and faith healing.[11]

In 1960, the charismatic movement, a neo-Pentecostal development, emerged, emphasizing gifts of the Spirit manifested through
private revelations, prophecies, and visions. "Pentecostalism spilled
over denominational lines," when Dennis Bennett, rector at St.
Mark's Episcopal Church in Van Nuys, California, experienced what
he believes "was the baptism of the Holy Spirit and the gift of
tongues. In appropriating these experiences, Charismatics sought to
restore authenticity and power to strayed Methodist, Baptist, and
Presbyterian traditions." One Charismatic goal is the union of various Protestant movements with Catholics through a common
emphasis on the gifts of the Spirit. Not surprisingly, this movement
is regarded with skepticism and suspicion by other members of the
religious right—especially by fundamentalists.[12]

Fundamentalists

By the 1920s, the larger evangelical movement split between liberalism and conservatism. According to religious scholar Stephen W. Carson, "On the one hand were theological liberals who, in order to maintain better credibility in the modern age, were willing to modify some central evangelical doctrines such as the reliability of the Bible or the necessity of salvation only through the atoning sacrifice of Christ. On the other hand were conservatives who continued to believe the traditionally essential evangelical doctrines."[13]

The fundamentalist movement, which has been called "a militant wing of the conservatives" and "the militant and faithful defenders of biblical orthodoxy," began in the late nineteenth and early twentieth centuries but came into its own in the early 1920s. The movement took its name from a series of pamphlets published in 1909, *The Fundamentals: A Testimony of Truth*. Their authors—representing Presbyterians, Methodists, and Episcopalians from the United States and abroad—attempted to identify the fundamental doctrines of the Christian faith "which were under attack from the then-current tides of scientific inquiry."[14] They settled on five:

1. The Bible as inspired and infallible.
2. Christ as divine.
3. Christ's substitutionary atonement. Liberal theologians had begun arguing that Christ was a man who had died a martyr's death, thereby providing a moral influence on society and setting an example from which all people could benefit. Fundamentalists saw this as downgrading Jesus's status and denying the heart of Christianity and the soul of the gospel. They insisted that, by dying a voluntary and substitutionary death, He provided an infinite atonement for all of humankind's sins.
4. Christ's literal resurrection. Liberal theologians took the position that the resurrection was spiritual and metaphorical rather than literal, while the fundamentalists argued strenuously for the opposite posit.

5. The second coming. Fundamentalists also took the position that Christ's second coming would be a literal, bodily return to earth.[15]

Many fundamentalists during the 1920s believed that liberals (or "modernists") "were plotting the overthrow of conservative Christianity in favor of materialistic and agnostic philosophies." Viewing themselves as defenders of "true" Christianity, fundamentalists were, in part, protesting "German rationalism (reflected in the higher critical theories of the Bible) and evolution."[16] Its apparent increase in popularity and power simply hastened the inevitable confrontation with liberalism—which it lost.

The Scopes Trial

In July 1925, the Scopes "Monkey Trial" took place in Dayton, Tennessee. Tennessee, like Mississippi and Oklahoma, had passed laws forbidding the teaching of evolution in public schools. In Tennessee, the recently formed American Civil Liberties Union had asked for teachers who agreed to raise the constitutional issue. John T. Scopes, a twenty-four-year old biology teacher at Dayton's Central High School, was coaxed into volunteering; he and Dayton town officials agreed to his arrest and charging.

The trial "became a national obsession and media circus" as reporters and partisans from around the country invaded Dayton. Although it was an economic boon to the small community, the "circus" aspect erupted. "Owners of chimpanzees and monkeys hurried downtown for photo opportunities, while flappers sparked a short-lived fashion trend by donning simian stoles. Radio, rapidly spreading into American homes, brought the trial to people's firesides, and newsreels showed it to moviegoers."[17]

Scopes's conviction was expected and even encouraged. He had, after all, broken the law. What Scopes, the ACLU, and others wanted was the conviction's appeal to the U.S. Supreme Court, which they expected would overturn the law. The real fight was for public opinion. Leading Scopes's team of lawyers was Clarence Darrow, perhaps the most famous trial lawyer of the twentieth century. A self-described agnostic, he was widely believed to be an atheist. On the prosecution's side was thrice-failed presidential candidate and former Secretary of State William Jennings Bryan. A champion of religious conservatism, Bryan was known as "the Great Commoner" and had almost legendary status. He agreed to participate, at the Dayton city attorney's request, and the straightforward case took on the aura of a battle or "duel to the death" as Bryan called it.[18]

The trial itself, which lasted about eight days, was unremarkable except for the hype and sensationalism that both preceded and followed it. The exception occurred near the trial's end when Darrow called Bryan as an expert witness. Bryan, surprisingly, agreed. During the examination, Darrow grilled him for about two hours on such biblical questions as Jonah and the whale, the age of the Earth, whether Joshua made the sun stand still, and whether Eve was created from Adam's rib. After two hours, the judge called a halt to the testimony and had it expunged as irrelevant. Furthermore, Darrow's courtroom grandstanding had offended some who felt it lacked decorum and had "cheapened legal procedure." In fact, "popular resentment against Darrow had become so strong that law enforcement officials met secretly with the judge and cautioned against any further examination." They explained that the questioning should be stopped before someone got hurt, that someone being Clarence Darrow. After that, the judge brought the examination to a close.[19]

The next day Darrow surprised the court by asking the jury to find Scopes guilty. This tactic meant that he forfeited his closing argument but, more importantly, also deprived Bryan of a closing argument. Bryan was outraged since he considered his planned remarks to be the most important speech of his life—a composite of his earlier arguments against evolution.[20]

The jury duly found Scopes guilty, and the judge fined him $100 instead of the required $500 imposed by law. Bryan and the fundamentalists declared the trial a victory and delivered a number of speeches and press releases on that theme for five days. Then Bryan died while napping after attending Sunday church services. Although he had suffered from diabetes and heart problems for some time, the trial had no doubt taken a greater toll than anyone realized.[21]

Darrow appealed the case to the Tennessee Supreme Court, which overturned it on technical grounds. The claims of victory further eroded in the court of public opinion, as the stereotype of backward southern religion fighting "enlightened science" solidified.[22] H. L. Mencken, the acid-penned spokesman of the liberal establishment, had a field day in describing Darrow's examination of Bryan concerning the evolution of man and ape from a common ancestor: "I allude to his astounding argument against the notion that man is a mammal. I am glad I heard it, for otherwise I'd never believe it. There stood the man who had been thrice a candidate for the Presidency of the Republic. . . . There he stood in the glare of the world, uttering stuff that a boy of eight would laugh at! The artful Darrow led him on: he repeated it, ranted for it, bellowed it in his cracked voice. A tragedy, indeed! He came into life a hero, a Galahad, in bright and shining armor. Now he was passing out a pathetic fool."[23]

According to an anonymously authored analysis of the Scopes trial's negative effect on evangelicalism, it became "a victory for free speech over censorship, of reason over faith, of the modern over the primitive."[24] Thirty years later, Jerome Lawrence and Robert Edwin Lee's 1955 play, *Inherit the Wind*, and its 1960 screen adaptation portrayed Bryan as a pompous, ignorant buffoon, outwitted and outreasoned by Darrow, again reinforcing the popular view that science and intelligent thought had triumphed over backward religion. In fact, some from the religious right believe they are still trying to overcome the negative stereotyping that resulted from the Scopes trial.[25]

They may have a point. In their introduction to the 1987 book *Piety and Politics: Evangelicals and Fundamentalists Confront the World*, Richard John Neuhaus, the well-known Catholic theologian and author, and Michael Cromartie of the Ethics and Public Policy Center, announced: "Not since the so-called Scopes Monkey Trial in 1925 have American Evangelicals and Fundamentalists received so much public attention as they are getting in the mid-1980s. They have emerged from a half-century of exile from the mainstream of

American life every bit as controversial as they were when William Jennings Bryan was defending the Genesis story of creation against the teaching of evolution in Tennessee public schools."[26] The Scopes trial was not the only setback for the religious right, particularly the fundamentalists. The later 1920s continued to portray them in the press as ignorant and hypocritical. Adding to the negative view of both evangelicals and fundamentalists was the dismal failure of their most ambitious political experiment—Prohibition.

In 1919 the Eighteenth Amendment, prohibiting the production, transportation, and sale of alcoholic beverages, had been ratified. Members of the temperance movement, most of whom were evangelical and fundamentalist Protestants, had worked long and hard for its passage, arguing that it would "reduce crime and corruption, solve social problems, reduce the tax burden created by prisons and poorhouses, and improve health and hygiene in America."[27] Ratification was seen as a moral and social victory.

Initial euphoria turned to frustration and dismay as alcohol consumption per capita went from a low in 1921 to an all-time high by the end of the decade. Not only had drinking increased, but bootlegging and official corruption were widespread. Moralists were arguing that Prohibition was undermining respect for all laws and causing a general breakdown of society. In 1933 the Twenty-first Amendment cancelled the "noble experiment."[28]

This second blow quickened the retreat of the religious right from politics and the public scene. According to Joel Carpenter's *Revive Us Again: The Reawakening of American Fundamentalism*, the movement turned inward, using the thirties and forties to create a network of Bible institutes, fellowships, and radio gospel hours. It also produced a large body of literature supporting conservative beliefs about the gospel and society.[29]

The evangelical and fundamentalist retreat from public activism coincided with what political commentator Jacques Berlinerblau has called "the Golden Age of American Secularism," which he dates at 1925 to 1973 when *Roe vs. Wade* ignited the activist fires of the religious right. Many of those who desired a greater separation of church and state were Protestants, Catholics, and Jews who had suffered by evangelical Protestantism's dominion over America's political life. Thus, for a large part of the twentieth century, "routine public activism and aggressive Bible-believing Protestantism" were kept apart.[30] The desirability of this goal was underscored by fundamentalists' limited "participation in sporadic rearguard actions through fringe movements and extremist crusades like those of the Ku Klux Klan during the 1920s, and segregationist[s] and anti-Communists during the 1950s. Those links between the Christian Right and regressive political movements fixed the Christian Right with a public image as narrow-minded, bigoted, and backward looking—an image that obscured earlier associations between the same religious community and progressive political causes."[31] Support tended to be localized and personality-driven, never official or national-scale. Nevertheless, the image of fundamentalism "working hand in glove" with the Klan was created at that time and has been hard to overcome.[32]

The Southernization of American Culture and Religion

Another characteristic of evangelical and fundamentalist Christianity, at least in the minds of many critics, is its link with America's South. Some scholars have argued that the last half of the twentieth century saw a Southernization of America or, as *New York Times* editor Peter Applebome wrote, "the fingerprint of the South on almost every aspect of the nation's soul." In support, they cite the popularity of country music, the nation's turn to conservative politics, the rise of states' rights, and particularly, the spread of evangelical religion.[33]

Historian Paul Harvey, in *Redeeming the South*, stated, "In the twentieth century, with the SBC [Southern Baptism Convention] becoming the largest Protestant denomination in the United States, it became increasingly apparent that white southerners had lost the war but won the peace." Commenting on the SBC's status as the fastest growing major denomination in the United States, Kevin

Phillips cynically asked if it was the "State Church of the ex-Confederacy."[34]

In 1979, the conservative fundamentalist faction captured and consolidated the Convention's leadership, a landmark victory that had immediate political consequences.[35] Even in the 1920s, some 80 percent of the Southern Baptist Convention's membership were farmers, who are traditionally conservative. While the nation's percentage of rural dwellers has declined steadily since the 1950s, the Southern Baptist Convention still manifests a strong rural influence. Furthermore, it followed southern agrarian migration patterns into the North and West. Impressively, it has been able to retain many of its populist characteristics. The convention is "a 'folk' church determined to keep its relationship with southern farmers and country people."[36]

The Religious Right's Political Rise

By the 1960s and 1970s, the national setting was perfect for the reemergence of the Christian right. While most historians say this happened sometime in the 1970s, some point to the 1960 presidential election as a key moment when "large numbers of white, church-going southern Protestants," who traditionally voted Democrat, expressed their "long-standing antipathy toward Roman Catholics" by abandoning John F. Kennedy and "defecting to the Republican candidate, Richard Nixon."[37]

Even so, the nation at large considered the Christian right as still wandering in the political wilderness until the 1970s. In the 1972 election, active church-going Christians, offended by the tumultuous counterculture of the sixties and encouraged by Richard Nixon's appeal to the "traditionalist views of the nation's 'silent majority,'" gave him a ten-point advantage in the election.[38]

Newsweek declared 1976 to be the "Year of the Evangelical." Gary Wills wrote that born-again Southern Baptist Jimmy Carter's "automatic evangelical vote [was] probably in the vicinity of 40 million." Although a majority of white southerners voted for Gerald Ford, Carter won; and most evangelicals expected his administration to reflect their concerns over moral and social issues. When it did not, many evangelicals became disillusioned, seeing the country's traditional religious and economic values as under attack.[39] These disillusioned elements took action. The National Christian Action Coalition, the first national organization of the Christian right, was organized in 1978, followed by the Rev. Jerry Falwell's Moral Majority in 1979. Evangelicals and fundamentalists had once again ventured into politics in force. Stephen W. Carson commented wryly, "They were not welcomed with open arms by either the political or religious establishments. Rather, they kicked down the door and marched in with such fury that they sent panic through most sectors of American society."[40]

The Moral Majority

The Moral Majority, which took its name from Richard Nixon's earlier reference to a "silent majority," was founded with the idea of staying focused on issues of concern to Christians but maintaining negotiating distance from any particular political party.[41] The original 1978 platform had nine "belief" statements:

1. We believe in the separation of church and state.
2. We are pro-life.
3. We are pro-traditional family.
4. We oppose the illegal drug traffic in America.
5. We oppose pornography.
6. We support the state of Israel and Jewish people everywhere.
7. We believe that a strong national defense is the best deterrent to war.
8. We support equal rights for women.
9. We believe the Equal Rights Amendment is the wrong vehicle to obtain equal rights for women. We feel that the ambiguous and simplistic language of the amendment could lead to court interpretations that might put women in combat.

The Moral Majority also explained what it was not:

1. We are not a political party.
2. We do not endorse political candidates.
3. We are not attempting to elect "born again" candidates.
4. Moral Majority, Inc., is not a religious organization attempting to control the government.
5. We are not a censorship organization.
6. Moral Majority, Inc., is not an organization committed to depriving homosexuals of their civil rights as Americans.
7. We do not believe that individuals or organizations that disagree with Moral Majority, Inc., belong to an immoral minority.[42]

Conservative columnist Cal Thomas remembered Jerry Falwell as the most intriguing man he had ever met, a larger-than-life personality. While a number of influential people were involved in the Moral Majority's founding and growth, it was, in large part, Falwell's dynamism that generated the Moral Majority's early successes. He approached politics with the same zeal he approached religion, often overlapping the two. He would say, "Get saved, get baptized, and get registered to vote."[43]

Falwell, a fundamentalist Baptist from Lynchburg, Virginia, was, in many ways, a bundle of contradictions. His grandfather was an avowed atheist, and his father was an agnostic who "hated preachers and ran a moonshine operation during Prohibition." Yet Falwell chose the ministry as his profession, graduated from Baptist Bible College in Springfield, Missouri, established a congregation in Lynchburg, and founded what is now Liberty University. Falwell later explained that he had founded the Moral Majority with the goal "to engage the religious right and, in return, to change the direction of the country on its moral and social dilemmas." In other words, the Moral Majority was founded "as a reaction against a secular society that was increasingly hostile to conservative Christians," and the Moral Majority's message appealed to these conservative Christians across the country. Unified in a common goal, they began working with the 1980 presidential election in mind.[44]

As Ronald Reagan triumphed, critics claimed that the Moral Majority and Christian conservatives had little effect, a dismissive attitude summarized in the bumper stickers: "The Moral Majority Is Neither." Although probably not decisive in Reagan's victory, the Moral Majority, nevertheless, had a significant impact. Cal Thomas later commented, "Had we not been Baptists we would have danced in the streets." He remembered the intense publicity and praise for the Moral Majority as heady times. "The aphrodisiac of political power descended on Lynchburg, Virginia, with the impact of an asteroid."[45] Even more significantly, the Moral Majority represented the new political activism of Christian right groups who were tired of being ridiculed and marginalized. Furthermore, they were better organized and more motivated than other political groups.[46]

Ed Dobson, speaking for the conservatives, termed the "Reagan-Bush landslide" as "the greatest moment of opportunity for conservative Christians in [the twentieth century]. We had been disgraced in 1925 at the Scopes trial. But now we were vindicated. We had helped elect our man to the White House, and he openly praised the efforts of Falwell and the Moral Majority."[47]

Although the religious right helped Reagan to a second landslide in 1984, it could not extract all of the moral and economic legislation on its agenda. Notwithstanding such disappointments, they again backed the Republican candidate in the 1988 election, an election openly permeated with religion. Two ministers ran for president, Pat Robertson as a Republican candidate on the right and left-leaning Jesse Jackson as a Democrat. George H. W. Bush, an Episcopalian and the successful Republican candidate, claimed to have been born again and made sure his speeches included "God words" to shore up his political base. Democratic candidate Michael Dukakis claimed to have "sought religious benefits from his association with the Greek Orthodox Church," but there was no evidence that he regularly attended services. Furthermore, his liberal stand on social issues and affiliation with the ACLU earned him the appelation of the "first truly secular candidate" for president.[48] In the end, it may very well have been votes against Dukakis rather than votes for Bush that decided the election.

The religious tone of the election surprised and dismayed some commentators and scholars. Southern historian C. Vann Woodward characterized it as "thoroughly saturated with religious issues, conflicts, personalities, fanatics, candidates, scandals and demagogues."[49] Many evangelicals were skeptical of Bush's sincerity in claiming to be born again. His policies and judicial selections tended to be moderate at best and openly liberal in other cases. Critics noted that he apparently lacked familiarity with scripture when he told the National Religious Broadcasters that his favorite Bible verse was the somewhat irrelevant John 16:3 ("And these things will they do unto you, because they know not the Father, nor me") rather than the evangelical favorite, John 3:16 ("for God so loved the world that he gave his only begotten Son . . . ").[50]

Furthermore, Falwell disbanded the Moral Majority in 1989. Although he claimed that it had achieved all of its goals, the harsh reality was that it had lost the political clout of the early 1980s and had been able to change very little, even during its heyday. Former Moral Majority board member Ed Dobson conceded that "despite all the time, money, and energy—despite the political power—[it] failed." Social conditions actually got worse during the late eighties and certainly during the nineties.[51]

Perhaps the longest lasting legacy of the Moral Majority was its transition role from the 1930s to the '50s when evangelicals and especially fundamentalists tended to be apolitical, if not downright hostile to the political process, to greater participation in mainstream politics. "In some respects," observed the University of Akron's Dr. John Green, "the Moral Majority represented a pragmatic step for evangelicals."[52]

The Christian Coalition

To fill the vacuum created by the disbanding of the Moral Majority, Pat Robertson, in the wake of his failed 1988 presidential bid, created the Christian Coalition in 1989. Its mission statement staked out a clear political agenda:

1. Represent the pro-family point of view before local councils, school boards, state legislatures and Congress.

2. Speak out in the public arena and in the media.

3. Train leaders for effective social and political action.

4. Inform pro-family voters about timely issues and legislation.

5. Protest anti-Christianity bigotry and defend the rights of people of faith.[53]

Despite his public persona as a simple, faithful servant of God, Robertson was much more complex. The son of a Democratic U.S. Senator from Virginia, he grew up in a life of privilege and studied at the "best schools," then "heard the call to the ministry." Robertson bought a "a dilapidated UHF channel in Portsmouth, Virginia, for $37,000" and turned it into the Christian Broadcasting Network in 1960. The flagship program was his immensely popular *700 Club*, named for the first seven hundred donors they needed to keep the program running, Robertson projected down-home, folksiness in his sermons, building a multi-million dollar empire in the process. In 2004, the Christian Broadcasting Network had a revenue of over $186 million, up to $236 million the next year. His personal wealth is estimated at $140 million, and he lives in a luxurious estate with its own private airstrip on top of a Virginia mountain.[54]

Robertson's 1988 presidential campaign, while short-lived, had moments of controversy and excitement, beginning with his announcement that God had told him he should run for president. Robertson's campaign accused fellow Republican Jack Kemp of favoring pornography and claimed that one of Kemp's daughters had an abortion. Robertson's supporters disrupted the Georgia Republican convention by shouting down speakers so vehemently that it "adjourned in chaos."[55]

Although Robertson withdrew months before the national convention, his army of ardent evangelical supporters was a natural foundation for his Christian Coalition. Through a network of members working on the local, state, and national levels and by skillfully using voter education courses and publications, the Christian Coalition created "the largest and most active conservative grassroots political organization in America." Their success has been both applauded and jeered, even among the religious right. Ed Dobson complained that "the most blatant attempt to co-op God is the Christian Coalition. The very name places the divine stamp of approval on their agenda."[56]

The Christian Coalition could not, however, save Bush in 1992. Bill Clinton carried three-fourths of the secular vote, while two-thirds of Bush's votes came from the traditionalists.[57] During the first two years of Clinton's administration, many conservative legislative accomplishments were rewritten or repealed, much to the chagrin of Pat Robertson and other conservative Christians.

By 1994, Clinton's administration had alienated several traditionally Democratic constituencies, angered conservative voters over taxes and gun issues, and "enraged the Christian right with his stem-cell and military policies." The Republican Party had begun to do very well in the Sunbelt states of the South and West. The religious right remobilized, and many conservative voters who had stayed home in 1992 came to the polls, giving the Republicans a huge victory in Congressional races and control of both bodies of Congress that lasted until 2006.[58]

In the 2000 presidential race, religion played an important role. George W. Bush, like his father, claimed to have been born again; but his claim had more credibility. Religion seemed to permeate every aspect of his life, and the moralistic and religious rhetoric that peppered his speeches seemed authentic. Although this style drew criticism in Europe, largely considered to be a secularist, post-Christian society, it attracted a large portion of the American voting population.[59]

In both 2000 and 2004 a majority of the religious right not only voted but actively campaigned for Bush. In 2004 white evangelicals, who constituted 23 percent of the electorate, gave Bush 78 percent of their votes. Their high turnout was a major factor in Bush's control of swing states like Florida and Ohio.[60] A majority of those attending religious services at least weekly, regardless of religious affiliation, voted Republican. (The only exceptions were weekly-attending black Protestants, 83 percent of whom voted for John Kerry, while 72 percent of less-observant evangelical Protestants still voted for Bush. Thus, evangelicalism per se constituted the main predictive factor in voting.[61])

The success of the religious right did not, however, depend on the Christian Coalition. In 2001 Pat Robertson stepped down from its leadership; and in 2007, newspaper journalist Steven Thomma described the Christian Coalition as "a shell of its former self." In 1996, its high point in terms of membership, the Christian Coalition had a budget of $26 million. In 2007, the budget was a paltry $1 million. Furthermore, state chapters in Alabama, Georgia, Iowa, and Ohio separated from the national organization, claiming that it was too liberal.[62]

In fact, the ultimate Bush legacy may be faithful conservatism. In spite of his flagging popularity, he has, for the most part, retained the support of religious conservatives. As a president with a proud and public Christian foundation, Bush has assured that "the evangelical movement will have a foothold in Washington well after he returns to Crawford, Texas. Indeed, the Bush White House teaches young believers how to be true to their faith within the confines of the nation's capital."[63]

Notes

1. Michael Lienesch, "Right-Wing Religion: Christian Conservatism as a Political Movement," *Political Science Quarterly* 97, no. 3 (Autumn 1982): 407.

2. Janet Moore Lindman, "Acting the Manly Christian: White Evangelical Masculinity in Revolutionary Virginia," *The William and Mary Quarterly*, 3rd Series, 57, no. 2 (April 2000): 397; see also Steven Waldman, "The Framers and the Faithful: How Modern Evangelicals are Ignoring Their Own History," *Washington Monthly* (April 2006), http://www.washingtonmonthly.com/features/2006/0604 .waldman.html (accessed April 29, 2008).

3. Waldman, "The Framers and the Faithful"; and Steven Waldman, "The Evangelical Founding Fathers," *Christianity Today*, March 25, 2008, http://www .christianitytoday.com/ct/2008/marchweb-only/113-22.0.html (accessed April 26, 2008).

4. Waldman, "The Evangelical Founding Fathers."

5. Bryan F. Le Beau, "The Political Mobilization of the New Christian Right," http://are.as.wvu.edu/lebeau1.htm (accessed September 10, 2007).

6. Hart, as quoted in Terry Eastland, "Saving Souls—and Society," *Weekly Standard*, January 21, 2003, http://www.weeklystandard.com/Content/Public/Articles/000/000/002/125vuami.asp (accessed September 5, 2007).

7. Donald Scott, "Evangelicalism, Revivalism, and the Second Great Awakening," National Humanities Center, October 2000, http://nationalhumanitiescenter.org/tserve/nineteen/nkeyinfo/nevanrev.htm (accessed October 20, 2007).

8. Kevin Phillips, *American Theocracy: The Peril and Politics of Radical Religion, Oil, and Borrowed Money in the 21st Century* (New York: Viking, 2006), 100, 104.

9. Eastland, "D. G. Hart Examines Evangelical Christianity's Place."

10. Martin E. Mrty, "Insiders Look at Fundamentalism," Religion Online, n.d., http://www.religion-online.org/showarticle.asp?title=1706 (accessed April 26, 2008).

11. Milton V. Backman Jr., *Christian Churches of America: Origins and Beliefs*, rev. ed. (New York: Charles Scribner's Sons, 1976), 214–15; Roger Finke and Rodney Stark, *The Churching of America, 1776–1990: Winners and Losers in Our Religious Economy* (1992; rpt., New Brunswick, N.J.: Rutgers University Press, 1997), 164.

12. Backman, *Christian Churches of America*, 218–20; "The Charismatic Movement," Jeremiah Project, http://www.jeremiahproject.com/prophecy/charis1.html (accessed November 4, 2007).

13. Stephen W. Carson, "Christians in Politics: The Return of the 'Religious Right,'" LewRockwell.com, October 30, 2003, http://www.lewrockwell.com/carson/carson17.html (accessed November 4, 2007).

14. Cal Thomas and Ed Dobson, *Blinded by Might: Can the Religious Right Save America?* (Grand Rapids, Mich.: Zondervan Publishing House, 1999), 31; Marty, "Insiders Look at Fundamentalism."

15. Thomas and Dobson, *Blinded by Might*, 31–32.

16. Gerald L. Priest, "William Jennings Bryan and the Scopes Trial: A Fundamentalist Perspective," *Detroit Baptist Seminary Journal* 4 (Fall 1999): 54, 55.

17. David Greenberg, "The Legend of the Scopes Trial," *Slate*, September 8, 2005, http://www.slate.com/id/2125492/ (accessed October 11, 2007).

18. "The Greatest Trials of All Time: The Scopes Monkey Trial," Court TV Online, http://www.courttv.com/archive/greatesttrials/scopes/making.html (accessed October 22, 2007); Priest, "William Jennings Bryan and the Scopes Trial," 64.

19. "The Greatest Trials of All Time"; Norman F. Furniss, *The Fundamentalist Controversy, 1918–1931* (New Haven, Conn.: Yale University Press, 1954), 91, quoted in Priest, "William Jennings Bryan and the Scopes Trial," 70 and 71.

20. Priest, "William Jennings Bryan and the Scopes Trial," 71.

21. "The Greatest Trials of All Time"; Priest, "William Jennings Bryan and the Scopes Trial," 71–72.

22. Greenberg, "The Legend of the Scopes Trial."

23. H. L. Mencken, *Baltimore Evening Sun*, July 27, 1925, as quoted in "The 'Declension' of Evangelical Protestantism: The Scopes Trial, Fundamentalism, and the 'Acids of Modernity,'" http://www.assumption.edu/ahc/scopes/default.html (accessed October 24, 2007).

24. Ibid.

25. Phillips, *American Theocracy*, xiv.

26. Richard John Neuhaus and Michael Cromartie, eds., *Piety and Politics: Evangelicals and Fundamentalists Confront the World* (Washington, D.C.: Ethics & Public Policy Center, 1987), vii. It is interesting to note the shift in historical perspective. This statement assumes that it was Bryan and the Bible that were on trial (hence, on the defensive) rather than the teaching of evolution, which was actually the focus of the trial (and, hence, on the defensive).

27. Thomas and Dobson, *Blinded by Might*, 67; Mark Thornton, "Alcohol Prohibition Was a Failure," Cato Policy Analysis No. 157, http://www.cato.org/pubs/pas/pa-157.html (accessed October 24, 2007).

28. Thomas and Dobson, *Blinded by Might*, 68.

29. Joel Carpenter, *Revive Us Again: The Reawakening of American Fundamentalism* (New York: Oxford University Press, 1997), xii.

30. Jacques Berlinerblau, *Thumpin' It: The Use and Abuse of the Bible in Today's Presidential Politics* (Louisville, Ky.: Westminster John Knox Press, 2008), 8–9. The Jehovah's Witnesses also played a major role, particularly in the courts, in the separation of church and state. While these denominations and groups had varying reasons for encouraging a more secular society, "the promulgation of nonbelief was not foremost among them."

31. Le Beau, "The Political Mobilization of the New Christian Right."

32. Robert Moat Miller, "A Note on the Relationship between the Protestant and the Revived Ku Klux Klan," *Journal of Southern History* 22, no. 3 (August 1956): 356.

33. Phillips, *American Theocracy*, 139–40.

34. Paul Harvey, *Redeeming the South: Religious Cultures and Racial Identities among Southern Baptists, 1865–1925* (Chapel Hill: University of North Carolina Press, 1997), as quoted in Phillips, *American Theocracy*, 132, also p. 148.

35. Phillips, *American Theocracy*, 149, 153, 156. According to Ed Dobson and Ed Hinson, *The Fundamentalist Phenomenon: The Resurgence of Conservative Christianity* (New York: Doubleday-Glailee, 1981), as quoted by Marty, "Insiders Look at Fundamentalism," Dobson and Hinson explained, "The bulk of today's Fundamentalists are certainly Baptists, but the majority of Baptists are not necessarily Fundamentalists."

36. Marty, "Insiders Look at Fundamentalism," 153, 155, 157. In spite of its status as the largest Protestant denomination in the United Sates and its powerful presence throughout many parts of the country, the Southern Baptist Convention, according to the Associated Press, "Ranks of Southern Baptists Are Still Growing Thinner," *New York Times*, April 25, 2008, http://www.nytimes.com/2008/04/25/us/25baptists.html?ex=1366862400 (accessed May 2, 2008), the number of people baptized in Southern Baptist churches "fell last year for the third straight year." In fact, "total membership dropped by nearly 40,000." While this was part of a greater national trend of declining membership in mainline Protestant churches, the Rev. Frank Page, the convention's president, blamed in part the "perception that Baptists are 'mean-spirited, hurtful and angry people.'" The ratio of annual baptisms has dropped sharply in the last fifty years from a high of one person baptized for every nineteen members in 1950 to one baptism for every forty-seven members in 2007. Such unfortunate and troubling news has, not surprisingly, caused significant debate and some second-guessing within the convention. Trevin Max, "Finger-Pointing, Divisions and the Decline of the SBC," *Baptist Press*, May 1, 2008, http://www.bpnews.net/printerfirndly.asp?ID=27967 (accessed May 2, 2008), placed the major blame on the factions in the church that have been arguing and fighting for decades. He ended by writing, "Let's end the fighting, reunite around the Gospel, love those with whom we disagree, and continue to cooperate."

37. Le Beau, "The Political Mobilization of the New Christian Right."

38. Kevin P. Phillips, "Politics Good for Religion," *Montana Standard*, January 1, 1974, 4; Phillips, *American Theocracy*, 184.

39. Gary Wills, "The God Election," *Oakland Tribune*, June 23, 1976; Le Beau, "The Political Mobilization of the New Christian Right"; and Thomas and Dobson, *Blinded by Might*, 11.

40. Carson, "Christians in Politics." See also "Presidential Politics and the Evangelical Movement," ReligionLink: Religion Story Ideas and Sources, http://www .religionlink.org/tip_040503a.php (accessed August 31, 2007) and Le Beau, "The Political Mobilization of the New Christian Right."

41. Thomas and Dobson, *Blinded by Might*, 36.

42. Le Beau, "The Political Mobilization of the New Christian Right."

43. Quoted in Thomas and Dobson, *Blinded by Might*, 13; see also Sarah Pulliam, "Falwell, Megachurch Pastor Who Organized Religious Right, Dead at 73," *Christianity Today*, May 16, 2007, http://www.christianitytoday.com/ct/2007/mayweb-only/120-32.0.html (accessed October 26, 2007).

44. "A Biography of Jerry Falwell," CBS News, May 15, 2007, http://www .cbsnews.com/stories/2007/05/15/national/main2806425.shtml (accessed April 26, 2008); Pulliam, "Falwell," 14, 21. Jacques Berlinerblau, *Thumpin' It*, 12, commented that the reemergence and rise of the Religious Right was called by some "the Fourth Great Awakening."

45. Thomas and Dobson, *Blinded by Might*, 21, 26.

46. Arthur H. Miller and Martin P. Wattenburg, "Politics from the Pulpit: Religiosity and the 1980 Elections," *The Public Opinion Quarterly* 48, no. 1 (Spring 1984): 302, 315; Thomas and Dobson, *Blinded by Might*, 36.

47. Carson, "Christians in Politics."

48. Thomas and Dobson, *Blinded by Might*, 85.

49. Ibid.; James L. Guth and John C. Green, eds., *The Bible and the Ballot Box* (Boulder, Colo.: Westview Press, 1991), 116, 39 as quoted in Phillips, *American Theocracy*, 188, 187.

50. Thomas and Dobson, *Blinded by Might*, 93.

51. Quoted in Carson, "Christians in Politics."

52. Interview with John Green, *The Jesus Factor*, Frontline PBS documentary, http://www.pbs.org/wgbh/pages/frontline/shows/jesus/interviews/green.html, aired October 18, 2007.

53. "About Us," Christian Coalition of America, http://www.cc.org/about.cfm (accessed October 26, 2007).

54. "Robertson's Grand Design," *U.S. News & World Report*, February 22, 1988, 14–18; Daniel Roth, "Pat Robertson's Quest for Eternal Life," *Fortune*, June 10, 2002, http://money.cnn.com/magazines/fortune/fortune_archive/2002/06/10/324534/index.htm (accessed April 29, 2008); Rob Boston, "Religious Right Power Brokers: The Top Ten," Americans United for Separation of Church and State, June

2006, http://www.au.org/site/News2?page=NewsArticle&id=8253&news_iv_ctrl=0&abbr=cs_&JServSessionIdr007=upfjq55gc2.app13a (accessed February 27, 2008); "Religious Right Funding Increases, AU Research Shows," Americans United for Separation of Church and State, October 15, 2007, http://www.au.org/site/News2?abbr=pr&page=NewsArticle&id=9429 (accessed April 22, 2008); "Pat Robertson," http://www.geocities.com/CapitolHill/7027/dictator.html (accessed April 22, 2008).

55. Robert G. Fichenberg, "Robertson Must Separate Fact, Fiction," *Salt Lake Tribune*, February 28, 1988; also "State Convention Is Disrupted," *New York Times*, May 23, 1988. Scholarly articles on Robertson's run for the presidency include Stephen D. Johnson et al., "Pat Robertson: Who Supported His Candidacy for President?" *Journal for the Scientific Study of Religion* 28, no. 4 (December 1989): 387–99; Lisa Langenbach and John C. Green, "Hollow Core: Evangelical Clergy and the 1988 Robertson Campaign," *Polity* 25, no. 1 (Autumn 1992): 147–58; James M. Penning, "Pat Robertson and the GOP: 1988 and Beyond," *Sociology of Religion* 55, no. 3 (Autumn, 1994): 327–44.

56. "About Us"; Thomas and Dobson, *Blinded by Might*, 102.

57. Phillips, *American Theocracy*, 189.

58. Joshua Zeitz, "How the Republicans Conquered the World in 1994 (Sound Familiar?)," American Heritage, January 4, 2007, http://www.americanheritage.com/events/articles/web/20070104-republican-party-newt-gingrich-congress-contract-with-america.shtml (accessed September 5, 2007).

59. Steve Waldman, Interview, *The Jesus Factor*, Frontline PBS documentary, http://www.pbs.org/wgbh/pages/frontline/shows/jesus/interviews/waldman.html (accessed October 18, 2007).

60. Peter Brown, "There's No Reason to Expect Dems to Win Over Evangelicals," *Real Clear Politics*, August 21, 2006, http://www.realclearpolitics.com/articles/2006/08/theres_no_reason_to_expect_dem.html (accessed August 31, 2007).

61. John C. Green, "Religion and the Presidential Vote: A Tale of Two Gaps," *Pew Forum*, August 21, 2007, http://pewforum.org/docs/?DocID=240 (accessed August 31, 2007).

62. Steven Thomma, "The Religious Right's Political Power Ebbs," *McClatchy Newspapers*, September 30, 2007, http://www.mcclatchydc.com/226/story/20062.html (accessed April 26, 2008).

63. Hannah Rosin, "Bush's Real Legacy: Faithful Conservatism," *USA Today*, October 1, 2007, A19.

Chapter 2
The Power of the
Religious Right

The rise (or, more correctly, the reemergence) of the religious right was a long, fitful, and not always pretty journey. Despite liberal claims of a well-organized, vast, right-wing conspiracy, it has been "by no means monolithic."[1] In fact, the religious right has always been an awkward coalition of many different groups and factions who, while commonly believing in and working together for a number of conservative social issues, are at odds with each other, not only over theology but even over what role they should play in America's political landscape. In a reversal of the U.S. motto, *E pluribus unum*, "out of many, one," the religious right seems to be out of many, not quite one. This predictable fragmentation is both helped and hindered—but definitely complicated—by the numerous religious traditions and claims represented by this significant segment of American society. In short, the political coalition that finds a home under the "religious right" rubric has been at best an uneasy alliance of like-minded people with significant theological differences and at worst a fractured assembly of retreating factions who call curses on each others' houses as they depart.

A major division in the religious right is between the evangelicals and fundamentalists. For the first several decades of the twentieth century, "there was not a practical distinction between fundamentalist and evangelical: the words were interchangeable," according to George Marsden, well-regarded conservative historian of religions. That changed, however, when "the sons of evangelical-fundamentalist preachers determined to create a 'New Evangelicalism.' They would not be fighters; they would be diplomats, positive rather than militant, infiltrators rather than separatists."[2]

Fundamentalism has been defined as "orthodox religious beliefs based on a literal interpretation of the Bible and regarded as fundamental to Christian faith." Fundamentalists see themselves as remaining "true to the Word of God"; they are contending for the faith, not passively letting true Christian doctrine be watered down to appease the various sects. From the fundamentalist perspective, New Evangelicals "have abandoned a militant Bible stance," refused to separate themselves from error, and have even developed a "toleration toward error." Therefore, "doctrinal corruption has permeated the movement."[3]

Of course, these religious divisions are far from monolithic. Numerous fundamentalists have evangelical tendencies, and many New Evangelicals are fundamentalists on some theological points. Furthermore, the coalition is not exclusively made up of Protestants but includes other religious groups. The extent to which these Protestants interact with people from other religious persuasions also reflects where they stand theologically.

Catholics

In general, fundamentalists believe that evangelicals are in a state of apostasy if they enter into dialogue with other denominations like Catholics and Latter-day Saints (Mormons). They are, as Catholic apologist Karl Keating puts it, in "dialogue with those who teach error rather than proclaim the Word of God boldly and without compromise." He continued his description of the two positions: "Most Evangelicals acknowledge that Catholics are Christians; most Fundamentalists doubt Catholics deserve the title." Even Jerry Falwell, a fundamentalist, was accused by other fundamentalists of having "departed from authentic and historic fundamentalist practices, sacrificing doctrinal purity on the altar of popularity and prominence" because he had reached out, albeit to a limited degree, to other conservative religions on behalf of the Moral Majority.[4] As a result, the Moral Majority and similar organizations during the late

1970s and early 1980s lost effectiveness. They were "built upon networks of fundamentalist churches and their leaders were unwilling to build coalitions with Pentecostals, evangelicals, mainline Protestants, and Catholics." In contrast, the Christian Coalition and Focus on the Family made a concerted and more effective effort to include conservative Catholics, mainline Protestants, and other groups.[5] While markedly successful when compared to the Moral Majority, the Christian Coalition's major effectiveness may not have been in attracting Catholics to formal membership but rather in the support they gave to social issues important to these organizations and to Christian Coalition candidates.[6]

Although the American Catholic Church has supported social welfare programs, opposed the death penalty, and resisted the proliferation of nuclear weapons, it has, nevertheless, worked with the Christian Coalition and other Protestant members of the Christian Right. Furthermore, "a small but not insignificant minority of Catholics have adopted evangelical styles of religiosity, and these are more likely to share evangelical political attitudes on issues where the Catholic church has not staked a position."[7]

Mormons

More conservative than Catholics and, in many ways, even more conservative in their social values than evangelicals and fundamentalists, are members of the Church of Jesus Christ of Latter-day Saints (Mormons). Theologically and historically, however, the LDS Church is so radical that many conservative denominations refuse to recognize it as Christian. The founding prophet, Joseph Smith of upstate New York, in 1829 translated the Book of Mormon, a compilation of ancient records inscribed on metal plates. This book is a thousand-year religious history of a people in the western hemisphere that includes prophets, the law of Moses, numerous cycles of repentance and backsliding, a visitation of the risen Jesus Christ, and eventual genocide. The book thus positions itself as a second witness of Christ's divinity, canonized as scripture, and a companion volume to the Bible. More radically, it stakes out a Mormon claim to ongo-

ing revelation and an open canon with new scripture. Joseph Smith
founded the Church in 1830, which has continued ever since under
a succession of prophet-presidents. Revelations to Joseph Smith and
his successors have been published in a third volume of scripture, the
Doctrine and Covenants.

Among additional claims that other churches were unwilling to
recognize was the Mormon assertion that the Church of Jesus Christ
of Latter-day Saints represented a restoration of Jesus Christ's pure
gospel and organization, lost in the "great apostasy" that followed the
martyrdom of the apostles and disciples in the first century. This
"apostasy" left believers without priesthood authority recognized by
God to perform saving ordinances (e.g., baptism) and to correctly in-
terpret the scriptures. While recognizing goodness in all humankind
and partial truth in all religious movements, the Latter-day Saints
(ironically, like fundamentalist Protestants) see themselves as the
only "true" church, a view by which members of other Christian denominations are inevitably offended. Particularly problematic for
most fundamentalists and evangelicals were the Book of Mormon's
acceptance as scripture and an expansive view of humankind's potential that did not stop short of deification in the eternities. Because of
these theological differences and a history of interdenominational violence (Joseph Smith and his brother were murdered by nonbelievers
in 1844 in Illinois), distrust and even antipathy have long characterized Mormon relationships with other Christians.

The irony of this situation has not gone unnoticed by scholars
and political pundits. If it were not for their intense theological disagreements, Latter-days Saints would naturally be evangelicals' and
fundamentalists' best political allies. In terms of social characteristics,
lifestyle, and attitudes, evangelicals and fundamentalists share a
closer kinship with Latter-day Saints than with any other Christian
church.

A number of significant social characteristics demonstrate the
conservative, family-oriented LDS lifestyle:

- 87 percent of LDS adults have been married, a higher perecn-
  tage than Protestants, Catholics, and Jews.[8]

- The Mormon divorce rate is lower than that of Protestants but higher than that of Catholics and Jews.[9]
- 58 percent of LDS members said that premarital sex is always wrong while 34 percent of mainline Protestants and 25 percent of Catholics gave the same answer. 90 percent of LDS said extramarital sex and homosexuality are always wrong compared to about three-fourths of Protestants and two-thirds of Catholics.[10]
- Utah has the highest birthrate and lowest rate of out-of-wedlock births.[11]
- Only 28 percent of Latter-day Saints drink alcohol compared to 65 percent of Protestants, 85 percent of Catholics, and 86 percent of Jews. 14 percent of Mormons smoke compared to 36 percent of Protestants, 38 percent of Catholics, and 28 percent of Jews. (Unlike the other groups, Mormons have a strict health code flatly prohibiting alcohol and tobacco.)[12]
- Over 86 percent of LDS high school seniors' religious views were similar to their parents'. The next highest rate of youth conformity occurred among Baptists (almost 75 percent).[13]
- LDS youth were the most engaged in practicing their faith, followed, in this order, by evangelical Protestants, black Protestants, mainline Protestants, Catholics, and Jews.[14]
- Utah is the only state in the nation to not have any "dropout factories" (high schools in which no more than 60 percent of its freshmen make it to their senior year and actually graduate).[15]
- 18 percent of LDS women and 22 percent of LDS men have graduated from college, a rate "significantly higher than the comparable percentages among Protestants and Catholics, but lower than among Jews and those with no religious affiliation."[16]
- Latter-day Saints give more to their church than any other denomination (an average of 5.2 percent of their income). The next highest were evangelical Protestants (1.8 percent).[17]
- Because of the LDS Church's extensive welfare and self-help program, Utah spends 14 percent of its budget on public welfare in contrast to the national average of about 22.4 percent.[18]

Latter-day Saints, like many conservative Protestants, believe the United States is a divinely appointed nation with Judeo-Christian values. It is, or should be, as John Winthrop and the early Puritans proclaimed, "a city sette upon a hill." For Mormons, however, the special place of the American continent in general and the United States in particular are theologically grounded in the Book of Mormon and the Doctrine and Covenants. The Book of Mormon refers to America is referred to as a "land of promise" and "a land which is choice above all other lands" (1 Ne. 13:30). Doctrine and Covenants 101:77 praises U.S. laws and its Constitution as being established "for the rights and protection of all flesh, according to just and holy principles." Participation in the political process by informed voting, running for political office, and supporting good public causes therefore is a religious as well as a civic responsibility.

Although the voting history of Mormons displays broad variations over time, at present they overwhelmingly vote Republican, another factor that should create a strong alliance with the religious right. As of 2000, about 69 percent of white evangelicals were Republican (or leaned in that direction), and a strong majority believe that evangelical Christians influence George W. Bush's administration. In 2000, 88 percent of Mormon voters cast their ballots for George W. Bush, the largest percentage of any religious group. Even religiously active white evangelical Protestants trailed with 84 percent, while practicing Catholics gave Bush 57 percent. In 2004, 71.5 percent of Utahns voted for Bush, his highest percentage in any state; overall, 85–90 percent of Latter-day Saints lined up behind Bush.[19]

An analysis of the thirty-one red and twenty blue states (including the District of Columbia) from the 2004 presidential election, compared to a 2001 survey of red and blue states, quickly concluded: "The higher the percentage of the population that identifies as Protestant or Mormon, the greater the likelihood that the state voted Republican." All of the thirteen states that were at least 60 percent Protestant or Mormon were red. Of the twenty-eight states that were 40-50 percent Protestant or Mormon, sixteen were red and twelve were blue. In those sixteen red states, the Protestant or Mormon majority successfully garnered support from Catholics and other conservative voters.[20]

So many Latter-day Saints vote Republican that, as early as 1992, people were voicing fears that the Utah Republican Party would eventually become the Mormon party and the Democratic Party the non-Mormon party. During the 1980s, up to 70 percent of the active Latter-day Saints voted Republican while the same percentage of non-Mormons voted Democrat. A national study conducted by New York University found that Mormons were "the most Republican of any church membership in the country."[21]

Mormon block voting is not new, but the party affiliation is. When the Republican Party was founded in 1854, one of its purposes was to end "the twin relics of barbarism"—southern slavery and Mormon polygamy. Until the 1890s when the Church dissolved its own "Peoples Party" and influential General Authorities began recruiting Mormons into the Republican Party, the relationship between the Republican Party and the LDS Church was confrontational. Former affiliates of the Peoples Party did not have to be recruited into the Democratic Party, which granted Utah its long-awaited statehood in 1896. It wasn't until the first decade of the twentieth century that the Utah Republican Party had large numbers of Latter-day Saints. After that time, Utah continued to be very conservative; but it was also a closely bipartisan state, often splitting its statewide and congressional offices between the two parties.

But that changed in the late 1960s. During this volatile period, large numbers of Mormons, like their conservative Protestant counterparts, reacted negatively to the perceived radicalization of the Democratic Party. Many felt that it no longer reflected mainstream Utah values. As Congressman Rob Bishop (R-UT) explained in 1998, the national Democratic Party became so liberal that "the Democrats got out of the stream, up on the left bank and waved as the majority of Utahns floated by." Indeed, more than one Latter-day Saint has commented, "I didn't leave the Democratic Party, the party left me."[22]

Republican dominance continued to worry LDS Church leaders throughout the 1990s and into the new century. On at least one occasion, in 1998, leaders assured Church members that there are also conservatives in the Democratic Party and that good Church members could be Democrats. Church leaders, who are very sensitive about being publicly neutral in political races, were "troubled" that one-party dominance would undermine the checks-and-balances principle of democratic government.[23] Of even greater concern to Church leaders was the possible long-term damage of tying the Church to one political party. Some fundamentalists express similar concerns. Ed Dobson wrote, "When pastors become entangled too deeply with politics, they harm the gospel of Jesus Christ. Jesus becomes synonymous with a political party or platform."[24]

Like conservative Catholics and Protestants, members of the LDS Church have been attracted to the conservative Republican social and family values from the 1960s on. And while the LDS Church takes a very strict neutrality stance on political campaigns, Church leaders assert the right to speak out on "moral issues." Throughout the 1970s and into the 1980s, the LDS Church encouraged a well-organized campaign against the ratification of the Equal Rights Amendment on moral grounds. In the process, Church members joined both Catholics and conservative Protestants in fighting the amendment.

In the early 1990s, the Church also issued formal statements of opposition to assisted suicide and pornography in Oregon and against legalized gambling in several states. Also in the 1990s and in the twenty-first century's first decade, the LDS Church has teamed up with the Catholic Church and other conservative denominations in well-organized campaigns to stop the legalization of gay marriage. In California the Church strongly encouraged fundraising and campaigning by members in support of Proposition 22 (the "Knight Initiative"), which recognized only heterosexual marriages as "valid." This proposition passed. The Church directed similar campaigns in a number of states including Colorado, Hawaii, Nevada, and Oregon, and pushed for a constitutional amendment in "defense" of heterosexual marriage.[25]

In the process of taking on the ERA in Nevada and other states, the Latter-day Saints and Catholics formed an "old right coalition" and worked on a limited basis with other religious denominations. As the Moral Majority and the new Christian Right gained momentum, political pundits and scholars began to discuss the possible Mormon-religious right coalition.[26] Given Jerry Falwell's attempt to attract other conservative organizations like Sun Myung Moon's Unification Church into the Moral Majority, some observers felt that the Latter-day Saints and the new religious right would inevitably form permanent bonds. Their positions on so many social issues from abortion to pornography have been "virtually indistinguishable." In fact, conservative Protestants "were generally closer to the Mormons than to Mainline Protestants."[27]

Nevertheless, such an alliance has not emerged, possibly because the differences are significant. While Latter-day Saints are conservative, they are generally well educated and middle-class, two traits that keep most of them from being radically right-wing.[28] The Moral Majority, in contrast, are mainly southern, fundamentalist, less educated, and lower-middle class. Falwell's gestures of inclusiveness probably exceeded the actual hospitality his members were willing to extend, and Mormons' "non-Christian" differences were a theological and ideological chasm that could not be bridged. According to some critics, fundamentalists are "militant extremists who demand that others embrace their way or hit the highway."[29] "Among the various inter-religious hostilities in American history, probably none has been so violent or prolonged as that between Mormons . . . and assorted fundamentalist/Baptist . . . groups." The LDS Church has been attacked as "a cult in a variety of books, tracts, and films. . . . The Mormons, conversely, have had little love for the persecution and impugning of their right to call themselves Christians that has resulted from such unremitting criticisms."[30] Furthermore, according to Anson Shupe and John Heinerman, two conservative critics of Mormonism, "Protestants have traditionally outnumbered the Mormons and had the upper hand politically," resulting in ideological friction between them and physical violence perpetrated upon the Mormons (but not, apparently, by Mormons upon other denominations). Patrick Q. Mason cited 320 documented cases of violence against Mormons in the South between 1876 and 1900: beatings, clubbing, whippings, destruction of churches and meeting places, tarring and feathering, and even murder. Mormons shared the unpleasant distinction of being social pariahs, with local law winking at violations of their protection. In 1886 the *Alabama Baptist* editorialized: "It is Mormonism itself that is to be hated, to be feared, to be crushed."[31] Although in more contemporary times Mormon missionaries have been kidnapped and murdered in the former Soviet Union and in South America, and even though LDS chapels in South America have been the targets of bombings and vandalism, these assaults overseas seem to have been more anti-American than anti-Mormon.

Although stopping short of bloodshed, some animosity continues to the present. A 1987 survey of conservative Protestants, mainline Protestants, Catholics, Mormons, and Jews found that "the greatest degree of intolerance or social distance manifest by any one religious group towards another [was] that of the Conservative Christians [Protestants] for the Mormons." Mormons were more tolerant of conservative Christians, but not by much.[32] Observers who confidently predicted an alliance between the religious right and the Latter-day Saints either ignored or underestimated the strength of this mutual distrust. What they should have been paying attention to was the fact that collaboration on specific projects with Southern Baptists, conservative Protestants, and Catholics has continued, thanks in large part to LDS leaders' pragmatic approach to politics.

An Anti-Religious-Right Bias and Shifting Trends

Given the religious right's traditional willingness to dish it out to Mormons, its own feelings of persecution are a little ironic. "Feeling persecuted has special resonance for Christians," notes Steven Waldman, editor-in-chief of Beliefnet, because "it's Christ-like." They are probably not wrong in claims of being attacked verbally and in the media. Such portrayals reinforce "tired and false elitist stereotypes about religious believers." What especially angers members of the religious right is that the media not only ignores blatant examples of anti-evangelical bias but sometimes seems to encourage it.[33]

The rather unsettling results of a survey conducted by the Institute for Jewish and Community Research among university faculty across the country in the spring of 2007 showed that over half of non-evangelical university professors hold unfavorable views of evangelical Christians. Only 30 percent hold favorable views, and a startling 71 percent agreed with the statement, "This country would be better off if Christian fundamentalists kept their religious beliefs out of politics."[34] Another straw blowing in the anti-evangelical wind was reaction to the HBO documentary, *Friends of God*, which was a visual attempt to discover and understand American evangelical Christians by visiting areas with evangelical dominance (i.e., the South) and interviewing a number of individuals about their faith and lifestyle. After the documentary aired, *New York Times* television critic Alessandra Stanley characterized the Bible belt as "the Loire Valley of American extremism," and Tom Shales of the *Washington Post* characterized the documentary as "a tour through another America that is sometimes funny, sometimes touching, and sometimes scary as hell." As evidence, "The Christians we see in this film are unyielding in the rightness of their ideas . . . and if someone challenges them, they simply say God has told them the truth."[35]

As another example, Mark Morford, a San Francisco newspaper columnist, linked the deplorable state of America's public schools with evangelicals: "We are now at a point where we are essentially churning out ignorant teens who are becoming ignorant adults and society as a whole will pay dearly, very soon, and if you think the hordes of easily terrified, mindless fundamentalist evangelical Christian lemmings have been bad for the soul of this country, just wait."[36]

While some evangelicals read these attacks as proof that they have been chosen to suffer for their fidelity to Christ, others have shifted to a more moderate stance, emphasizing issues like peace, taking care of the poor, and global warming. In the words of CBS News anchor Katie Couric, a "chasm" is appearing between "progressive" evangelicals and "traditional" evangelicals in "the God-war" about whose values will be represented in the national government.[37] According to Couric and some other commentators, some evangelicals see their best strategy as distancing themselves from the "traditional" agenda. Rev. Jim Wallis, founder of the left-leaning evangelical Sojourners, openly critiqued traditional evangelicals. "If I'm an unborn child and I want the support of the far religious right I better stay unborn as long as possible because once I'm born I'm off the radar screen. No health care, no child care, no nothing."[38]

Another critic of traditional evangelicals is the Rev. Gregory Boyd, a Minnesota mega-church pastor. In his May 2006 book, *The Myth of a Christian Nation: How the Quest for Political Power Is Destroying the Church*, and a series of sermons during the 2004 presidential campaign, he attacked the U.S. self-image of being "the light of the world and the hope of the world." He also "chastised the 'hypocrisy and pettiness' of evangelicals who dwell on 'sexual issues' like homosexuality and abortion. American evangelicalism, he said, 'is guilty of nationalistic and political idolatry.'" The politically conservative *Weekly Standard* suggested that he "may represent a trend among a new generation of evangelical clergy who want to overturn conservative stereotypes about the evangelical culture."[39]

Michael Luo and Laurie Goodstein, writing in the *New York Times*, heralded the evangelical shift "in potentially momentous ways in recent years" that has broadened the religious right's agenda, exposed new fissures, and produced "a new generation of leaders who have mostly avoided the openly partisan and confrontational approach of their forebears." They characterized the new leaders as "more likely to speak out about more liberal causes like AIDS, Darfur, poverty, and global warming than controversial social issues like abortion and same-sex marriage." That is because some evangelicals feel "the Christian Right moral agenda has been too narrow and too partisan."[40]

Wallis wrote exuberantly:

> Evangelicals—especially the new generation of pastors and young people—are deserting the Religious Right in droves. The evangelical social agenda is now much broader and deeper, engaging issues like poverty and economic justice, global warming, HIV/AIDS, sex trafficking, genocide in Darfur and the ethics of the war in Iraq. Catholics are returning to their social teaching; mainline Protestants are asserting

their faith more aggressively; a new generation of young black and Latino pastors are putting the focus on social justice; a Jewish renewal movement and moderate Islam are also growing; and a whole new denomination has emerged, which might be called the "spiritual but not religious."[41]

Yet despite announcements of this shift away from such evangelical standards as opposition to abortion and gay marriage to more moderate issues like global warming, other conservatives have declared the so-called shift to be mere wishful thinking by liberals. They insist that, while some evangelicals have branched out into other issues, the majority are steadfast in their defense of moral or family values. And as a majority counted in the millions, they are frustrated that only an aberrant minority is getting the positive press.[42]

Public image is not, however, the only frustration for the religious right. Apparently others are battling a more depressing demon—the feeling of failure and abandonment.[43] Republicans in both the executive and legislative branches have backed away from the very issues that helped elect them. Furthermore, many national leaders of the religious right seem out of touch with their members, no longer holding sway over the large followings they accumulated up through the new millennium.[44] As David Kuo of the *Washington Post* put it, the 2008 presidential primaries clearly demonstrated that "the old religious right, a hierarchical group dominated by larger-than-life figures who'd anointed themselves [as] Jesus's political representatives" were "becoming politically marginalized and out of touch with an increasingly independent evangelical flock."[45]

Problems between the Religious Right and the Republican Party

Religious right leaders and members alike grumble that the Republican Party courts them and flourishes "God talk" speeches during every election cycle, but promptly forgets them when the election is over. Donald Wildmon, chairman of the American Family

Association, commented bitterly in 2007, "Every six months before an election, Republicans are our best friends, and six days after the election, they don't even know us."[46] Conservative columnist Cal Thomas called leaders of the religious right "religious-political alchemists" and reported their complaints that "they had been faithful foot-soldiers for the Republicans, doing the grunt work necessary to get any candidate elected, from knocking on doors to staffing phone banks. And what did they get for their efforts? They got nothing, or little more than lip service."[47]

The religious right had expected better from George W. Bush, a proud "born-again" evangelical. Yet Bush has angered fundamentalists and evangelicals by, for example, suggesting that Christians, Muslims, and other believers pray to the same god. Adding to their anger is what they perceive as Bush's inaction on values legislation. They may simply be expecting too much from a government designed to make changes slowly and to work in a system of give and take. The fact that Bush's approval ratings were at near-record lows nationally and that the Republicans lost both houses of Congress in 2006 meant that unpopular values-oriented legislation had to take a back seat to more critical and more demanding issues. Even in Mormon Utah, the reddest state in the union, support for Bush and his policies fell from 56 percent in January 2007 to 47 percent in October 2007, but this approval rating was still well above the national average, which stood at a paltry 24 percent in October. Furthermore, Bush was still receiving a 65 percent approval rating among Utah Republicans in October.[48]

Religious right dissatisfaction boiled over into the 2008 presidential race which quickly became the most religion-riven race since 1960 when John F. Kennedy became the first and, so far, only Catholic elected president. A fall 2007 Pew poll on religion and politics reported that 70 percent of Americans wanted a president with strong religious beliefs. Claims of America's rapid secularization notwithstanding, "there [was] more mixing of religion and politics" than in 1960. Furthermore, the "high level of discussion on faith and values" was occurring in both parties, not just among Republicans.

The impact of religion on a person's worldview became an especially hot topic among Democratic candidates and their supporters.[49] While members of the religious right should have been happy with the renewed emphasis on religion in the presidential campaigns, they were not. For one thing, some segments disliked their selections in both major parties. The early first-tier Republican candidates were lapsed Catholic Rudolph ("Rudy") Giuliani, former mayor of New York City, and practicing Mormon W. Mitt Romney, former governor of Massachusetts. Senator John McCain, who had a history of difficulties with evangelicals and whom conservatives had never trusted, was a distant third in most polls.[50] Dissatisfied members of the religious right coaxed Fred Thompson, who infrequently attended the Church of Christ, into the race. A former moderate U.S. Senator from Tennessee, he retired a few years ago after a rather undistinguished career to return to acting. He came in as an embarrassing third behind both Huckabee and Romney in the Iowa caucus as a result of a lackluster campaign that disappointed conservatives.[51] His presidential aspirations had essentially ended by January 22, 2008.

Whispers of a religious right revolt began in September of 2007. Tony Perkins, president of the Family Research Council, based in Washington, D.C., publicly declared that Giuliani was virtually "indistinguishable" from Hillary Clinton, then the Democratic front-runner. Particular concern focused on Giuliani's liberal position on such social issues as abortion and gay rights.[52] Conservative Christian leaders met in Salt Lake City the first weekend in October to interview GOP candidates and discuss who, if any, they should support. After intense discussion, they announced that they would not then declare support for any of the candidates but would seriously think about fielding a third-party candidate if Giuliani were nominated.[53] Wildmon acknowledged, "The only reason to go third party is to hurt another party, as Ross Perot did and Ralph Nader did."[54] That is exactly what the religious right was in the mood to do.

Editorialist Kathleen Parker recognized the irony of their decision: "Evangelical Christians never had it so good, but they seem not to know it. Instead of supporting the candidate who most shares their values—Mitt Romney—they seem hell-bent for the proverbial cliff."

Wildmon presented a less destructive explanation: "They [the Republicans] may not win with us, but they cannot win without us. The leadership needs to think seriously and long about that proposition."⁵⁵ However, purposely hurting the Republican Party would only "further marginalize them [the religious right] and their cause," as Roger Simon, chief political columnist of *Politico*, pointed out. In the following weeks, some religious right leaders agreed, backpedaled a little, and began to consider the advantages of supporting Romney, even though he was considered to be a cultist.⁵⁶

Once again demonstrating both the fragmentation and the seething discontent among the rank and file of the religious right, many of them attached themselves to former Arkansas governor Mike Huckabee, who billed himself as a "Christian leader."⁵⁷ After having traveled the long, often frustrating, and bitter road to political power, members of the religious right have experienced victories and defeats. By the spring of 2008, with Romney out of the race, they again faced the unpleasant prospect of candidates they would rather not support. Although they were spared from Mormon Mitt, a "non-Christian cultist" from a religion they have traditionally despised, the other Republican choice was John McCain, a candidate whose previous voting record and outspoken dislike for the Christian conservative leadership had offended their conservative values. They had the choice of looking elsewhere for political and religious relief or dancing with the devil.

Notes

1. Michael Lienesch, "Right-Wing Religion: Christian Conservatism as a Political Movement," *Political Science Quarterly* 97, no. 3 (Autumn 1982): 418.

2. George M. Marsden, *Reforming Fundamentalism: Fuller Seminary and the New Evangelicalism* (Grand Rapids, Mich.: William B. Eerdmans, 1987), 48; "Fundamentalist View of New Evangelicalism," http://wayoflife.org/fbns/fundamen1.htm (accessed October 22, 2007).

3. Ibid.; "Fundamentalism: Militant vs. Passive," Pilgrim Fundamentalist Baptist Press, http://www.pfbaptistpress.org/102.htm (accessed October 18, 2007).

4. Karl Keating, "Fundamentalist vs. Evangelical vs. Protestant," *Catholic Answers* 117 (June 2003), http://www.catholic.com/newsletters/kke_030617.asp (accessed October 18, 2007); "Fundamentalist View of New Evangelicalism"; Bruce Buursma, "Dissension Is Growing among Fundamentalists," *Chronicle-Telegram*, September 3, 1981.

5. Mary Bendyna et al., "Catholics and the Christian Right: A View from Four States," *Journal of the Scientific Study of Religion* 39, no. 3 (September 2000): 321–22.

6. Ibid., 324–26, 330.

7. Mary E. Bendyna and Mark J. Rozell, "Uneasy Alliance: Conservative Catholics and the Christian Right," *Sociology of Religion* 62, no. 1 (Spring 2001): 52.

8. Tim B. Heaton and Kristen L. Goodman, "Religion and Family Formation," *Review of Religious Research* 26 (1985): 343–59, as quoted in Stephen J. Bahr, "Mormon Statistics," *Light Planet*, http://www.lightplanet.com/mormons/daily/social _eom.htm (accessed October 19, 2007).

9. Bahr, "Mormon Statistics."

10. Ibid.

11. Lee Davidson, "Utah's Birthrate Is Highest in the Nation: But Out-of-Wedlock Birthrate Is Lowest," *Deseret Morning News*, April 18, 2001, as quoted in "Sampling of Latter-day Saint/Utah Demographics and Social Statistics from National Sources," Adherents.com (September 16, 2005), http://www.adherents.com /largecom/lds_dem.html (accessed 10 June 2008).

12. Bahr, "Mormon Statistics."

13. Christian Smith et al., *Are American Youth Alienated from Organized Religion?* (Chapel Hill: National Study of Youth and Religion, University of North Carolina at Chapel Hill, 2004), 15.

14. "Study: Most U.S. Teens Serious about Religion," MSNBC, posted February 23, 2005, http://www.msnbc.msn.com/id/7019023 (accessed October 27, 2007).

15. Nancy Zuckerbrod, "1 in 10 Schools Are 'Dropout Factories,'" ABC News (October 30, 2007), http://abcnews.go.com/US/wireStory?id=3790483 (accessed June 10, 2008). While Utah has low poverty rates and fewer minorities, one of the main reasons for the high graduation numbers is the culture of education encouraged by the LDS Church.

16. Bahr, "Mormon Statistics." According to Terrell H. Bell, former U.S. Secretary of Education, "Latter-day Saints have a significantly higher level of edu-

cational attainment than does the population of the United States as a whole." Bell, "Educational Attainment," *Encyclopedia of Mormonism* vol. 1 (New York: Macmillan, 1992) as quoted on Light Planet, http://www.lightplanet.com/mormons /daily/education/Attainment_EOM.htm (accessed October 30, 2007). According to Anna Greenberg and Jennifer Berktold, "Evangelicals in America," April 5, 2004, http://www-tc.pbs.org/wnet/religionandethics/week733/results.pdf (accessed June 14, 2008), 2, approximately 22 percent of white evangelicals have a four-year college degree, in contrast to approximately 40 percent of the total LDS population.

17. Daniel L. Chen and Jo Thori Lind, "The Political Economy of Beliefs: Why Fiscal and Social Conservatives and Liberals Come Hand-in-Hand," Appendix Table 3, http://folk.uio.no/jlind/papers/Political%20Economy%20of%20Beliefs.pdf (accessed October 18, 2007).

18. Maria Titze, "Utah's Budget Slice for Schools Highest in Nation," *Deseret News*, April 28, 2000 as quoted in "Sampling of Latter-day Saint/Utah Demographics and Social Statistics from National Sources." The LDS Church emphasizes self-sufficiency. Members temporarily unable to provide for themselves are expected to go to their family and church before seeking public welfare. The Church maintains farms, ranches, factories, canneries, and other facilities throughout the United States and Canada where members volunteer their time in processing food and making other supplies for needy members. It also maintains a chain of thrift shops that act as sheltered workshops in teaching trades to the physically or mentally handicapped and which encourages donations of clothing, furniture, appliances, books, etc., from members. Between 1985 and 2007, the Church provided humanitarian assistance in 165 countries with totals estimated to be almost $260 million in cash and $750 million in material assistance. In the process, it has cooperated with other religious and relief organizations including the Adventist Development and Relief Agency, Catholic Community Services, Catholic Outreach, First African Methodist Episcopal Church, Islamic Relief Worldwide, Japanese Church of Christ, and Lutheran Social Service of Utah. The Church of Jesus Christ of Latter-day Saints, "Welfare Services Factsheet—2007," http://www.providentliving.org/welfare/pdf/ 2006WelfareFactSheet.pdf (accessed April 30, 2007); "Humanitarian Activities Worldwide," Provident Living webpage, http://www.providentliving.org/content/ display/0,11666,4600-1-2323-1,00.html (accessed April 30, 2008). According to David Haldane, "U.S. Muslims and Mormons Share Deepening Ties," *Los Angeles Times* April 2, 2008, http://www.latimes.com/news/local/la-me-morlims2apr02,1, 2488142.story (accessed April 2, 2008), the Mormon Church has become the

biggest contributor to Islamic Relief and has donated $20 million in goods and services since 2004.

19. "LDS Vote Went to Bush," *Deseret News*, January 26, 2001; David Finkel, "Utah Town Has Question about President: 'What's Not to Like?'" *Washington Post*, http://www.washingtonpost.com/wp-dyn/content/article/2006/01/30/AR200601 3001608.html (January 31, 2006); Kevin Phillips, *American Theocracy: The Peril and Politics of Radical Religion, Oil, and Borrowed Money in the 21st Century* (New York: Viking, 2006), 413. While 88 percent of Mormons voted for Bush in 2000, numerically they accounted for only 2 percent of the total vote; white evangelical Protestants constituted 26 percent of the total votes for Bush while Catholics accounted for another 19 percent.

20. James D. Davidson, "Red States, Blue States: It's about Religion," http://www.the-tidings.com/2004/1112/signs_text.htm (accessed October 29, 2007).

21. Paul Rolly, "Mormon Democrats Fear Parties Dividing along Religious Lines," *Salt Lake Tribune*, February 16, 1992.

22. Bob Bernick Jr., "GOP Doesn't Pander to LDS Voters, State Leader Says," *Deseret News*, May 1, 1998, B2; Ralph Wakley, "Bishop: Mormons Went GOP during the '60s," *Ogden Standard Examiner*, May 2, 1998, 1C, 2C. At the time of these articles, Rob Bishop was the chairman of the Utah Republican Party. He was elected to Congress in 2002.

23. Dan Harrie, "GOP Dominance Troubles Church," *Salt Lake Tribune*, May 3, 1998, A1, A20.

24. Dobson's chapter in Cal Thomas and Ed Dobson, *Blinded by Might: Can the Religious Right Save America?* (Grand Rapids, Mich.: Zondervan Publishing House, 1999), 80. See also Martha Sonntag Bradley, *Pedestals and Podiums: Utah Women, Religious Authority, and Equal Rights* (Salt Lake City: Signature Books/ Smith-Pettit Foundation Book, 2005).

25. Peggy Fletcher Stack, "LDS Church Takes Stand on Suicide, Pornography Ballot Measures in Oregon," *Salt Lake Tribune*, October 1, 1999; Carrie A. Moore, "LDS Church Joins Gay-Marriage Fight," *Deseret News*, October 4, 1998; "Vote to Eliminate Lottery, Arizona LDS told," *Deseret News*, October 4, 1998; Peggy Fletcher Stack, "Gays Oppose LDS California Activism," *Salt Lake Tribune*, July 10, 1999, D1, D2; Jan Ferris, "Mormons Take 'Family Values' to Polls," *Sacramento Bee*, September 27, 1999; Affirmation: Gay & Lesbian Mormons, http://www.affirmation.org/news/1999_52.shtml (accessed June 10, 2008); Hallye Jordan, "Churches Defend Role in Campaign," *San Jose Mercury News*, December 27,

1999; Robert Gehrke, "Bush, LDS Church Unite on Marriages," *Salt Lake Tribune*, June 6, 2006, http://www.sltrib.com/portlet/article/html/fragments/print_article.jsp ?article=3903718 (June 6, 2006); Richley H. Crapo, "Chronology of Mormon/LDS Involvement in Same-Sex Marriage Politics," 1997, http://cc.usu.edu/~fath6/ldschron .htm (accessed October 31, 2007). In May 2008 the California Supreme Court struck down the ban on same-sex marriage. The LDS Church was quick to respond by issuing an official statement on May 16, 2008 that read, "The Church of Jesus Christ of Latter-day Saints recognizes that same-sex marriage can be an emotional and divisive issue. However, the Church teaches that marriage between a man and a woman is ordained of God and that the family is the basic unit of society. Yesterday's California Supreme Court decision is unfortunate." See "Church responds to California Supreme Court Same-Sex Marriage Decision," LDS Newsroom, May 16, 2008, http://newsroom.lds.org/ldsnewsroom/eng/commentary/church-responds-to -california-supreme-court-same-sex-marriage-decision (accessed June 10, 2008).

26. O. Kendall White, "A Review and Commentary on the Prospects of a Mormon New Christian Right Coalition," *Review of Religious Research* 28, no. 2 (December 1986): 180.

27. Anson Shupe and John Heinerman, "Mormonism and the New Religious Right: An Emerging Coalition?" *Review of Religious Research* 27, no. 2 (December 1985): 154; Merlin B. Brinkerhoff et al., "Mormonism and the Moral Majority Make Strange Bedfellows? An Exploratory Critique," *Review of Religious Research* 28, no. 3 (March 1987): 236; and White, "A Review and Commentary," 183.

28. Peggy Fletcher Stack and Jessica Ravitz, "The LDS Church in America: Redefining the Mormon Empire," *Salt Lake Tribune*, March 30, 2008, http://www .sltrib.com/utah/ci_8732985 (accessed April 1, 2008), reconfirmed the middle-class make-up of the Latter-day Saints. Over half of the American Mormons have had at least some college education and over half of the members earn $50,000 or more.

29. White, "A Review and Commentary," 183; Shupe and Heinerman, "Mormonism and the New Religious Right," 152; Phillips, *American Theocracy*, 156.

30. Shupe and Heinerman, "Mormonism and the New Religious Right," 146.

31. Ibid., 155; Patrick Q. Mason, "Sinners in the Hands of an Angry Mob: Violence against Religious Outsiders in the U.S. South, 1865–1900" (Ph.D. diss., Notre Dame University, 2005), 281, 127. He is citing an editorial in the Selma *Alabama Baptist*, April 22, 1886.

32. Brinkerhoff et al., "Mormonism and the Moral Majority Make Strange Bedfellows?" 240–42.

33. Steven Waldman, "The Real Reasons Evangelicals Love Bush," Beliefnet, 2006, http://www.beliefnet.com/story/152/story_1521.html (accessed November 2, 2007); and Kristen Fyfe, "Friends of God *Not* Friendly to Evangelicals," *Culture and Media Institute*, February 5, 2007, http://www.cultureandmediainstitute.org/articles /2007/20070205141805.aspx (accessed October 30, 2007). See also Colleen Raezler, "Media Ignores Study Revealing Anti-Evangelical Bias," *Culture and Media Institute*, May 8, 2007, http://www.cultureandmediainstitute.org/articles/2007/ 20070508135600.aspx (accessed October 30, 2007).

34. Audrey Barrick, "Survey Suggests University Faculty Bias against Evangelicals," *Christian Post*, May 9, 2007, http://www.christianpost.com/article/ 20070509/survey-suggests-university-faculty-bias-against-evangelicals.htm (accessed October 19, 2007). The Institute for Jewish & Community Research was created, according to its home page found at http://www.jewishresearch.org/about .htm (accessed June 10, 2008), to conduct survey research on religious prejudice.

35. Robert Knight and Kristen Fyfe, "TV Critics Smear 'Scary' Bible Belt," *Culture and Media Institute*, January 29, 2007, http://www.cultureandmediainstitute .org/articles/2007/20070129124015.aspx (accessed October 30, 2007).

36. Mark Morford, "American Kids, Dumber than Dirt: Warning: The Next Generation Might Just Be the Biggest Pile of Idiots in U.S. History," SFGate, October 24, 2007, http://www.sfgate.com/cgi-bin/article.cgi?f=/g/a/2007/10/24/ notes102407.DTL&hw=&sn=002&sc=749 (accessed October 30, 2007); Kristen Fyfe, "'Easily Terrified, Mindless Fundamentalist Evangelical Christian Lemmings': Columnist Links Religious Belief and 'Dumber than Dirt' Generation of Teens," *Culture and Media Institute*, October 24, 2007, http://www.cultureandmediainstitute .org/articles/2007/20071024181552.aspx (accessed October 30, 2007). Examples of attacks against the character and purposes of those in the religious right by scholars, media, and bloggers are plentiful in both print and electronic format.

37. Kristen Fyfe, "CBS, ABC Embrace Left-Wing Christians, Greet Conservatives with Skepticism," *Culture and Media Institute*, October 19, 2007, http:// www.cultureandmediainstitute.org/articles/2007/20071019174131.aspx (accessed October 30, 2007); Sven Erlandson, "The Irony of Evangelical Political Growth and Waning Spiritual Influence," Associated Content, 2007, http://www.associatedcontent .com/article/354487/the_irony_of_evangelical_political.html?cat=34 (accessed August 31, 2007).

38. Quoted in Fyfe, "CBS, ABC Embrace Left-Wing Christians."

39. Mark D. Tooley, "The Evangelical Left," *Weekly Standard*, August 10, 2006, http://www.weeklystandard.com/Content/Public/Articles/000/000/012/534ymruw.asp (accessed September 17, 2007).

40. Michael Luo and Laurie Goodstein, "Emphasis Shifts for New Breed of Evangelicals," *New York Times*, May 21, 2007; Jane Lampman, "Signs of a Truce in America's Divisive Cultural War?" *Christian Science Monitor*, October 11, 2007, 2.

41. Jim Wallis, "The Religious Right's Era Is Over," *Time*, February 16, 2007, http://www/time.com/time/nation/article/0,8599,1590782,00.html (accessed March 28, 2008).

42. Colleen Raezier, "Are Evangelicals Really Becoming Environmentalists? Wishful Thinking from the *Washington Post*," *Culture and Media Institute*, August 8, 2007, http://www.cultureandmediainstitute.org/articles/2007/20070808192348.aspx (accessed October 30, 2007); Hugh Hewitt, "Is the Religious Right Finished?" Townhall.com, October 10, 2007, http://hughhewitt.townhall.com/blog/g/11b3c310-4c96-4309-b6c7-577328152e90 (accessed October 10, 2007).

43. Bill Murchison, "Fall of the Religious Right?" Townhall.com, October 30, 2007, http://www.townhall.com/columnists/BillMurchison/2007/10/30/fall_of_the_religious_right (accessed October 30, 2007).

44. Marc Ambinder, "Republicans and Evangelicals: Yes, This Marriage Can Be Saved," *Weekly Standard*, September 18, 2006, http://www.weeklystandard.com/Utilities/printer_preview.asp?idArticle=12680&R=138EEF68F (accessed September 5, 2007).

45. David Kuo, "It's Not Your Father's Religious Right," *Washington Post*, February 24, 2008, http://www.washingtonpost.com/wp-dyn/content/article/2008/02/22/AR2008022202383.html (accessed February 25, 2008).

46. Quoted in Micelle Vu, "Presidential 'God Talk' Not Enough, Says Evangelical Leader," *Christian Post*, August 6, 2007, http://www.christianpost.com/article/20070806/presidential-god-talk-not-enough-says-evangelical-leader.htm (accessed August 31, 2007); Ralph Z. Hallow, "Religious Right Aims 'to Hurt' GOP," *Washington Times*, October 5, 2007, http://www.washingtontimes.com/news/2007/oct/05/religious-right-aims-to-hurt-gop (accessed 6 October 2007).

47. Thomas's chapter in Thomas and Dobson, *Blinded by Might*, 140.

48. Cal Thomas, "The Same God?" Townhall.com, October 9, 2007, http://www.townhall.com/columnists/CalThomas/2007/10/09/the_same_god (accessed October 10, 2007); "Under the Weather," *The Economist*, August 9, 2007, http://www.economist.com/world/na/displaystory.cfm?story_id=9619083&CFID=139663

76&CFTOKEN=93953816 (accessed August 31, 2007); Matthew D. LaPlante, "Even in Republican Utah, Support for Iraq War and Bush Fading," *Salt Lake Tribune*, November 2, 2007, http://www.hinckley.utah.edu/events/media/eveninRepublicanUtah.pdf (accessed June 10, 2008); and John Whitesides, "Voters Unhappy with Bush and Congress," *Reuters*, October 17, 2007, http://www.reuters.com/article/topNews/idUSN1624620720071017?feedType=RSS&feedName=topNews&rpc=22&sp=true (accessed June 11, 2008).

49. Jane Lampman, "Faith's Role on the Rise in Campaign 08," *Christian Science Monitor*, September 12, 2007, http://www.csmonitor.com/2007/0912/p13s02-lire.htm (accessed September 14, 2007); "Religious Adherence of 2008 Candidates High on Voters' Minds," FoxNews.com, July 30, 2007, http://www.foxnews.com/story/0,2933,291434,00.html (accessed August 21, 2007).

50. Donald Lambro, "In Search of the Right Candidate," *Washington Times*, October 18, 2007, http://www.washingtontimes.com/news/2007/oct/18/in-search-of-the-right-candidate/ (accessed October 18, 2007); and Ralph Z. Hallow, "Christians Riven by '08 GOP Field," *Washington Times*, October 18, 2007, http://www.washingtontimes.com/news/2007/oct/18/christians-riven32by-08-gop-field/ (accessed October 18, 2007); Donald Lambro, "For GOP, a Paradox in the Polls," Townhall.com, October 4, 2007, http://www.townhall.com/columnists/DonaldLambro/2007/10/04/for_gop,_a_paradox_in_the_polls (accessed October 8, 2007).

51. Iowa Caucus Results," *New York Times*, January 3, 2008, http://politics.nytimes.com/election-guide/2008/results/states/IA.html (accessed June 10, 2008).

52. "Religious Right Leader: Giuliani Same as Hillary," NewsMax.com, October 10, 2007, http://www.newsmax.com/insidecover/giuliani_hillary/2007/10/10/39725.html (accessed October 11, 2007).

53. Carol Platt Liebau, "Dobson's Ultimatum," Townhall.com, October 15, 2007, http://www.townhall.com/columnists/CarolPlattLiebau/2007/10/15/dobsons_ultimatum (accessed October 16, 2007). The irony that their decision was made in Salt Lake City, LDS Church headquarters, did not go unnoticed either by political pundits or Romney supporters.

54. Hallow, "Religious Right Aims 'to Hurt' GOP."

55. Kathleen Parker, "Christians for Self-Defeat," Townhall.com, October 5, 2007, http://www.townhall.com/columnists/KathleenParker/2007/10/05/christians_for_self-defeat (accessed October 8, 2007).

56. Roger Simon, "GOP Rift Sends Christian Right Adrift," *Politico*, October 11, 2007, http://www.politico.com/news/stories/1007/6300.html (accessed October

11, 2007); Michael Luo, "Letter Urges Conservative Christians to Support Romney," *New York Times*, October 11, 2007, http://www.nytimes.com/2007/10/11/us/politics/11repubs.html?_r=1&sq=&st=cse&adxnnl=1&oref=slogin&scp=1&adxnnlx=1216495465-kB3RRMikzZwkP1Cl0B8SnA (accessed July 19, 2008); Ralph Z. Hallow, "Evangelicals Warming to Romney," *Washington Times*, October 11, 2007, http://www.washingtontimes.com/news/2007/oct/11/evangelicals-warming-to-romney/ (accessed on October 12, 2007).

57. "Christian Leader," *Washington Post*, December 21 2007, A34. The newspaper editorial mentioned, "An earlier Huckabee ad in Iowa opened with the words 'Christian leader' emblazoned on the screen."

Chapter 3
A Political History of the Latter-day Saints

In the Doctrine and Covenants, a compilation of revelations, doctrinal instructions, and ecclesiastical procedure, the Lord, speaking through his prophet, Joseph Smith, declared: "All things unto me are spiritual."[1] Nineteenth-century members of the Church of Jesus Christ of Latter-day Saints interpreted that statement literally. As a result, all aspects of life—society, commerce, domestic relations, politics, and government—were within the purview of Church control. While this approach to the gospel of Jesus Christ tightened the bonds of loyalty among adherents, it also proved detrimental for their interaction with their non-Mormon neighbors.

Early Latter-day Saints espoused a millenarian view of their place in time and society. Not only were they living in the end-time before Jesus Christ's second coming, they had the privilege of preparing for that glorious event by preaching the good word and establishing the kingdom of God. They, as heirs of the restored gospel, would set all things in order that the "kingdom of heaven may come" and "the millennial reign of Jesus Christ begin."[2]

Primary to Mormon doctrine was the belief that the United States was the only country with sufficient freedom to allow the gospel of Jesus Christ to be restored in preparation for God's kingdom. In fact, it had achieved freedom from Great Britain to fulfill this divine destiny. And while the United States government was certainly not the kingdom of God, it nevertheless had an inspired foundation and a special status above all other nations.

Mormons were not the only Americans who ascribed special status to the United States. From the founding of New England to the present, many conservative Protestants have viewed the United States as a divinely appointed nation with Judeo-Christian values— or, as John Winthrop and the early Puritans proclaimed, "a city sette upon a hill." For Mormons, however, the special place of the American continent and the United States, in particular, goes beyond sentiment and theory. Both the Book of Mormon and the Doctrine and Covenants contain affirmations of the nation's special status in LDS theology. The Book of Mormon frequently refers to America as a "land of promise" or "a land which is choice above all other lands" (e.g., 1 Ne. 2:20, 1 Ne. 13:30, Ether 2:12, Ether 13:2). The concept of a choice land is reinforced in the Doctrine and Covenants, in which the Lord announces: "For this purpose have I established the Constitution of this land, by the hands of wise men whom I raised up unto this very purpose, and redeemed the land by the shedding of blood . . . for the rights and protection of all flesh, according to just and holy principles (D&C 101:77, 80). Joseph Smith reinforced these teachings in a prayer, now canonized, for the protection of Mormons then being harassed in Missouri: "May those principles which were so honorably and nobly defended, namely, the Constitution of our land, by our fathers, be established forever" (D&C 109:54). Joseph Smith also taught that "the Constitution of the United States is a glorious standard; it is founded in the wisdom of God. It is a heavenly banner."[3]

Because American Latter-day Saints in particular, but also many Latter-day Saints in other countries, believe in the inherent greatness and goodness of this nation and the Constitution as divinely inspired, much has been spoken and written over the years celebrating this nation and form of government. For example, Wilford Woodruff, fourth president of the LDS Church, declared in 1889, that "those men who laid the foundation of this American government were the best spirits the God of heaven could find on the face of the earth. They were choice spirits . . . [and] were inspired of the Lord." In the twentieth century, Ezra Taft Benson, Secretary of Agriculture in Dwight D. Eisenhower's administration (1953–61) and thirteenth president of the LDS Church (1985–94), taught that America is "a consecrated land" chosen by God to be "a place of many great events" for spreading the gospel of Jesus Christ.[4]

While Mormons placed great love and trust in the Constitution, they also had significant concern about evil and corrupt people in positions of power. Because of the persecution early Latter-day Saints experienced, they recognized the truth in the revelatory utterance, that "it is the nature and disposition of almost all men, as soon as they get a little authority, as they suppose, they will immediately begin to exercise unrighteous dominion" (D&C 121:39). This point has been repeatedly emphasized in Mormon speeches and publications. For example, in 1835 a general assembly of church members adopted a declaration of belief regarding governments and laws. The very first point reads: "We believe that governments were instituted of God for the benefit of man; and that he holds men accountable for their acts in relation to them, both in making laws and administering them, for the good and safety of society" (D&C 134:1).

At another point, Joseph Smith recorded: "When the wicked rule the people mourn." Therefore, "honest men and wise men should be sought for diligently . . . otherwise, whatsoever is less than these cometh of evil" (D&C 98:9-10). The fear that the Constitution might be overthrown and their rights trampled on was compounded by neighborly tensions so severe that the Latter-day Saints had to leave New York, Ohio, Missouri (twice), and Illinois, always accompanied by violence or threats of violence. Despite federal refusal to intervene in these contretemps, Mormon devotion to the Constitution remained strong. Joseph Smith reportedly even prophesied at one point that the day would come "when the destiny of the nation will hang upon a single thread. At this critical juncture, this people will step forth and save it from the threatened destruction."[5]

To the present, Church members have speculated about this time of Constitutional peril, usually in the context of what they see as a current threat. It even entered Mitt Romney's campaign briefly. While there are various interpretations of this "hang by a thread" concept, practically all agree that the Constitution and country will be saved through Mormon efforts. Brigham Young, second Church president, commented in 1854, "Will the Constitution be destroyed? No: it will be held inviolate by this people; and, as Joseph Smith said, 'The time will come when the destiny of the nation will hang upon a single thread. At that critical juncture, this people will step forth and save it from the threatened destruction.' It will be so."[6]

Coupled with this time of danger to the Constitution is a prophecy allegedly received by Joseph Smith which foretold a time of turmoil and conflict immediately preceding the second coming of Jesus Christ. While this view is generally held by all believers in New Testament descriptions of the apocalypse, the purported Joseph Smith revelation symbolizes future events and conditions using the Apostle John's imagery from Revelation 6:1-8, describing the four horsemen. As a result, the alleged Joseph Smith prophecy is known as the White Horse Prophecy. The prophecy itself is controversial. On the one hand, it uses idioms and language Joseph Smith is known to have used in his sermons and teachings. Moreover, its two witnesses, Edwin Rushton (1824–1905) and Theodore Turley (1801–71), were well-respected Mormons in Nauvoo and, hence, were in a position to have heard Joseph Smith make the statement.

Raising questions about its veracity, however, is the fact that their accounts were not recorded until the mid-1850s, more than a decade after the event. Several copies of these accounts are archived in the LDS Church Historian's Office, while another copy of Edwin Rushton's version appears in the unpublished diary of John J. Roberts of Paradise, Utah, as cited by George Cobabe but without the date of Roberts's diary entry. John J. Roberts (1854–1922) (who actually appeared to have been John T. Roberts) did reside in Paradise, Utah, located in Cache Valley near the Idaho border. Although Cobabe cites Roberts's diary, the diary itself is not known to be available. According to Cobabe's posting on his website, Roberts's diary entry quoting Rushton reads:

> On or about the sixth day of May, 1843, a Grand Review of the Nauvoo Legion was held in Nauvoo. The Prophet Joseph complimented them for their good discipline and evolutions performed. The weather being hot, he called for a glass of water. With the glass of water

in his hand he said, "I will drink to your toast to the overthrow of the mobocrats," which he did in the following language:

"Here's wishing they were in the middle of the sea in a stone canoe with iron paddles and that a shark swallowed the canoe and the Devil swallowed the shark and himself locked up in the northwest corner of Hell, the key lost and a blind man hunting it."

The next morning a man who had heard the Prophet give the toast returned to visit the mansion of the Prophet and so abused him with bad language that the man was ordered out by the Prophet. It was while the two were out that my attention was attracted to them, and hearing the man speaking in a loud tone of voice, I went towards them, the man finally leaving. There were then present the Prophet, Theodore Turley and myself [Edwin Rushton]. The Prophet began talking to us of the mobbings and deriding and persecutions we as a people had endured, "but we will have worse things to see. Our persecutors will have all the mobbings they want. Don't wish them any harm, for when you see their sufferings you will shed bitter tears for them."

While this conversation was going on we stood by his south wicket gate in a triangle. Turning to me he said: "I want to tell you something of the future. I will speak in a parable like unto John the Revelator. You will go to the Rocky Mountains, and you will be a great and mighty people established there, which I will call the White Horse of peace and safety." When the Prophet said, "You will see it," I asked him, "Where will you be at that time?" He said, "I shall never go there. Your enemies will continue to follow you with persecutions and will make obnoxious laws against you in Congress to destroy the White Horse, but you will have a friend or two to defend you to throw out the worst part of the law so they will not hurt much. You must continue to petition Congress all the time, but they will treat you like strangers and aliens and they will not give you your rights, but will govern you with strangers and commissioners. You will see the constitution of the United States almost destroyed; it will hang by a thread as fine as a silk fiber." At that time the Prophet's countenance became sad, because as he said, "I love the constitution; it was made by the inspiration of God; and it will be preserved and saved by the efforts of the White Horse, and by the Red Horse who will combine in its defense. The White Horse will find the mountains full of minerals and they will become rich (at this time, it must be remembered, the precious metals were not known to exist in either the Rocky Mountains or California). You will see silver piled up in the streets. You will see the gold shoveled up like sand. Gold will be of little value then, even in a mercantile capacity; for the people of the world will have something else to do in seeking for salvation. The time will come when the banks of every nation will fail and only two places will be safe where people can deposit their gold and treasures. These places will be the White Horse and England's vaults. A terrible revolution will take place in the land of America, such as has never been seen before; for the land will be literally left without a Supreme Government, and every specie [*sic*] of wickedness will be practiced rampantly in the land. Father will be against son and son against father; mother against daughter and daughter against mother. The most terrible scenes of bloodshed, murder and rapine that have ever been imagined or looked upon will take place. [Peace] will be taken from the earth and there will be peace and love only in the Rocky Mountains. This will cause many hundreds and thousands of the honest in heart to gather there, not because they would be Saints, but for safety and because they will be so numerous that you will be in danger of famine, but not for want of seed, time and harvest [*sic*], but because of so many to be fed. Many will come with bundles under their arms to escape the calamities for and the[re] will be no escape except only by escaping and fleeing to Zion.

"Those that come to you will try to keep the laws and be one with you for they will see your unity and the greatness of your organization. The Turkish Empire or the Crescent will be one of the first powers that will be disrupted, for freedom must be given for the Gospel to be preached in the Holy Land. The Lord took of the best blood of the nations and planted them on the small islands now called England and Great Britain, and gave them great power in the nations for a thousand years and their power will continue with them that they may keep the balance of power; and they will keep Russia from sweeping her power over all the world. England and France are now bitter enemies, but they well [*sic*] be allied together and be united to keep Russia from conquering the world. The two Popes, Greek and Catholic, will eventually come together in their decline and be united. The Protestant Religions do not know how much they are indebted to Henry the VIII for throwing off the Pope's bill and establishing the Protestant faith. He was the only monarch who could do so at the time and he did it because the nation was at his back to sustain him. One of the peculiar features in England is the established Red-coat; a uniform making so remarkable a mark to shoot at, and yet they have conquered wherever they have gone. The reason for this will be known to them some day as red is seen in a different color threading through in under [sic] all history. The lion and the unicorn of England comes from there being so much blood of Israel in the nation. While the terrible things of which I have mentioned are going on, England will be neutral until it becomes so inhuman that she will interfere to stop the shedding of blood and history will be more properly understood. England and France will unite together to make peace, not to subdue the nations. She will find this nation so broken up and so many claiming government, till there will be no reasonable government. Then it will appear to the other nations, or powers, as though England had taken possession of the country. The Black Horse will flee to the invaders and will join them for they have fear of becoming slaves again; knowing that England did not believe in slavery, they will flee to them that they believe will make them safe. Armed with British bayonets, the doings of the Black Horse will be terrible." Here the Prophet said he could not bear to look longer upon the scenes as shown to him in vision and he asked the Lord to close the scene.

Continuing, he said, "During this time the great White Horse will have gathered strength, sending out Elders to gather the honest in heart among the Pale Horse, or people of the United States, to stand by the Constitution of the United States, as it was given by the inspiration of God. In these days which are yet to come God will set up a Kingdom never to be thrown down, but other Kingdoms to come in to it, and those Kingdoms that will not let the Gospel be preached in their lands will be humbled until they will.

"England, Germany, Norway, Denmark, Sweden, Switzerland, Holland and Belgium have a considerable amount of blood of Israel among the people which must be gathered out. Those nations will submit to the kingdom of God. England will be the last of these kingdoms to surrender, but when she does she will do so as a whole in comparison as she threw off the Catholic power. The nobility knows that the Gospel is true, but it has not pomp enough, and grandeur and influence for them to yet embrace it. They are proud and will not acknowledge the kingdom of God or come unto it until they see the power which it will have. Peace and safety in the Rocky Mountains will be protected by the Guardians, the White and Red Horses. The coming of the Messiah among his people will be so natural that only those who see him will know that he has come, but he will come and give his laws unto Zion and minister unto his people. This will not be his coming in the clouds of Heaven to take vengeance on the wicked of the world.

"The Temple in Jackson county, Missouri, will be built in that generation. The saints will think that there will not be time to build it, but with all the help you can receive, you can put up a great temple quickly. They will have all the gold, silver, and precious stones you need, for these things will only be for the beautifying of the temple. Also, all the skilled mechanics you want, and the Ten Tribes of Israel will help build it. When you see this land bound with iron, you may look forward to Jackson County."

At this point he made a pause, and looking up as though the vision were still in view, he said, "There is a land beyond the Rocky Mountains that will be invaded by the heathen Chinese unless great care and protection be given." Speaking of the heathen nations, he said, "Where there is no law there is no condemnation; this will apply to them. Power will be given to the White Horse to rebuke nations afar off, and you obey it, for the laws go forth from Zion. The last great struggle that Zion will ever have to contend with will be when the whole of America will be made the Zion of God. Those opposing will be called Gog and Magog. The nations of the earth will be led by the Russian Czar and his power will be great, but all opposition will be overcome and then this land will be the Zion of our God. Amen."[7]

Some aspects of this quotation from Roberts's diary call into question its accuracy and credibility. Even more problematic is that the details in the text reflect the events and worldview of the later nineteenth century rather than the early middle of the century, thus bring into question when the events were actually supposed to have taken place.[8] While Joseph Smith prophesied as early as 1842 "that the Saints would yet go to the Rocky Mountains" where they would become a great people,[9] he was not known to have ever compared them to the white horse in John's Revelation. Smith was also reliably reported to have mentioned danger to the Constitution but, again, did not associate this event with the four horsemen. Furthermore, Rushton was in his seventies in the 1890s, and Turley had died in 1871. Although Rushton obviously took it seriously, it is not known whether Smith stated that his comments were an actual revelation or just a hypothesis on his part.[10] Another factor that could arouse skepticism is the extreme detail of this account—not only Joseph's exact words in a prolonged speech but also his actions and facial expressions throughout. While such an experience would have been very impressive to Rushton and Turley, it is unusual for human memory to preserve such minute details for so long a period of time. More importantly, later leaders of the Church refused to accord it status as a valid revelation.

Some who accept the prophecy as valid have interpreted the "White Horse" as a single individual who would step forward to preserve the Union, but the text clearly shows that the White Horse (assuming the prophecy to be genuine) represents the Mormons as a whole. In other words, the Constitution would be saved by the Church as a body, not just by one member. Furthermore, the Mormons would not usurp or replace the U.S. government; rather, they would come to its rescue, shoring it up and defending it from its enemies.[11] In short, even during this predicted time of crisis, the Latter-day Saints would not impose their rule on anyone else. They would, as a church, cooperate with the state in preserving liberty and democracy.

In Mormonism's early years, most Latter-day Saints could best be described as Jacksonian democrats.[12] Joseph Smith and other early members were also enthusiastic about the democratic process—with a religious twist, of course. Ironically, it was the democratic process that proved to be so difficult for the Mormons. Mormon historian

Thomas G. Alexander noted, "Few things caused the LDS church as much difficulty during the nineteenth century as single-party politics."[13]

While a number of factors caused controversy and conflict between the Latter-day Saints and others, politics was unquestionably one of the more volatile. In Missouri, for example, the abolitionist views of many Mormons offended the slave-holding majority. Even more troubling to the original settlers was the potential Mormon power that resulted from the large numbers of Latter-day Saints, many of them destitute but full of millennial expectations, moving into the western portion of the state. Mormons did not alleviate these fears when they began to purchase large tracts of Jackson County property and publicly discussed their millennial expectations of Jackson County as the Saints' gathering place. As historian Kenneth H. Winn explained, "Both the poverty and zeal of the Mormon immigrants stirred the anger and resentment of the old settlers."[14] Further exacerbating the problem with non-Mormon settlers was Mormon political activity in other western Missouri counties.[15]

For example, in Gallatin, Daviess County, Missouri, a fight broke out on election day in August 1838 between Mormons and other Missourians. Election days on the frontier were not infrequently characterized by whiskey and fisticuffs, but the fight that day developed on religious rather than party lines, as non-Mormons were determined to prevent the Mormons from voting. Already angry about a summer filled with threats of mob violence against them, Latter-day Saints had declared they would fight back and did so energetically at Gallatin. This altercation was the beginning of the so-called Mormon War of 1838 which resulted in deaths on both sides, a massacre of unarmed men and boys at Haun's Mill, the calling-up of numerous Missouri militia units, the incarceration of Joseph Smith and other leaders for up to six months, and the forced removal of thousands of Latter-day Saints during the winter of 1838–39.[16]

By the time the Latter-day Saints settled in Nauvoo, Illinois, in the spring of 1839, they believed that one of their main problems in Missouri had been a lack of political and judicial control. Therefore, they worked hard to convince the Illinois state legislature to grant a city charter that allowed sufficient powers, such that they created, in essence, a city-state. Smith and the Saints were overconfident that the city charter protected them legally and politically. Over the next few years, they did not hesitate to push their newly gained powers to the limit to establish a safe haven for their religion. Furthermore, they used their new political clout as a voting bloc to play the Whigs and the Democrats against each other in local and state elections.[17]

Not surprisingly, Mormon manipulation of local politics was extremely unpopular with non-Mormon residents in surrounding communities, leading to a cycle of confrontation, further alienation, and heightened tensions. Unfortunately, the Latter-day Saints' effort to ensure their own peace and safety backfired. Joseph Smith was assassinated with his brother in June 1844, and the Saints, under threat of further violence, crossed the Mississippi River and moved west in 1846.[18]

Added to the tension was the expanding concept of church and state as explained by Joseph Smith. For example, in 1842 a Mormon newspaper article announced, "Nauvoo, then, is the nucleus of a glorious dominion of liberty, peace, and plenty; it is an organization of that government of which there shall be no end—of that kingdom of Messiah which shall roll forth, from conquering and to conquer, until it shall be said, that 'the kingdoms of this world are become the kingdoms of our Lord, and of his Christ.'"[19] Acting in accordance with these views, Joseph Smith endeavored to lay the theological and organizational foundation for a political kingdom of God. Non-Mormons in surrounding communities, understandably, claimed that the Mormons were trying to take over that part of Illinois.

As a part of the kingdom of God's political governance, Joseph Smith, in the spring of 1844, established "the Kingdom of God and His Laws with the keys and powers thereof and judgements in the hands of his servants." Because there were a few more than fifty members of this exclusive committee, it was commonly called the Council of Fifty, but it also appears in the records as the "special council," the "general council," or "the Living Constitution." The latter name derived from the belief that they held the power and authority to act in the name of God and that their deliberations and decisions would be governed by divine inspiration.[20] Joseph was crowned king by this council. This act and the general secrecy of the Council of Fifty's activities have generally been interpreted as manifesting Joseph's political aspirations. However, as one unidentified LDS scholar explained:

> Joseph was never anointed King over the earth in any political sense. The Council of Fifty, while established in preparation for a future millennial government under Jesus Christ (who is King of Kings) was to be governed on earth during this preparatory period by the highest presiding ecclesiastical authority, which at the time was the Prophet Joseph Smith. Joseph had previously been anointed a King and Priest in the Kingdom of God by religious rites associated with the fullness of the temple endowment, and was placed as a presiding authority over this body in his most exalted position within the Kingdom of God (as a King and a Priest). The fact that Joseph's prior anointing was referenced in his position as presiding authority over this body creates the confusion that he had been anointed King of the Earth. He was in fact only anointed as the presiding authority over an organization that was to prepare for the future reign of Jesus Christ during the millennium.[21]

In other words, Mormons, like other Christians, accept Jesus Christ as the King of Kings and Prince of Peace. Mormons believe that, like Melchizedek of the Old Testament, who was a king and priest to the Most High God (Heb. 7:1), subsequent prophets have been spiritually crowned kings and priests to help administrate Christ's kingdom on earth. Part of the LDS temple endowment ceremony confers the potential status on those who keep their covenants of being kings and queens, priests and priestesses, but "to the Most High God," not in any earthly, political sense. Nevertheless, they and all others are subordinate to the true King of Kings.

Furthermore, the Council of Fifty, as a political committee, was subordinate to the Church president and Quorum of the Twelve, several of whom were also members of the Fifty. The Fifty, as established by Joseph Smith, had two main purposes for the council. The first was to gain further understanding of government, the United States Constitution, and Christ's kingdom. (As a amatter of fact, because of Joseph Smith's teachings about the Constitution, Mormon historian D. Michael Quinn has called him "Mormonism's greatest Constitutionalist."[22]) The second purpose was to help find a new gathering place for the Saints, a growing necessity as a result of the problems they were experiencing in Illinois.[23]

Even before Joseph Smith's assassination, Smith and other Church leaders authorized representatives from the Council of Fifty to investigate moving the Latter-day Saints to the Pacific Northwest, the Rocky Mountains, or to Texas, then an independent republic. An intriguing "what if?" chapter in Mormon history is President Sam Houston's encouragement for the Mormons to move into the largely unsettled area known as the Nueces Strip, then a contested area between the fledgling republic and Mexico. In this scheme, the Mormons would have provided a buffer against Mexico with their Nauvoo Legion. But ultimately, negotiations failed, and the Saints moved to the Rocky Mountains and Great Basin.[24]

The Council of Fifty was also heavily involved in Joseph Smith's short-lived and ill-fated 1844 presidential campaign. However, it was never the leading body of the LDS Church, it always operated under the direction of the Quorum of the Twelve, and it never exerted any political governing authority, even in Nauvoo.[25]

The Mormons left Illinois carrying, alongside their reverence for the U.S. Constitution, a strong persecution complex and an intense sense of injustice for the federal government's failure to protect their religious rights. Documents of the time express a sense of relief at their escape from U.S. boundaries (the Great Basin was then a Mexican territory) and celebrated an "unfolding sense of liberty" as they traveled into the West, believing they were free from persecution and oppression.[26] It was only natural, then, that the new Mormon community in the Great Basin set up a government modeled on how they believed the millennial kingdom of God would be organized. The original government, which operated for fifteen months, was a theocracy, with the stake high council assuming both political and ecclesiastical functions.

In 1849 the Council of Fifty, acting under the direction of Brigham Young and the Quorum of the Twelve Apostles, helped organize a more permanent government, consisting of local probate judges, the first legislature, and a formal government entity named the State of Deseret.[27] At that point it was a theodemocracy, which meant that church and state were intertwined as "rule by God, from the top down, and government of the people, from the bottom up." The Saints, like the Puritans in seventeenth-century New England, saw no conflict with this admixture. In fact, the alternative would have been undesirable. Although a theocracy, the State of Deseret recognized "the right of liberty of conscience for all," both in politics and religion." Brigham Young explained, "We would not make everybody bow down to our religion, if we had the power; for this would not be Godlike."[28]

The Council of Fifty had always included a few nonmembers, reflecting strong Mormon beliefs concerning individual rights. This same pattern was followed in Utah. Few non-Mormons agreed to work with what they viewed as an un-American theocracy. Ironically, Latter-day Saints viewed themselves as exemplary patriots because they believed they were defending the Constitution against those in the government who were dishonoring it. According to Mormon historian David L. Bigler, "Mormons considered themselves the true inheritors of the [Constitution] because they were carrying out the divine purpose for which it was intended."[29] Brigham Young drew a sharp distinction between the Constitution and "the damned rascals who administer the government."[30]

Originally, the Latter-day Saints hoped to create a self-sustaining, independent nation where they would be free to worship as they pleased. With that in mind, they selected the beehive (*Deseret* means "honeybee") as "a symbol and model—of unified . . . orderly, cooperative work for the public well-being." From the Church's beginnings, the Saints had accepted as the best social and religious model a community that covered "all aspects of life" and encouraged "unity" between human beings and God and also between each other.[31] This view led to early attempts at communal living, first in Kirtland, then in Missouri (but not Nauvoo) during Joseph Smith's lifetime, and sporadically under Brigham Young's direction in Utah. Latter-day Saints recognized the difficulties in living the law of consecration, as it was known. Only a small percentage of members ever entered this order, and at best such communities lasted for only a few years. Their idealistic goal was to achieve unity and equality among the members, to eliminate poverty, to provide for the needs of all, and to expand the kingdom of God on Earth. While the emphasis was on meeting the needs of all, this plan did not destroy individuality. On the contrary, its basis was the energetic efforts of individuals who would selflessly share the results of their productivity. The system assumed that everyone had individual talents whose exercise would benefit the common good.[32]

Perhaps its most successful moment came in the early 1870s under Brigham Young's leadership when about 150 LDS communities entered local United Orders. There was some variation in the level of communal living they were willing to attempt. For example, the Brigham City United Order did not require members to consecrate their private property and labor to the order. Instead, the program emphasized community ownership and operation of particular enterprises. The most extreme form of the United Order, in which everyone in the community had all things in common, was practiced by only a handful of communities, Orderville in southern Utah being the best known.[33]

Perhaps one of the most controversial forms of Mormon communitarianism was the cooperative movement, also launched by Brigham Young in the late 1860s. He was contemplating the economic changes that would follow in the wake of the transcontinental railroad, completed in Utah in 1869. Zion's Cooperative Mercantile Institution (ZCMI) was created as the country's oldest department store (sold to the Frank May department store company in December 1999), and it acted as the parent company product distributor for hundreds of branch stores throughout the Great Basin.[34] Presenting a solid economic front developing home industries and patronizing them to keep cash in the territory was a sound economic policy, but it came with the inevitably hostile gesture of discouraging Church members from shopping at non-Mormon businesses. Brigham Young openly preached that non-Mormon merchants were a threat to Mormons' economic and social well-being; sometimes, Mormons who did not join the boycott were disfellowshipped by their local ecclesiastical officers.[35] There was, in fact, some evidence that some non-Mormon "merchants actually were trying to undermine the Church" by speaking out and encouraging rebellion against Church economic policies.[36] Such actions on the part of the non-Mormon merchants may have been partly because of their disdain for Church teachings and especially its leaders but were mostly because of concern for their own economic survival. The policy of boycotting non-Mormon merchants endured well into the 1880s and became a point of suspicious inquiry during the U.S. Senate committee hearings (1904–7) to investigate whether Apostle-Senator Reed Smoot should keep his seat.

Utah's isolation, which was not completely alleviated by the completion of the railroad, necessitated the Church's involvement in numerous business enterprises, both to provide capital and also to encourage necessary but costly infrastructure. During the rest of the nineteenth century, the Mormons launched, usually with limited success, a number of enterprises to help make themselves self-sufficient. These ventures included banking, communication, transportation, mining and smelting iron, cotton growing and manufacturing, silk making, sugar manufacturing, and papermaking. They also developed a highly successful and innovative cooperative irrigation system that transformed their desert kingdom. This last development was particularly significant since, for the first time, they were able to establish communities largely without competition from other settlers. They met comparatively little resistance from Native Americans, and other whites in the area had mostly been trappers and traders. Historical geographer D. W. Meinig explained, "They were thus able to apply an orderly system of colonization under centralized Church authority essentially unrestrained by United States laws and, in a word, initiate a nation-state essentially on their own terms."[37]

Because of the Mormons' physical isolation and as an extension of their desire to create their own nation-state, Mormons printed their own currency and created their own coinage. All of the gold coins had religious symbolism and were stamped with the temple motto, "Holiness to the Lord." The 1860 five-dollar gold coin had that motto written in the Deseret Alphabet, an experiment also fostered by Brigham Young that attempted to simplify the English language for the benefit of the numerous Scandinavian converts then immigrating to Utah. The goal was to create an alphabet that had "one letter for every sound, and only one sound for every letter." Despite considerable effort, "the cumbersome alphabet characters failed to capture the imagination of the church membership" and the alphabet eventually died.[38] Still, the experiment stands as evidence of how earnestly the Mormons attempted to establish their own distinctive culture, separate from that of the United States.

Another demonstration of Latter-day Saint independence was the "Deseret National Flag." While there appears to have been several versions, the most popular displayed twelve blue and white stripes and twelve blue stars, on a field of white, circling a larger blue star. The stripes represented the twelve tribes of Israel, the twelve stars the apostles, and the large star in the center Jesus Christ. The flag was flown on various occasions from the early 1850s until at least 1880.[39]

The State of Deseret was short-lived. By the terms of the Treaty of Guadalupe Hidalgo, the United States took possession of this former Mexican territory in late 1848. Nevertheless, during its short existence, the provisional government of Deseret was the Great Basin's governing entity and a functioning theodemocracy. Mormon leaders, recognizing the inevitability of U.S. control over their new homeland, in late 1849 quickly created a constitution and officially sought entrance into the union as a state.[40] This request (and five that followed) were rejected. The Territory of Utah was created with federal oversight that vexed the Latter-day Saints for the next forty-six years until it finally achieved statehood under the Democratic administration of Grover Cleveland in 1896.

Because of the State of Deseret's continued structures and the strong affiliation of its citizens, it was inevitable that the Mormon "nation" would come into conflict with the United States government. Federal appointees frequently displayed neither moral rectitude nor adequate competence, further exasperating the already reluctant LDS citizens of Utah Territory. Almost universally, these appointees were imports from the East (contemptuously called "carpetbaggers") and, therefore, often were both ignorant of and indifferent toward the territory's social and political conditions. Utah historian Everett Coolley lamented that "the Mormons were forced to put up with as unpopular a set of federal officials as ever collected a government pay check."[41]

Unfortunately, these social and ideological conflicts quickly assumed political shape. In 1857, as a result of wild tales related by federal officials who abandoned their Utah posts, claiming they were in fear of their lives, James Buchanan's administration sent a large army to Utah to put down a non-existent rebellion. Although the paucity of official records from the Buchanan administration makes an exact reconstruction of motivations difficult, a primary cause seems to have been the politicization of the slavery issue. The Republican Party, which had been founded in 1854 with the goal of ending the "twin relics of barbarism" (slavery and polygamy), had made an impressive showing in the 1856 presidential election. Because the Democratic Party was pro-slavery, it was good strategy to look tough on at least one of the two main Republican issues while diverting attention from the slavery-related violence of "Bleeding Kansas." It seems likely that Buchanan hoped to make suppressing a Mormon "rebellion" into a common cause that would unite the divided nation.[42]

Many of the troops raised from the standing army headquartered in Kansas came from the Latter-day Saints' old nemesis, Missouri. Because Washington officials refused to communicate with the Latter-day Saints in Utah about the approaching army and because of the past history of persecution, Mormons expected the worst. This time, however, they decided to stay and fight.

What became known as the Utah War of 1857–58 was, for the most part, bloodless because of Brigham Young's orders to avoid direct conflict as much as possible. Nevertheless, members of the Nauvoo Legion were able to force the troops to winter in Wyoming instead of making it all the way to Salt Lake Valley. Guerilla raids on the plains by Mormon legionnaires burned acres of prairie grass in Wyoming, making it difficult for the livestock to graze, stampeded horses and cattle, and captured and burned supply wagons.[43] Over the winter, both Mormons and non-Mormons tried to find a peaceful solution to the crisis. In the end, the Latter-day Saints allowed the army to enter the Salt Lake Valley in the late spring of 1858 and pass through to a camp southwest of the main population center of the Saints.

For their part, more than thirty thousand Mormons living north of Salt Lake City left their homes that spring and fled into Utah Valley to the south, prepared to move deeper into the mountains and fight a guerilla war against the U.S. Army. Their willingness to flee, coupled with their willingness to fight, represented the ambivalence of a basically peace-loving, religious people worked upon by the fear and anger experienced during a traumatic past of beatings, rapes, burned-out homes, and "drivings." Symbolizing their determination, they spread straw on their floors, and a few men, lit torches in hand, remained behind, prepared to burn Salt Lake City if the U.S. troops deviated from the line of march.[44]

Although the army had been informed that the city had been abandoned, they were, according to Elizabeth Cumming, wife of Governor Alfred Cumming, "not prepared for the death like stillness which existed" in the abandoned city. For its part, the army marched "in the strictest order and discipline" without breaking rank. Philip St. George Cooke, one of the army officers, removed his cap as he rode through the city "as a token of respect for the Mormon Battalion" that he had commanded a decade earlier.[45]

Although actual warfare was averted in this crisis, conflict between the LDS Church and the federal government continued, sometimes accelerating, sometimes waning, for the next four decades. A crucial issue was the separation of church and state. One vocal critic of the Mormons stated that it was "the absolute subservience of the State to the Church . . . that makes Mormonism our enemy."[46] Though overstated, this critique accurately captures the inevitable conflict between the Mormon vision of the perfect society versus the American ideals of Pluralism and Democracy. As just one example, no political parties existed in Utah before 1870, when non-Mormons in Utah formed the Liberal Party.[47] Latter-Saints reacted by forming the People's Party, but both parties simply codified denominational affiliations. "For many Liberals," observed historian Ronald W. Walker, "victory at the polls was less important than maintaining a strong doctrinaire anti-Mormonism. . . . For them, politics was not a process of building coalitions but a crusade."[48]

The Mormons also steadily sought statehood, primarily because it would bring them more autonomy than they had as a federally administered territory. Six attempts between 1849 and 1887 were rebuffed, with success coming only in 1896, after the Mormon Church had given up, at least symbolically, the strongest elements of its theocracy: its own political party, its communitarian-living experiments that held out against capitalism, and above all, plural marriage.

Opponents of the LDS Church on both the local and national level realized that plural marriage, or the plurality of wives, was an excellent rallying point in their fight against the Church's perceived power and influence. Although numerous American religious and communal experiments throughout the nineteenth-century had flourished (and usually failed), involving different interpretations of marriage and sexuality, the Mormons, according to legal historian Sarah Barringer Gordon, were "the largest, the most powerful, the most explicitly political and the best organized."[49]

"The Protestant majority in the United States responded with a series of laws, court tests, and political activities designed to break the back of the Mormon community and reshape it in the image of the remainder of the United States," summarized Thomas G. Alexander.[50] Unlike today's society, nineteenth-century Americans did not tolerate ethnic identity, including religious minorities, instead emphasizing conformity to the mainstream—pluralistic, Protestant, capitalistic, and above all, monogamous.

From the 1870s through 1887, the years D. W. Meinig described as the height of American intolerance of ethnic identity, the LDS Church and its members were the target of federal legislation aimed at forcing their submission.[51] The Edmunds Act of 1882 was followed by the Edmunds-Tucker Act in 1887, which western historian Howard Lamar described as "one of the most far-reaching pieces of federal legislation ever passed in peacetime history."[52] Legal historians Edwin B. Firmage and R. Collin Mangrum were even more critical: "Even under the most generous standards of legislative latitude, the Edmunds-Tucker Act skirted the boundaries of constitutionality. It was legislation that nakedly attacked a religious institution and imposed civil punishments on an entire group of people solely for their religious beliefs."[53]

Together these acts "disfranchised all polygamists, took control of Utah's Mormon-dominated public school system, abolished the territorial militia, disfranchised Utah women who had been given the vote in 1870, provided for the imprisonment of those practicing plural marriage, and confiscated virtually all of the Church's property." The acts also disincorporated the LDS Church and froze all assets above $50,000, which essentially bankrupted the Church; replaced local judges with federally appointed judges; required voters, jurors, and public officials to take an oath rejecting polygamy; and forced plural wives to testify against their husbands. The 1887 act even declared "all children of plural marriages to be illegitimate in the eyes of the government."[54]

The effect of this legislation on the Saints and their Church was catastrophic. Families were torn asunder as husbands and even wives had to go into hiding to avoid arrest for practicing plural marriage. To go into hiding meant not only trying to hide near their homes but sometimes living in other states, moving frequently, and changing their names. Church leaders, constantly in hiding, were seriously hampered in directing Church affairs. The ultimate threat was the proposed confiscation of the temples.[55]

To save the Church, President Wilford Woodruff issued the Manifesto in September 1890, withdrawing official approval of new plural marriages. It did not dissolve the plural unions that already existed, although Wilford Woodruff, testifying to the master in chancery in 1891 to recover Church property, when pressed, conceded that he meant for husbands to stop living with more than one wife. New plural marriages, secretly authorized by members of the First Presidency and Twelve and usually performed outside the boundaries of the United States, still continued for a period of time after the Manifesto.[56] However, the Manifesto was a watershed moment in Latter-day Saint history and introduced a new era of better, albeit not perfect, relations between the Mormons and American society.[57]

The second step toward "Americanization" was disbanding the People's Party in 1891 and encouraging members to affiliate with the two major political parties. Recognizing that Mormons tended to favor the Democrats because the Republican Party had sponsored most of the anti-Mormon legislation, LDS leaders made great efforts to create a strong two-party atmosphere in Utah. The Liberal Party disbanded two years later.[58] The economic consequences of "the Raid" had done much toward dismantling the Church's efforts in the direction of communitarianism. Thus, in 1896, Utah became the forty-fifth state in the union, thereby gaining more autonomy from the federal government. But to achieve this goal, Mormons had reluctantly given up many aspects of the religion that had made them strangers in their own land.[59]

Utah's and Mormonism's heritage is unique. As Howard Lamar observed, "What other territory has been occupied by a federal army? What other continental territory has been the subject of so much special legislation, appointive commissions, and exceptional judicial control[,] . . . has had to abandon cherished domestic institutions by manifesto, formally declare separation of church and state, and deliberately create national parties in order to get into the union?"[60]

During the twentieth century, Mormons have not only become "Americanized" but have acquired the image of conservative, super-Americans. As Donald Meinig puts it, "Mormon life today is a bastion of respectability, of staid family values, and of rock-ribbed conservatism."[61] But Latter-day Saints have always seen themselves as true patriots, even in the darkest days of conflict with the federal government. Never did the Mormons question the divine origin of the United States nor the divinely inspired Constitution, whose purity and sanctity they defended.[62]

So enthusiastic about the Constitution are members of the LDS Church that in 1987, the bicentennial of the Constitution, a number of officially-sponsored events celebrated it. These activities included speeches, a one-hour television special, museum exhibits, publication of a book about the Constitution as a divinely inspired document, and a Constitutional Bicentennial Ball in Salt Lake City, which was telecast live to Church meetinghouses where similar celebrations were being held throughout the United States and Puerto Rico.[63]

Mormon political activity goes beyond simply celebrating and glorifying the founding fathers and documents of the United States. Like their spiritual forebears, modern Latter-day Saints are encouraged to participate in the political process by voting, running for political office, and supporting good public causes. Even though Mormons are no longer trying to physically establish the kingdom of God on earth, they still consider honoring the Constitution and performing their civic duty to be part of their religious duty in preparing for Christ's second coming and the establishment of His kingdom.

Notes

1. The Doctrine and Covenants (Salt Lake City: The Church of Jesus Christ of Latter-day Saints, 1981), Section 29, verse 34; hereafter cited in-text parenthetically as D&C by section and verse. Citations to the Book of Mormon also appear in-text parenthetically by abbreviated book, chapter, and verse.

2. J. Keith Melville, "Theory and Practice of Church and State during the Brigham Young Era," *BYU Studies* 3 (Autumn 1960): 33.

3. Joseph Smith et al., *History of the Church of Jesus Christ of Latter-day Saints*, edited by B. H. Roberts, 2d ed. rev., 7 vols. (Salt Lake City: Deseret Book, 1978), 3:304.

4. Ezra Taft Benson, "Our Divine Constitution," *Ensign*, November 1987, 5; and Ezra Taft Benson, "A Witness and a Warning," *Ensign*, November 1979, 31. Other examples of speeches and articles making this point by LDS Church General Authorities are Mark E. Petersen, "The Church and America," *Ensign*, April 1970, http://www.lds.org/pa/display/0,17884,4892-1,00.html (accessed June 12, 2008); Ezra Taft Benson, "Civic Standards for the Faithful Saints," *Ensign*, July 1972, 59–61; Marion G. Romney, "America's Fate and Destiny," May 2, 1976, http://speeches .byu/reader/reader.php?id=6150 (accessed September 10, 2007); Ezra Taft Benson, "The Constitution—A Heavenly Banner," September 16, 1986, http://speeches.byu

/reader/reader.php?id=6985 (accessed September 10, 2007); Dallin H. Oaks, "The Divinely Inspired Constitution," *Ensign*, February 1992, 68–74; M. Russell Ballard, "Religion in a Free Society," devotional, America's Freedom Festival at Provo, Utah, July 5, 1992; and Dallin H. Oaks, "Some Responsibilities of Citizenship," devotional, America's Freedom Festival at Provo, Utah, July 3, 1994; photocopies in my possession. Mormon scholars publishing on the same topic in the Church's official publication are Frank W. Fox and LeGrand L. Baker, "Wise Men Raised Up," *Ensign*, June 1976, 27–38, and Robert K. Thomas and Shirley Wilkes Thomas, "Declaration of Dependence: Teaching Patriotism in the Home," *Ensign*, June 1976, 39–45.

5. Joseph Smith, quoted in Brigham Young, *Journal of Discourses*, 26 vols. (London and Liverpool: LDS Booksellers Depot, 1855–86), 7:15.

6. Ibid.

7. John J. Roberts, Diary, n.d., quoted in George Cobabe, "The White Horse Prophecy," 3, 8–9, http://www.fairlds.org/pubs/whitehorse.pdf (accessed February 18, 2008); single quotation marks standardized to double.

8. For a more detailed analysis of the White Horse Prophecy, see Appendix B of Newell G. Bringhurst and Craig L. Foster, *The Mormon Quest for the Presidency*, 282–92.

9. Roberts, *Comprehensive History of the Church*, vol. 2, 181.

10. Cobabe, "The White Horse Prophecy."

11. Ibid., 5–6.

12. Marvin S. Hill, *Quest for Refuge: The Mormon Flight from American Pluralism* (Salt Lake City: Signature Books, 1989), 56.

13. Thomas G. Alexander, *Mormonism in Transition: A History of the Latter-day Saints, 1890–1930* (Urbana: University of Illinois Press, 1986), 16.

14. Kenneth H. Winn, *Exiles in a Land of Liberty: Mormons in Amerca, 1830–1846* (Chapel Hill: University of North Carolina Press, 1989), 89.

15. James B. Allen and Glen M. Leonard, *The Story of the Latter-day Saints* (1976; 2d ed., rev. and enlarged, Salt Lake City: Deseret Book, 1992), 92–93.

16. Ibid., 133–40.

17. Ibid., 168, 190–93; and Hill, *Quest for Refuge*, 106.

18. Allen and Leonard, *The Story of the Latter-day Saints*, 224–34.

19. "Government and Institutions of Nauvoo," *Millennial Star* 3 (August 1842): 69; emphasis Smith's.

20. Klaus J. Hansen, *Quest for Empire: The Political Kingdom of God and the Council of Fifty in Mormon History* (1967; rpt., Lincoln: University of Nebraska Press, 1974), 61, 68.

21. "The Council of Fifty," FAIR Mormon, http://en.fairmormon.org/The_Council_of_Fifty (accessed February 14, 2008). FAIR Mormon is a part of FAIRlds.org.

22. D. Michael Quinn, "The Council of Fifty and Its Members, 1844 to 1945," *BYU Studies* 20, no. 2 (1980): 163.

23. Allen and Leonard, *The Story of the Latter-day Saints*, 199–201.

24. Ibid.; Hansen, *Quest for Empire*, 82–84; Michael Scott Van Wagenen, "Lyman Wight and the Texas Option of 1844: A Forgotten Mormon Alternative," in *Scattering of the Saints: Schism within Mormonism*, edited by Newell G. Bringhurst and John Hamer (Independence, Mo.: John Whitmer Books, 2007), 80–82, 84.

25. "The Council of Fifty," FAIR Mormon.

26. Richard E. Bennett, "'The Star-Spangled Banner Forever Be Furled': The Mormon Exodus as Liberty," *Nauvoo Journal* 10, no. 1 (Spring 1998): 29, 33. For the Mormon Battalion's march to California, see Norma Baldwin Ricketts, *The Mormon Battalion: US Army of the West, 1846–1848* (Logan: Utah State University Press, 1997).

27. Melville, "Theory and Practice of Church and State," 46; Allen and Leonard, *The Story of the Latter-day Saints*, 263–64, 270–71; and Hansen, *Quest for Empire*, 128–30.

28. Brigham Young, quoted in David L. Bigler, *Forgotten Kingdom: The Mormon Theocracy in the American West, 1847-1896*, Vol. 2 of KINGDOM IN THE WEST: THE MORMONS AND THE AMERICAN FRONTIER (Spokane, Wash.: Arthur H. Clark, 1998), 48; Melville, "Theory and Practice of Church and State," 54.

29. Bigler, *Forgotten Kingdom*, 36.

30. James R. Clark, "The Kingdom of God, The Council of Fifty, and the State of Deseret," *Utah Historical Quarterly* 26 (April 1958): 137; Klaus J. Hansen, "The Political Kingdom of God as a Cause for Mormon-Gentile Conflict," *BYU Studies* 2, no. 2 (Spring-Summer 1960): 251.

31. Eugene England, "Brigham's Gospel Kingdom," *BYU Studies* 18, no. 3 (1978): 10.

32. Allen and Leonard, *The Story of the Latter-day Saints*, 84–88.

33. Ibid., 365–72. See also Leonard J. Arrington, Dean L. May, and Feramorz Y. Fox, *Building the City of God: Communication and Cooperation among the Mormons*, 2d ed. (Urbana: University of Illinois Press, 1992).

34. Allen and Leonard, *The Story of the Latter-day Saints*, 331–33.

35. Ibid., 342–43.

36. Ibid., 340–42.

37. Meinig, "The Mormon Nation and the American Empire," 42.

38. William G. Hartley, "Mormon Money," in *Encyclopedia of Latter-day Saint History*, edited by Arnold K. Garr, Donald Q. Cannon, and Richard O. Cowan (Salt Lake City: Deseret Book, 2000), 774. See also M. Scott Reynolds, "The Deseret Alphabet," http://www.deseretalphabet.com (accessed February 12, 2008); Glenn N. Rowe, "Can You Read Deseret?" *Ensign*, March 1978, 60–61; and Douglas D. Alder, Paula J. Goodfellow, and Ronald G. Watt, "Creating a New Alphabet for Zion: The Origin of the Deseret Alphabet," *Utah Historical Quarterly* 52, no. 3 (Summer 1984): 285.

39. Bigler, *Forgotten Kingdom*, 48; "LDS Flag," http://www.ldsflag.com/Information.htm (accessed February 6, 2008); D. Michael Quinn, "The Flag of the Kingdom of God," *BYU Studies* 14, no. 1 (Autumn 1973): 111.

40. Peter Crawley, "The Constitution of the State of Deseret," *BYU Studies* 29, no. 4 (1989): 7–22; Edwin R. Keedy, "The Constitutions of the State of Franklin, the Indian Stream Republic, and the State of Deseret," *University of Pennsylvania Law Review* 101, no. 4 (January 1953): 526–28.

41. Everett L. Cooley, "Carpetbag Rule Territorial Government in Utah," *Utah Historical Quarterly* 26 (April 1958): 107. See also Leonard J. Arrington, ed., "Crusade against Theocracy: The Reminiscences of Judge Jacob Smith Boreman of Utah," *Huntington Library Quarterly* 24, no. 1 (November 1960): 1.

42. Allen and Leonard, *The Story of the Latter-day Saints*, 299–315. See also William P. MacKinnon, *At Sword's Point, Part 1: A Documentary History of the Utah War to 1858*, Vol. 10 of KINGDOM IN THE WEST: THE MORMONS AND THE AMERICAN FRONTIER (Norman, Okla.: Arthur H. Clark, 2008).

43. Ibid., 314–15. While the Utah War was essentially bloodless in northern Utah (for a contrary view, see William P. MacKinnon, "'Lonely Bones': Leadership and Utah War Violence," *Journal of Mormon History* 33, no. 1 (Spring 2007): 121–78), fear and general hysteria about the approaching army was a main cause for the Mountain Meadows Massacre which took place in southwest Utah. On September 11, 1857, over 120 men, women, and children were brutally murdered by

Mormon settlers and Paiute Indians. This tragedy has continued to haunt and disgust members of the Church of Jesus Christ of Latter-day Saints to the present. See Ronald W. Walker, Richard E. Turley, and Glen M. Leonard, *Massacre at Mountain Meadows* (New York: Oxford University Press, 2008).

44. Allen and Leonard, *The Story of the Latter-day Saints*, 316.

45. Ray R. Canning and Beverly Beeton, eds., *The Genteel Gentile: Letters of Elizabeth Cumming, 1857–1858* (Salt Lake City: Tanner Trust Fund of the University of Utah Library, 1977), 76; and Norman F. Furniss, *The Mormon Conflict, 1850–1859* (New Haven, Conn.: Yale University Press, 1960), 201–2.

46. J. H. Beadle, quoted in Hansen, "The Political Kingdom of God as a Cause for Mormon-Gentile Conflict," 258.

47. Ronald W. Walker, *Wayward Saints: The Godbeites and Brigham Young* (Urbana: University of Illinois Press, 1998), 225.

48. Ibid., 217–18, 225. Unfortunately, like politics in other cities and states during this volatile period in American history, contests between candidates and parties went beyond verbal exchanges. For example, according to Martha Sonntag Bradley, *Sandy City: The First 100 Years* (Sandy, Utah: Sandy City Corporation, 1993), 37, in 1875, railroader and LDS leader John Sharp, territorial chairman of the People's Party, was severely beaten by Liberal Party members outside a polling booth in Sandy City, Utah. He would probably have been killed if one of Sharp's employees on the Utah Central Railroad had not come to his aid.

49. Sarah Barringer Gordon, quoted in, Elaine Jarvik, "Visiting Professor Ties Polygamy to Constitutional Law," *Deseret News*, February 7, 2003, http://findarticles .com/p/articles/mi_qn4188/is_20030207/ai_n11377036/pg_1 (accessed June 12, 2008). For a detailed account of anti-polygamy judicial prosecution and its impact on the larger church-state issue, see Sarah Barringer Gordon, *The Mormon Question: Polygamy and Constitutional Conflict in Nineteenth-Century America* (Chapel Hill: University of North Carolina Press, 2002).

50. Alexander, *Mormonism in Transition*, 4; see also Meinig, "The Mormon Nation and the American Empire," 36.

51. Meinig, "The Mormon Nation and the America Empire," 47. Interestingly, 1887 was also the year of the Dawes Act, which, according to Meinig, "forced Native Americans to accept individual parcels of land, allow the remainder of their lands to be taken by whites, and submit to a comprehensive program of cultural change . . . and systematic suppression of Native American languages, religious ceremonies, and marriage practices," 36.

52. Howard R. Lamar, *The Far Southwest, 1846–1912: A Territorial History* (New York: Norton, 1970), 398.

53. Edwin Brown Firmage and R. Collin Mangrum, *Zion in the Courts: A Legal History of the Church of Jesus Christ of Latter-day Saints, 1830–1900* (Urbana: University of Illinois Press, 2001), 202.

54. Dennis Gafney, "Early Mormon History Explained," *Antiques Roadshow*, http://www.pbs.org/wgbh/roadshow/fts/saltlakecity_200602A18.html (accessed June 14, 2008). See also Firmage and Mangrum, *Zion in the Courts*, 202–6. Mormons termed this period of intense judicial prosecution during the 1880s "the Raid."

55. Alexander, *Mormonism in Transition*, 4.

56. See Joseph F. Smith's testimony, *U.S. Senate, Committee on Privileges and Elections, Proceedings . . . in the Matter of the Protests against the Right of Hon. Reed Smoot, a Senator from the State of Utah, to Hold His Seat*, 59th Congress, 1st session, Senate Report No. 486, 4 vols. (Washington, D.C.: Government Printing Office, 1904–7), 1:98–100. For an edition of excerpts, see Michael Harold Paulos, *The Mormon Church on Trial: Transcripts of the Reed Smoot Hearings* (Salt Lake City: Signature Books, 2008); D. Michael Quinn, "LDS Church Authority and New Plural Marriage, 1890–1904," *Dialogue: A Journal of Mormon Thought* 18, no. 1 (Spring 1985): 1–105; B. Carmon Hardy, ed., *Doing the Works of Abraham: Mormon Polygamy: Its Origin, Practice, and Demise*, Vol. 9 of KINGDOM IN THE WEST: THE MORMONS AND THE AMERICAN FRONTIER (Norman, Okla.: Arthur H. Clark Company, April 2007).

57. Allen and Leonard, *Story of the Latter-day Saints*, 418–22.

58. Ibid., 417–23; Jean Bickmore White, "Prelude to Statehood: Coming Together in the 1890s," *Utah Historical Quarterly* 62 (Fall 1994): 312–13. Church leaders were so concerned about encouraging political activity in both the Democratic and Republican parties that, according to Mormon folklore, some congregations were divided down the middle with one half of the seating assigned to the Republican Party and the other the Democratic Party.

59. Rick Philips, "The 'Secularization' of Utah and Religious Competition," *Journal for the Scientific Study of Religion* 8, no. 1 (March 1999): 75; Meinig, "The Mormon Nation and the American Empire," 51.

60. Howard R. Lamar, "Statehood for Utah: A Different Path," *Utah Historical Quarterly* 39 (Fall 1971): 308.

61. Meinig, "The Mormon Nation and the American Empire," 50.

62. Bigler, *Forgotten Kingdom*, 36, 205. Even the non-Mormon *Oakland Tribune*, October 15, 1911, noted that "the 'Mormon' people have always been true and loyal Americans. . . . All Latter-day Saints, whatever their nativity, are taught by their leaders and by their sacred books, to revere the Constitution of the United States as a divinely inspired instrument."

63. "Church Celebrates Bicentennial of U.S. Constitution," *Ensign*, November 1987, 102–3.

Chapter 4

Mitt Romney:

From Mormon Missionary to

Man with a Mission

The impact of the two cars hitting almost head-on that summer day in 1968 was instantaneous and violent. The luxury silver Citroën was crushed into a tangled heap of metal by the Mercedes which had been traveling at a high speed on the winding mountain road near Bordeaux. Leola Anderson, wife of the LDS mission president and one of the six American Mormon missionaries riding in the Citroën "suffered crushed lungs and died." The Citroën's driver was knocked unconscious and thrown from the car.[1]

The driver was still lying unconscious in the misty rain when a French gendarme found him on the side of the road. Assuming he was dead, the officer fished in the young missionary's pocket, found the passport of Willard Mitt Romney, and scrawled in pencil, *Il est mort,* "He is dead." Romney had been nearing the end of his two-and-a-half-year proselytizing mission when the accident occurred, and his parents, George and Lenore Romney, were informed by telephone that their son had been killed. It was in the middle of the night before Sargent Shriver, a personal friend of the family and U.S. ambassador to France, called to let the Romney family know Mitt was alive.[2]

George Romney had not believed his son was dead; and during those terrible hours of waiting, he never stopped having faith that Mitt was alive. Perhaps this was just a parent's intuition, but it could very well have been that the Romneys felt Mitt Romney had a special destiny.

A Heritage of Faith and Service

Romney comes from a heritage of service and sacrifice on behalf of the Church of Jesus Christ of Latter-day Saints. In fact, among Mitt Romney's forefathers was Parley Parker Pratt, one of the Church's original twelve apostles and a close associate of founding prophet Joseph Smith Jr. Pratt was killed while serving a mission.

The first Romneys in the family tree to join the LDS Church were Miles Romney and Elizabeth Gaskell Romney. Baptized in England in 1837, they immigrated to America in 1841. They then made the long, arduous journey to Utah where, in 1862, they went south to settle the desert community of St. George near the Utah-Arizona border. One of their sons, Miles Park Romney, practiced plural marriage as taught by the LDS Church. He eventually moved his plural wives and children to Mexico to escape what Mormons believed was government-sponsored religious persecution.[3]

Mitt Romney's father, George, was forced to flee from Mexico with his parents in 1912 during the Mexican civil war. While some members of the extended Romney family returned to what is known among Mormons as "the Colonies," George and his immediate family did not. They eventually made their way to Salt Lake City where they lived in poverty, having lost almost everything in their flight to safety. These experiences of tribulation and suffering strengthened, rather than weakened, the Romney resolve.[4]

"Faith can be passed from father to son, of course," comments Hugh Hewitt, "but when that faith has been upheld against persecution and treasured even through very difficult times, it becomes even more deeply ingrained in a family." Such was the case with the Romney family. They, as well as Mormons generally, view their history of persecution and hardship as evidence that their faith is "divinely ordained."[5]

Not only did the Romney family inherit a deep faith in Jesus Christ and the LDS Church, but they also inherited a strong determination to do—and to do well. In a church known for a strong work ethic and "can-do" attitude, the Romneys appear to out-do the average "can-do" attitude. In fact, so well-known are the Romneys for hard work and determination that a common saying in the Colonies was: If a Romney drowns, look upstream for the body.[6] Mitt Romney exemplifies this combination of faith and determination. What is more, he believes in himself and his mission in life. Latter-day Saints believe that God has a personal mission for each one of them; if they do all they can spiritually, emotionally, educationally, then God will guide them and, if necessary, intervene to be sure they achieve it. In other words, Latter-day Saints believe that every human being has been selected to accomplish certain things during mortality. They are not, however, predestined to succeed. Rather, success depends upon each person's faith and hard work. Mitt Romney's faith and drive are based, in great part, on his family's faith in him and his important purpose in life.

Early Years, Mission, Marriage, and Schooling

Mitt Romney should not have survived that accident almost forty years ago. In fact, he shouldn't even have been born on March 13, 1947, in Michigan, the fourth of George and Lenore Romney's children.

The pregnancy had been precarious; doctors had warned Lenore several years previously that she would not be able to have more children. Even so, as George Romney wrote at the time of his son's birth, Lenore "had a lot of faith." After delivery, "the doctor examined Lenore and announced in amazement, 'I don't see how she became pregnant, or how she carried the child.' Romney summed it up this way: 'We consider it a blessing for which we must thank the Creator of all.' From then on, Lenore referred to Mitt as 'my miracle baby.'"[7]

Continuing from what the family believed to be a miracle, other events and experiences reinforced the idea of Mitt's special destiny and shaped his worldview. Romney's LDS mission was a pivotal, life-changing experience. Many Latter-day Saints who have served a proselytizing mission say that "a mission either makes you or breaks you." Mitt Romney pretty much said the same thing when he explained, "On a mission, your faith in Jesus Christ either evaporates or it becomes much deeper. For me it became deeper."[8]

Romney's faith deepened further in the face of constant rejection. It was, needless to say, a humbling experience to work up to twelve hours a day, day after day, and to face continual disinterest in one's message. Romney had a sheltered, even privileged, childhood and youth, apparently succeeding in just about everything he attempted. In contrast, he recalled, his mission was the only time in his life when "most of what I was trying to do was rejected."[9]

Before his mission, Mitt Romney was known as a light-hearted, fun-loving jokester who entered the mission as "the free spirit of his crowd" and bent some mission rules. He described himself as "a half-hearted Mormon whose beliefs, as he recalled recently, were 'based on pretty thin tissue.'" Despite his youthful pranks and free spirit, he threw himself into his mission with the usual family zeal. Two and a half years later, he was a mature, sober, and ambitious man.[10]

The tragic 1968 car accident certainly played a role in his sudden maturation. Mitt Romney had cheated death while his mission president's wife had not. Furthermore, he had been driving the car, and while there was absolutely nothing he could have done to prevent the collision, he probably suffered some degree of survivor's guilt and depression. One way to deal with the trauma was to work even harder. While H. Duane Anderson returned to the United States with his wife's body to see to the funeral and other necessary duties, Romney, still recovering from his own injuries, helped direct the mission. It was during this difficult time and as a result of his surviving the car accident that his leadership and organizing abilities were revealed and refined.[11]

Romney's renewed zeal appears to have had a long-lasting effect. "There's nothing like hard work and time to heal the pain and sorrow of a tragic loss," he later explained. But the near-death experience also impressed on his mind that life is fragile and instilled in him a burning desire to accomplish whatever he was meant to do. Like many who have narrowly escaped death, he had a different perspective on life and mortality. Only those who have been to the edge of mortality and have, even if for only an inexplicable and uncertain moment, stared into the dark unknown of death, can truly understand the driving force that leaves a soul restless to live life to the fullest—and not only to live life to the fullest, but to achieve, to leave behind a legacy of some kind before once again standing at the edge of mortality and finally stepping through that thin veil separating life and death. "What we do with our time is not for frivolity," Romney once emphasized, "but for meaning."[12]

Mitt Romney returned from his mission with an intense desire to achieve, and the next several pivotal events that shaped his life were focused on that desire: marriage, schooling, and career choice. His first major act was to marry his high school sweetheart, Ann Davies. He later recalled that the closest he came to "a personal religious crisis" was when he was trying to decide to go on a mission. He was desperately in love with her and wasn't sure he wanted to be away from her for two and half years. In the end, it was Ann, "a convert to Mormonism from having been a once-a-year churchgoing Episcopalian," who talked him into going on his mission.[13]

Their separation, bridged only by letters, did not dampen the ardor of Mitt's feelings for Ann, and he proposed to her on the way home from the airport where she had joined his family in waiting for his plane to land from France. They were married March 21, 1969, in a civil service so that Ann's parents, who were not members of the LDS Church, could witness the ceremony. The newlyweds then flew to Salt Lake City where they were sealed "for time and all eternity" in the Salt Lake Temple.[14]

Mitt had attended Stanford University before his mission but transferred to Brigham Young University, nestled at the foot of the Wasatch Mountains in Provo, Utah, after his mission. While his year at Stanford had been less than stellar academically, he attacked his post-mission schooling with boundless energy. He graduated from the College of Humanities in 1971 and delivered two commencement speeches, one to the College of Humanities and the other to the entire graduating class. From there, he entered a joint MBA/JD program at Harvard University. He graduated in 1975 cum laude with his law degree and as a Baker Scholar in the Harvard Business School. The Baker Scholar designation is bestowed on the top 5 percent of each entering class of approximately five hundred students.[15]

Business Career

As Mitt neared graduation, he was in high demand. Charles Faris of Boston Consulting Group (BCG) recalled him as "an outstanding recruit with exceptional grades, and he was the very charming, smooth, attractive son of a former presidential candidate. So everybody was bending over backwards to get their hands on him." According to an article by Robert Gavin and Sacha Pfeiffer on Romney's business career, the young graduate hired on with BCG and quickly gained a reputation as a rising star because of his unique business skills.[16]

Romney "approached his consultant job with the complementary skills that had been sharpened during his parallel lives at Harvard. His legal training taught him to ask challenging questions, to play the role of devil's advocate, and to use an adversarial process in an effort to get answers. Business school developed his ability to reconcile conflicting data and differing points of view. It also shaped him as a leader and team builder." In the 1970s a rival Boston consulting firm began to eclipse BCG. In 1973, Bill Bain created Bain & Company which quickly became one of the top consulting firms in the nation. The vaunted "Bain way" was to do strategic audits of troubled companies from every imaginable angle, offer suggestions, and then work with the company until the recommendations were put in place. In 1977, Romney moved to Bain & Company and again began a rapid rise under the direction of his new mentor, Bill Bain.

In 1983, Bain & Company branched out and created Bain Capital, which bought promising or troubled companies, "retool[ed] them with Bain techniques," then sold them "at a profit." Mitt Romney was asked to run the new company as a partner to Bain. Known for being frugal with his own money, Romney was "especially careful with other people's money." Coleman Andrews, a Bain Capital partner, later recalled, "He never wanted to fall short on commitments or representations made to investors."

According to Gavin and Pfeiffer, the young company struggled for its first three years; but in 1986, Bain Capital made an initial investment of $650,000 in a start-up office supply company—Staples,

Inc. Today, Staples is an $18 billion company, and Bain saw an almost sevenfold profit when it sold several years later. Bain continued that same approach with other companies. In 1988, "Bain Capital used junk bonds from Drexel Burnham Lambert to finance the purchase of two Texas retailers. Junk bonds have low credit ratings and are therefore considered high risk, but also usually have high yields." The Securities and Exchange Commission had recently sued Drexel and "the man who had built its junk bond business, Michael Milken." Bain Capital went ahead and did business with them anyway. The deal was very profitable, converting a $10 million dollar investment into a return that exceeded $180 million. While the deal was profitable, the association with Drexel and Milken later came back to haunt Romney when he decided to run for office.

In the late 1980s, the parent company, Bain & Company, suffered serious financial setbacks that sent it reeling to the edge of bankruptcy. Asked to rescue the firm, Romney streamlined the company, made drastic cutbacks, renegotiated debt with banks and leases with landlords, and announced about two hundred layoffs. By 1991 he had stabilized the consulting firm, turned it over to new leadership, and returned to Bain Capital where the company continued its incredible record of financial success. Today the company manages about $9 billion in investments.[17]

A Political Family

In the midst of Romney's business successes, he also maintained a high level of ecclesiastical service in the LDS Church. Since all of its local offices are staffed by volunteers who are "called" to their positions by their ecclesiastical superiors, callings can require heavy time commitments. Beginning in 1982, Mitt Romney served for three years as a bishop in a local ward (the equivalent of a parish). Romney later described being a bishop as "a very weighty responsibility, which you take with a great deal of care and sobriety." In 1985 he was chosen as president of the Boston Stake, providing leadership and oversight to six to ten wards. He served in that position until 1994.[18]

By 1994 Mitt had seen significant success in his business career and was ready for something new. Like his father, he decided to expand his business career into politics. George Romney, after a successful business career, had served as governor of Michigan (1963–69), was a candidate for U.S. president in 1968, and then served as Secretary of Housing and Urban Development during the first Nixon administration.

Mitt, who was fifteen when his father first ran for governor, helped on both of George Romney's gubernatorial campaigns. He traveled with his father to all eighty-three Michigan counties, giving stump speeches at numerous county fairs. At the fair he would shout out, "You should vote for my father for governor. He's a truly great person. You've got to support him. He's going to help make things better."[19] Mitt then served as an intern in his father's office, even sitting in on some meetings. He also accompanied his father to the 1964 Republican National Convention where the elder Romney was treated as a rising star of the party. Although Mitt was in France during his father's unsuccessful presidential bid, he took time off from school to help his mother campaign for the U.S. Senate in 1970.[20] Politics was in his blood.

Another significant factor in Mitt's decision to enter into politics was his relationship with his father. All of his life, Mitt Romney has idolized his father, describing him as "the definition of a successful human." He explained his father's influence in an interview, "I pattern myself like him—his character, his sense of vision, his sense of purpose." "At every turn," agreed one writer in a profile, "Mitt Romney has steered his life into his father's groove, becoming a leader in the Mormon Church, a business whiz, a Republican Governor who defied his party's orthodoxy and won in a Democratic state." He even physically resembles his father, right down to the chiseled jaw and bountiful dark hair with graying temples.[21]

Finally, another important factor influenced Mitt Romney's decision to run for the U.S. Senate in 1994. Ann Davies Romney pushed him to run against Edward ("Ted") Kennedy. According to Ann's younger brother, Jim, Mitt was grumbling about Senator Kennedy's questionable escapades in Florida. Somebody needed to defeat him because he was an embarrassment to the state. Ann demanded, "Mitt, why don't you run against him?" Although Mitt demurred, she pressed him, telling him she was serious. She had faith he would win; and after analyzing the pros and cons, he jumped into the political arena.[22]

The 1994 Senatorial Campaign

By 1994, Ted Kennedy had been in the Senate for almost thirty-two years. In fact, there had been "at least one Kennedy brother in Congress for all but two of the last 48 years." The Kennedy name held, and continues to hold, great significance to a large portion of the American population. In Ted's previous reelection campaigns, he had averaged more than 66 percent of the vote, but 1994 was a difficult year for the Democratic Party with a backlash developing against the Clinton administration's policies. Congress slipped from Democratic control. Kennedy was personally struggling with some very public problems and family scandals, making 1994 the tightest race of his political career.[23]

In the early stages of the campaign, Romney appeared to have the advantage. He was close to Kennedy in the polls, even leading in some. He conveyed a well-polished public image of fitness, success, and finesse. Gerry Chervinsky of KRC Communications Research, who had been conducting campaign polling, explained, "He's younger, he's well spoken, he's good looking, and he's in shape. He has a pretty blond wife, and five kids. He doesn't smoke and he drinks milk. He's the perfect anti-Kennedy." In fact it was such a perfect image that some people questioned its genuineness. Even Chervinsky had to grudgingly admit, "His problem ultimately is that he's a little bit too slick and a little bit too light."[24] Kennedy, for one, didn't buy it. George Will reported that "Kennedy hired detectives to snoop into his past" only to discover that Romney "doesn't drink, not even Coca-Cola with caffeine. People who know him swear he never swears."[25]

Kennedy, recognizing his vulnerability, countered with an aggressive campaign. He made a number of public appearances, brought in big-name Democrats, including President Bill Clinton, and began picking at Romney's credibility. In July 1994, he launched a three-week, $650,000 television campaign that showed him "delivering the goods to his home state."[26] When Kennedy's campaign managers realized that they were not impacting Romney's campaign, they searched for other factors and found that Ampad, a company purchased in 1992 by Bain Capital, had recently purchased SCM, an office products company in Marion, Indiana. All 350 workers were laid off, then offered their old jobs back at reduced wages. The workers went on strike. Members of the Kennedy campaign traveled to Indiana, interviewed a number of disgruntled factory workers, and aired the interviews in commercials during the few weeks before election day.[27]

That was not Mitt Romney's only potential vulnerability, nor Kennedy's only negative tactic. Kennedy's campaign took its cue from John Lakian, Mitt Romney's opponent in the Republican primary. In September, as the candidates neared the primary election, Lakian sent a letter to the gay community urging them to vote against Romney, whom he called "a Mormon bishop," thereby suggesting Romney was anti-gay. The negative publicity resulting from the letter hurt Lakian more than Romney, since he had to back down and apologize. Romney beat him in the primary.[28]

Kennedy's use of the religion issue was a little more subtle than Lakian's. Even before the primary election, Kennedy had positioned himself with a liberal stand on women's issues by stating, "I count myself among the growing number of Catholics who support the ordination of women as priests." Kennedy's opinion was at odds with Roman Catholic policy, and the local Catholic newspaper criticized him for openly supporting such a position. C. J. Doyle, operations director for the Catholic League for Religious and Civil Rights, commented that Kennedy's statement was just one more example of "his lack of fidelity to Catholicism."[29]

Mitt Romney, in contrast, refused to comment. Pressed by a *Boston Globe* reporter, he simply said it would be inappropriate for him to lobby his church on liberalizing its patriarchal policies. "I do not consider it my place as a member of my church to fly out to Salt Lake City and say: 'You, who are people I believe in and trust, are wrong out here. Let me tell you how you should run your church.'"[30] Ultimately, voting Catholics and Protestants did not see women's ordination to the priesthood as sufficiently vital to be interested in the Mormon candidate's stand on that issue. So the Kennedy campaign turned next to the issue of race. Until 1978, the LDS Church did not ordain black men to the priesthood, although priesthood was freely bestowed on worthy men of every other ethnic and racial group beginning at age twelve. Speaking through Joseph Kennedy, Ted's nephew and a Democratic member of Congress, the Kennedy campaign attacked Romney and his religion for holding such arcane views on race and asked if someone of that religion should be elected to public office.[31]

Mitt Romney's response was swift and angry. He again refused to discuss his Church's policies on issues of sex and race. With his eighty-seven-year-old father standing next to him at a press conference, Romney excoriated Kennedy for stooping to religion bashing to win reelection, then declared, "In my view the victory that John Kennedy won was not for just 40 million Americans who were born Catholic, it was for Americans of all faiths. And I am sad to say that Ted Kennedy is trying to take away his brother's victory."[32]

Kennedy aides in turn responded with equal anger: "Invoking the Senator's dead brother for political purposes is reprehensible and unbecoming. This is about racial prejudice, and bias against women. No one is raising religion as an issue. What is being raised is [Romney's] indifference and silence in the face of religious bigotry and bias." In spite of Kennedy's protestations of innocence and altruism, neither the press nor the political pundits bought this attempt to deflect criticism.[33] "Of course it's about religion," commented *Boston Globe* reporter Martin F. Nolan. "Mormonism is an exotic concept in Massachusetts. It's part of [Kennedy's] game plan to create doubt about his opponent any way he can." Lou DiNatale, senior fellow in public policy at the McCormack Institute at the University of Massachusetts in Boston, agreed: "Everybody has always perceived one of Romney's fundamental weaknesses to be his high-visibility role in a church that has not traditionally had a strong position on racial and gender issues."[34] Conservative columnist Joseph Sobran was even blunter in his assessment of the Kennedy attack on Romney's religion: "The Kennedy people—such is their desperation—have calculatingly raised the religious issue. They are reasoning that the Mormon vote in Massachusetts is negligible." Sobran added: "Mormons . . . are clean-living, charitable and a little square. They all look wholesome and healthy, slim and fresh-complexioned. Their religion forbids all the things your doctor will eventually tell you to give up anyway: liquor, coffee, tobacco. The idea of a degenerate Mormon is almost a contradiction in terms." In contrast, "if there were a Least Likely to Be Mistaken for a Mormon award, Teddy would walk off with it most years."[35]

Perhaps more significantly, Senator Orrin Hatch of Utah smacked down on Kennedy for his negative campaigning. While the two are almost polar opposites in lifestyle and political leanings, they have had a strong "odd couple" friendship that has lasted for years and produced effective political alliances. According to "knowledgeable sources," however, Hatch telephoned both Ted and Joe Kennedy in separate conversations and rebuked them sharply. Hatch reportedly snapped at Kennedy, "There's no excuse for you running down my religion when you obviously have little or no knowledge about it." Both Kennedys apologized to Hatch, "but there's still tension between the two longtime lawmakers."[36]

Results among Massachusetts voters from Kennedy's attack of Mormonism showed mixed results. Some polls showed Kennedy losing ground for playing the religion card. Joseph Kennedy, who had even denounced Romney as "a member of the white boys' club," was heard to say he was struggling to dig himself out of a hole. Still, according to *Weekly Standard* publisher Terry Eastland, "The attacks had their desired effect," and Romney lost the race.[37]

Quoting Tagg Romney, the oldest of Mitt's five sons, "The defeat was jarring for Romney, who 'was embarrassed to have asked so many people to work for him without delivering results. . . . At that point he was so used to delivering—delivering shareholder results to investors, turning Bain & Company around. Losing the Senate race was a major experience with defeat.'"[38]

But the Romney campaign set to work analyzing what had gone wrong. The religious attack had taken them by surprise, perhaps because Romney advisor Charley Manning, who had "watched proudly a generation earlier when John Kennedy successfully fought off questions about his own Catholic faith," had assumed that Massachusetts and the United States were beyond using religion in politics. When he had begun advising Romney in his senatorial race, he had asked himself if religion would come up and had concluded, "No way. Even the Kennedys wouldn't sink that low." The Kennedys, however, had no such scruples and succeeded in making Mormonism seem "weird and exotic." In the future, Romney would see the Mormon question raised again and again.[39]

The 2002 Winter Olympics

After losing the race in 1994 Mitt Romney returned to Bain Capital the very next day and took up where he had left off. In 1998 Ann Romney was diagnosed with multiple sclerosis, which was a blow to Mitt and their five sons. At the time she was diagnosed, she was quite ill and had difficulty getting around. In early 1999 she took up horseback riding as a form of physical and psychological exercise. It worked wonders and, as long she doesn't get overtired, she has no physical problems. By following a very careful diet and exercise program, she was able to avoid taking drugs for the disease.[40]

By early 1999, however, the Romneys were living in Utah, where Mitt Romney was taking over as CEO and president of the Salt Lake Organizing Committee (SLOC) for the 2002 Winter Olympics. Salt Lake, after trying for more than three decades, had finally achieved its goal of hosting the Winter Olympics. Jubilation reigned when the announcement was made in Budapest in June 1995. By late 1998, however, the excitement had dissipated, and cold reality had set in. The cost of the games had been shockingly underestimated; the original projected budget of $800 million had been about one billion dollars too low. An international bribery and vote-buying scandal had erupted around the games. Consequently, potential sponsors were unenthusiastic and hard to find. State, local, and business leaders were desperately seeking a white knight to save the games and help salvage Salt Lake City's tarnished image.

In this situation, Romney's Mormonism was a plus. So was his well-deserved "reputation for business shrewdness and turnaround talent," commented Hugh Hewitt. "Because these games, like all Olympic Games, were so completely intertwined with the city that hosted, and because the city was so intertwined with the Mormon Church that founded it, an ability for the Games' leader to work with, trust, and be trusted by the LDS General Authorities was essential to the success of the Games." Romney had no interest in moving to Salt Lake and taking over the troubled games, but Ann talked him into at least visiting with the SLOC and other Utah leaders.[41]

The Romney family already owned a vacation house in Deer Valley, right next to Park City, in the Wasatch Mountains and had been planning a ski vacation to Utah for December 1998. Mitt agreed to meet with the relevant officials. Ultimately, he did more meeting than skiing. When he returned to Boston, he realized the magnitude of such an undertaking. Nevertheless, he accepted the herculean task when it was officially offered in early 1999.[42] Following the same modus operandi as on other troubled ventures, Romney immediately began an in-depth study of the situation, bringing in people he knew were up to the task. Most importantly, he worked to bring confidence and respect back to the Salt Lake Olympics, knowing that if he did not, he would not have the sponsors he needed to turn the games around.

The bidding scandal had, in Romney's words, "dispirited and devastated the psyche of this community [Utah] and probably the entire Olympic world." Inextricably tangled with the money problems were those of image. Refurbishing the games' image was crucial to reversing the hemorrhage of sponsors. Negative press across the world had given Salt Lake City and, by association, the LDS Church, a very large black eye.[43] Neither Church authorities nor Romney nor the others involved in the Olympics wanted that connection, but it was inevitable. Before the games even began, the press had coined the term "Mo-lympics." Some members of the press and other groups assumed that the LDS Church would milk the

Olympics for their PR benefit. Romney, SLOC, and the Church mutually agreed to work together, with the result that the Church received high praise from media around the world for "not proselytizing and [for] maintaining a restrained presence during the Games."[44]

And Romney had been the right man for the job. From being so deeply in debt, the Games actually earned $55 million, which is still being used to care for and promote winter sports. The negative publicity turned to positive coverage as luminaries, celebrities, Olympians, and the public weighed in with accolades. NBC Sports executive Dick Ebersol announced, "These Games surpassed my wildest expectations. Far and away the best Games I have ever been involved in." International Olympic Committee President Jacques Rogge of Belgium proclaimed them "superb Games."[45]

Romney had once again worked his magic. He and the people of Salt Lake City and surrounding communities had shown the Olympic community and the world what a community can do, and Mitt Romney had publicly announced that Salt Lake City had "shown its character, the character of the American West, independent but united if called upon to serve a greater purpose."[46]

What neither Romney nor LDS officials publicly admitted was how deeply the 2002 winter games really were the "Mormon Olympics." While the games would certainly have taken place and no doubt would have been very good, they would not have reached the level they did if it had not been for the Mormons. Recognizing the need for Church participation, Romney had worked well with top Church officials who made significant contributions in terms of money, equipment, and access to Church property and resources. Further demonstrating the Church's can-do approach, leaders encouraged Mormon members to volunteer. The SLOC had hoped for 22,000 volunteers and was dazzled by 67,000 applicants—the all-time record for volunteers at any Games.[47]

The 2002 Gubernatorial Race

As for Mitt Romney, he was named Utahn of the Year in 2001 and was being asked to run for public office even before the games had started. In fact, simultaneous talk in both Utah and Massachusetts claimed him as a candidate for governor. In Utah, he was considered a shoo-in, while even liberal Massachusetts seemed receptive to a Romney run for governor.[48] Massachusetts Republicans pressed him hard to say yes, especially since Republican governor Jane Swift's approval ratings had dropped to below 20 percent.

Romney considered the possibility with the same methodical calculation he would have applied to any business deal. He commissioned his own poll on Swift's chances. "The pollster, a longtime Massachusetts pro, said she was unelectable."[49] The Massachusetts Republican Party was reeling. In February 2002 several high-profile Massachusetts Republican activists started a "draft Romney" campaign. Polls put Romney ahead of even the Democratic candidates. Swift insisted she would run even if Romney entered the contest. By March, it was obvious Mitt Romney was going to run for governor, although he tactfully waited until Swift announced her withdrawal on March 9. Romney announced his candidacy the same day, and the two had a "show of unity" meeting in Swift's office the next day, marked by compliments and good wishes.[50] By maneuvering around Swift to become the Republican gubernatorial nominee, Romney demonstrated the shrewdness that had made him so successful in business and other ventures. By my appraisal, Romney is well-mannered, well-spoken, and charismatic. He makes friends easily and avoids making enemies. Perhaps more important, he has boundless energy and is very optimistic. In fact, the more difficult the goal, the more optimism he seems to have. He is also very tough. In business or politics, commented Larry Mankin of the Salt Lake City Chamber of Commerce, "he can be ruthless."[51]

The gubernatorial race between Mitt Romney and his Democratic opponent, state treasurer Shannon P. O'Brien, was close and heated. The Democratic Party tried to have Romney's name taken off the ballot because he had not resided in Massachusetts the previous three years. His tax records indeed showed that he was a legal resident of Utah; but he had also kept his residency in Massachusetts, thwarting that effort. Even so, his opponents did their best to portray him as a carpetbagger and again revived the 1994 portrayal of him as a heartless businessman.[52]

While taxes, budget, abortion, and gay rights formed topics of hot debate, Mitt Romney's Mormonism received only half of the news coverage it did in 1994, and O'Brian made no concerted effort to use it as a divisive factor. When Romney was elected by a 50 percent margin, Mark Shields, a CNN political commentator, exclaimed in amazement and with a hefty amount of hyperbole, "They [Massachusetts voters] just elected a Republican who's a Mormon who doesn't even live in the state." Professor Paul A. Djupe of Denison University also read religious results into the election: "Romney's election suggests that in one century we've come a long way, so that now it's perfectly acceptable to be Mormon. It also says something about the tolerance of the electorate."[53]

Mitt Romney was sworn in as the seventieth governor of Massachusetts on January 2, 2003. His four-year stint as governor was, like practically all political administrations, marked with ups and downs. Hugh Hewitt explained that Americans don't usually pay attention to the governing of other states unless there is a major disaster, and even then, successful managers don't get much credit. "By contrast Mitt Romney's four years have been unusually high profile, and for reasons mostly not of his doing." During his tenure, Romney welcomed the Democratic National Convention to Boston in 2004 and had a key speaking role at the Republican convention in New York City.[54] On the more controversial side, in 2003 when the Massachusetts Supreme Court ruled that same-sex marriage was legal, Romney became one of the decision's most outspoken opponents and a decided proponent of a constitutional amendment to ban gay marriage. On another liberal issue, he spoke out against Harvard's embryonic stem cell research as going "beyond the recognized limits of experimentation on human life in its cellular phase." This position rekindled suspicions over where Mitt Romney actually stood on such liberal issues as abortion and gay rights.[55]

While the LDS Church has been consistently opposed to abortion (except in cases of rape, sexual abuse, and danger to the mother's health) and gay rights, it takes a more neutral stand, neither opposing nor condemning, on stem cell research. In 1994 and 2002, Romney ran both of his Massachusetts campaigns as a pro-choice, pro-gay-rights candidate. He explained on more than one occasion that he was personally pro-life but respected and would defend "a woman's right to choice." It was only after the stem cell debate that Romney began to consistently refer to himself as pro-life and to claim, "My record as governor has been very clearly a pro-life record."[56]

The change has created a range of responses. Some argue that Romney had an epiphany of some sort that converted him to be strictly pro-life. Some feel he is just saying what he has to to win conservative votes. Others feel he never really was pro-choice. Shortly after a debate with Ted Kennedy in 1994, a political pundit called a friend and said, "Romney was good, but I think he might be more conservative than he let on. He seemed to be holding back." And after one of Romney's gubernatorial debates with Shannon O'Brien, she characterized Romney's abortion position as "flip-flop-flip." During the 1994 campaign, Kate Michelman of NARAL, a pro-abortion organization, demanded, "Mitt Romney, stop pretending. We need honesty in our public life, not your campaign of deception to conceal your anti-choice views."[57]

On the gay rights issue, the gay and lesbian community, as well as Romney's critics, accused him of changing his position from pro- to anti-gay rights for political expediency. Romney's office issued a statement: "Governor Romney believes Americans should be respectful of all people. What he opposes are the efforts by activist judges who seek to redefine the longstanding institution of marriage being between a man and a woman."[58]

Mitt Romney ended his governorship with mixed reviews. Fiscal concervatives were pleased with him, and his record was impressive in economic terms. When he entered the governor's office he inherited a $3 billion deficit. To alleviate the debt, Romney "cut spending, raised fees for such things as drivers' licences and gun licences and, with the help of a windfall in capital-gains taxes, turned the deficit into a $700m surplus by 2006."[59] He also made great strides regarding heath insurance and health care. On social issues, however, he seemed to alienate both sides of the spectrum with some believing he had not done enough and others thinking he had done too much. While his approval ratings earned high marks on some issues, overall, he had a 70 percent rating of fair to poor.[60]

The 2008 Presidential Campaign

Again, as with every other business, political, or personal venture Romney has considered, he carefully evaluated practically every imaginable angle of his presidential campaign and laid out the best way to win before ever embarking on the most ambitious of his ventures. As Paul M. Weyrich, social conservative and co-founder of the Moral Majority, explained, "I think he's thought through where he thinks he can win, how he thinks he can win, and what he's going to do about it."[61]

Nevertheless, campaign trails are beset with unforeseen problems, unintentional mistakes, and the whims of fate. In October 2006, even before declaring his candidacy, negative press erupted that Mitt Romney had contacted BYU alumni and Latter-day Saints through mailings and LDS-oriented periodicals for campaign donations. In fact, a large number of Latter-day Saints do appear to be supporting Romney. Although about 30 percent of Utahns are not Mormons, as of July 2007 he had raised almost $4 million for an average of $9 out of every $10 that Utahns have donated to all presidential candidates, and Provo, Utah, home of Brigham Young University, "is the top region in donations to Romney's presidential campaign." Nationally, Romney has raised 11 cents for every American, but in Utah he has raised $1.50 per person, fourteen times higher than the national average. Even more telling, six of the ten states that donated most to Romney's campaign have large LDS populations.[62]

Even so, Mitt Romney, who was described in November 2007 as "running the most traditional campaign for a Republican—raising a lot of money, concentrating on the early primary states, and paying a lot of attention to conservatives," appealed to voters across the country, particularly where he has been able to meet and talk with them in person. At that point, he was seen as the Republican candidate to beat.[63]

Romney's Competition

The 2008 presidential campaign quickly shaped up as an extraordinary one. For the first time in fifty-six years, there was no incumbent president or sitting vice-president running for president, although Hillary Clinton's campaign as the Democratic candidate has the penumbra of an incumbency. Both major parties fielded a host of candidates who tossed their hats into the ring. Diversity was the name of the game, since viable candidates at one point included a Hispanic,[64] an African American, an Italian American, a Mormon, and a woman.

Other candidates joining Mitt Romney on the Republican side included Sam Brownback, Rudolph Giuliani, Mike Huckabee, John McCain, and Fred Thompson. Sam Brownback, an attorney from Manhattan, Kansas, had been involved in state and federal government since the 1980s and was elected to the first of three terms as U.S. Senator from Kansas in 1996. His religious background is a fascinating pilgrimage. Raised a Methodist, Brownback had a pivotal religious experience in 1995 when he was diagnosed with cancer and had a tumor surgically removed. He and his family began attending a nondenominational, evangelical church called the Topeka Bible Church. In 2002 he converted to Catholicism, but his family did not. As a result, each Sunday he attends mass before accompanying his family to the Topeka Bible Church. While Brownback came in third in the Iowa straw poll, he was never able to get the money nor the support he needed and withdrew from the race in the middle of October 2007. After withdrawing, he threw his full support behind John McCain, sending out numerous emails encouraging former supporters to support McCain.[65]

Rudolph Giuliani, the two-term mayor of New York City, was often called "America's Mayor" because of his leadership on 9/11 when the World Trade Center towers were destroyed. Previous to his terms as mayor he was a U.S. district attorney. Giuliani was raised a Roman Catholic and even considered the priesthood before opting on a legal career.[66] At one point, he was seen as Romney's greatest competition, leading in the polls throughout most of 2007. He also brought a lot of personal baggage that hurt him politically. He has been married three times, had sexual scandals while mayor, and is estranged from his two children. Politically, he is pro-abortion, pro-gay rights, and anti-gun ownership. As Richard Land, president of the Southern Baptist Convention's Ethics and Religious Liberty Commission, said, "As [evangelicals] get to know him—not as the hero of 9/11 but as a supporter of tax-funded abortions—his support will decline precipitously." Moreover, he had been at odds at times with Catholic leadership.[67] After his strategy of not campaigning in Iowa in anticipation of winning big in Florida fizzled, he lost traction quickly and withdrew as a candidate at the end of January 2008.

Mike Huckabee, Arkansas's governor since 1996 and a Southern Baptist preacher, comes from Hope, Arkansas, and has a background in television and communications. Described as "a wise-cracking, guitar-strumming, Baptist preacher," he was also "an outspoken advocate of spending government money on education, and healthcare for poor children." While appealing to members of the religious right, he has also been attacked for his "liberal" record as governor of Arkansas. Political writer Robert Novak referred to him as "the false conservative" and "a high-tax, protectionist advocate of big government." Even so, in October and November of 2007, he overtook Mitt Romney in Iowa and led for the Republicans. Unfortunately, his spurt of popularity was strictly local. He remained near the bottom in national polling.[68]

John McCain, elected U.S. Senator from Arizona in 1986, came to his campaign with an impressive military record including over twenty years in the U.S. Navy. His controversial personal and political background, as well as his age (he turned seventy-two in 2008), scared away some voters, but he was a formidable candidate. He cinched the nomination by March 2008 by getting the crucial majority of superdelegates in his column. McCain was raised an Episcopalian and has repeatedly referred to himself as an Episcopalian but in 2007 began claiming to actually be a Baptist. He may have made that claim as a way of redeeming himself for his derogatory comments about the religious right during the 2000 presidential campaign.[69]

Interestingly enough, John McCain has garnered support among a significant group of Utah Mormons, including Governor Jon M. Huntsman Jr. and Utah Attorney General Mark Shurtleff. One reason for his attractiveness over Romney is that McCain, an Arizonan, has had more experience dealing with issues important to the West. Asked the predictable question about his religious preference, Huntsman explained, "Although dominated by one particular religion, I think we're heterogeneous in our thinking."[70] After dropping out of his own race, Romney, virtually without breaking stride, began campaigning and fund-raising for McCain, an impressive demonstration of party loyalty.

Fred Thompson entered the presidential race late, not officially declaring his candidacy until September 6, 2007, during a guest appearance on the *Tonight Show*, but riding a wave of great hopes from many in the religious right. A former U.S. Senator from Tennessee, he is a native of Lawrenceburg, Tennessee. He has had a varied and interesting career in government, as a lobbyist, and even as a movie and television actor, appearing most recently in a recurring role in *Law and Order*. Raised a member of the Church of Christ, he does not currently attend church. He was recently quoted saying, "I attend church when I'm in Tennessee. I'm in McLean right now. I don't attend regularly when I'm up there." Since he has been living in McLean for years, it seems to be a reasonable assumption that he is not currently associated with any church.[71]

Thompson was recruited by some on the religious right who were unhappy with the Republican selections available. They hoped that Thompson would be the "savior of the religious right" who would "galvanize the Christian conservatives" and snatch the lead from the likes of Guiliani and Romney.[72] Unfortunately, he proved to be a disappointment. His record was considerably less conservative than originally portrayed. In fact, he ran for the Senate in 1994 as a pro-choice candidate and supported some liberal legislation as a senator. Furthermore, critics have charged that some of his personal history and business transactions as a lobbyist were less than above board. Coming out in favor of abortion was probably the kiss of death as far as the religious right was concerned.[73] His brief campaign had withered by January 2008, and he ended his presidential bid after a poor showing in the South Carolina primary.

Romney's Strategy

Personal flaws and some political setbacks notwithstanding, these Republican candidates were a gifted and formidable group, and Romney recognized the difficulties in mounting a successful campaign to win the Republican nomination. Methodical as ever, he pulled together an expert campaign staff and carefully planned his campaign, right down to talking points and speeches. As early as March 2006, he had decided on the strategy of using humor to call attention to his conservative record: "Being a conservative in Massachusetts is a bit like being a cattle rancher at a vegetarian convention."[74] He also persistently used the strategy of deflecting the religion question until it became clear that he had to address it forthrightly. (See Chapter 5.)

Second, he excelled as a fund-raiser and demonstrated innovative ways to raise more. Third, Romney recognized he is not well known and spent considerable amounts of money on commercials and campaign literature to introduce and define himself to the voters. Fourth, as a related strategy, he has encouraged and even sought interviews, although almost every interview discussed his Mormonism.

For the most part, the interviews were positive toward Romney, if not always completely kind to his religion. In March 2006 the *America Spectator* had Mitt Romney on the front cover with the caption, "Romney Rocks!" The *Wall Street Journal* had an article titled, "Romney Rides High," while the *Times* of London had an article titled, "The Mormon Who Might Just Go All the Way." In May 2007 the *Washington Post* noted Romney's appeal to voters who have met with him one-on-one and, in June, announced, "Romney Gains Credibility In Early Primary States." CNN Money described Romney as "filthy rich, he's handsome, and he's the first honest-to-god businessman to have a real shot at the White House in 40 years." The *Daily Illini* declared Romney "the best solution to America's ills."[75]

While a good portion of the early news articles discussing Mitt Romney's attributes and qualifications to be president were favorable, political gadfly and satirist Joe Klein called Romney "the fastest talking presidential candidate I have ever seen" but a flip-flopper. Klein was certainly not alone in accusing him of switching positions depending upon the audience. Charges of flip-flopping and pandering plagued Romney's campaign to the end.[76]

Furthermore, many consider Romney's looks and lifestyle to be "too good to be true" and believe something must be wrong on a deeper level. One Iowa Republican complained, "With that perfect hair and those bright white teeth, Mitt is exactly the kind of polished politician I'm tired of. People want a candidate they can trust to talk truth." The "too perfect to be true" image wasn't helped when the media discovered that Romney paid almost $2,000 on makeup "consulting" during his four-year tenure as Massachusetts governor.[77]

Rudolph Giuliani capitalized on this uneasiness by warning voters to beware "this pretense of perfection." Romney responded by trying to show a more vulnerable side but didn't always seem sincere. In fact, body language expert Tonya Reiman described him as "not as committed but . . . very smooth, in a good sense. . . . It's all about charisma with him." Satirical *Radar* magazine polled Republicans on whether Mitt Romney "lies better" than Rudolph Giuliani.[78]

From the nicely coiffed hair that never seemed out of place to the tailor-made suits—even his casual clothes seemed to come straight out of *GQ* magazine—Romney's efforts to get every detail right backfired. He seemed unable to relate to the common voter. Another difficult detail was the $35 million of his own funds that he poured into his campaign.[79] Even his offer to donate his presidential salary if elected president was a reminder of his enormous wealth.[80] This image of a rich man, out of touch with common voters, combined with accusations of being a panderer and flip-flopper, were a lethal combination that Romney was unable to successfully counter.

According to friends and acquaintances, the real Romney was down-to-earth, authentic, and genuinely inspirational. In fact, even in the middle of his presidential campaign, Mitt Romney and Matt, one of his sons, went with other members of the LDS Church in the San Diego area to help clean up after fires ravaged the countryside in the fall of 2007. They spent the morning working, without fanfare or press attention, then continued campaigning that afternoon.[81]

Why did he come off in public as simultaneously stiff and slightly awkward but also glib and insincere? Presumably some of his discomfort came from portraying himself as a conservative when, in reality, he was more of a moderate with conservative leanings. By the middle of January 2008 as the failing economy replaced terrorism and the war in Iraq as the most pressing issues concerning voters, Romney was able to switch to a more comfortable role. At heart, according to political journalist and commentator Michael Scherer, Romney is a "geeky consultant, . . . a salesman and a number cruncher." Though socially stiff, he is a business genius with an enviable track record for turning around failing enterprises. This real Mitt Romney seemed to appeal to a larger number of people, but not enough to save his faltering campaign.[82]

Romney had led in the Iowa polls throughout most of the summer and into the early fall of 2007. Near the end of October, Mike Huckabee made an unexpected and very strong surge in the polls. Iowa's race promptly turned into a two-man race between Romney and Huckabee, with other Republican candidates trailing disconsolately. On January 3, propelled by the evangelical and female vote, Mike Huckabee handily won the caucuses.[83]

By the time Mitt Romney arrived in New Hampshire on January 8, 2008, the media were dismissing him as a loser, even though he had won the Wyoming county conventions and caucus on January 5. John McCain won in New Hampshire, ultimately garnering seven delegates. Although Romney received 32 percent of the vote and four delegates to McCain's 37 percent, the press described him as "suffering a humiliating loss," given the enormous time and money he had poured into a state where he had been leading by double digits only a month earlier.[84]

A week later on January 15, Romney pulled off a big and much-needed win in Michigan, topping McCain's 30 percent of the vote with a comfortable 39 percent. As a native son, it had been imperative that Romney show well. Even more importantly, Romney won 68 percent of the Republican vote, even breezing past Huckabee by five percentage points among born-again Christians. At his victory speech in Southfield, Michigan, Romney's relief was almost palpable as this win breathed new life into his campaign.[85]

On January 19, Mitt Romney experienced both triumph and defeat. The Nevada caucuses and South Carolina primaries were both held that day, and it was obvious early on that he would not do well in South Carolina. In fact, he came in a dismal fourth. Therefore, after his Michigan success he put great emphasis on Nevada rather than South Carolina where the other Republican candidates were focusing. Nevada was also the first state where the Latter-day Saints played a significant role.[86]

While 32 percent of Nevada voters are white Protestants, the 9 percent of Nevada voters who are Latter-day Saints appear to be politically involved, particularly as Republicans. In 2004, 62 percent of white Protestants voted for George W. Bush, but he garnered 82 percent of the Mormon vote. Mormons made up a quarter of the Republicans caucusing, and Romney ended up winning seventeen delegates. "Romney's strategy may have cost him some momentum nationally, however," one commentator observed, "as South Carolina's hotly contested primary received more media attention than Nevada's lightly contested GOP caucus." It was well that Romney won in Nevada given his fourth-place showing in South Carolina.[86]

Florida was the first winner-takes-all election, meaning that whoever won the majority of the vote took all of the delegates. With its diversity of race, ethnicity, and religions, Florida was also considered a good barometer for the country. Rudy Guiliani, employing a previously unheard of campaign strategy, had ignored the other primaries to put all of his efforts into Florida. Although he had held an early lead in this must-win state, by the primary on January 29, he was a distant third while Romney and McCain were virtually tied.

But in the end, McCain won—36 percent to Romney's 31 percent. Florida Governor Charlie Crist had come out in favor of McCain, which seemed to be decisive for a number of previously uncertain voters.[87]

While losing Florida was a serious setback for the Romney campaign, he soldiered on, but McCain's Florida momentum continued to move him ahead in the polls. The candidates jockeyed for position and vied for votes for Super Tuesday's election on February 5. Because twenty-four states were involved in primaries and caucuses, the day began to be called "Super Duper Tuesday" or "Tsunami Tuesday."[88] The Romney campaign pinned its hope on winning in the West, particularly in California, which had 173 delegates. Kirk Jowers, director of the University of Utah's Hinckley Institute of Politics and Romney supporter described the Golden State as "the new end-all, be-all," which would hopefully "counteract McCain's probable victories in New York and New Jersey."[89]

The Romney campaign got off to a bad start on Super Tuesday. Romney had the most delegates in the first round of West Virginia's voting but lost when John McCain's delegates threw their votes to Huckabee. It was a bitter disappointment, and the news only got worse. By that night, Mitt Romney had seven states, including Utah where 90 percent of the Republican voters voted for him. Unfortunately, California was not among them. McCain took nine states, including California, giving him more than twice the number of delegates Romney had. It struck a fatal blow to the campaign.[90]

On Thursday afternoon, March 7, Mitt Romney gave a prescheduled address at the annual Conservative Political Action Conference in Washington, D.C. Rumors were circulating among the media that he would announce the end of his campaign. The rumors were accurate, but Romney's announcement took most of his supporters by surprise.[91] He had obviously carefully evaluated the pros and cons of continuing his campaign and, ever the number cruncher, had decided that the investment had tipped past the possibility of profitable return. Romney was out of the race.

Evaluation

In retrospect, Romney's campaign suffered from a number of significant flaws. He was never able to shake the perception that he was reserving his position on crucial social issues and the related issue that he was portraying himself as more conservative than he actually was. Furthermore, he was unable to connect with a majority of the common voters. Although his ability to calculate odds and plan strategy was a genuine strength, it made him seem over-calculating.

He was also ill advised in trying to be "everything to everyone" with the result that he never settled into a natural, comfortable campaign style. More specifically, he had tried to remake himself into a Reagan conservative when he was actually a moderate, having only a dash of Reagan conservativism. When people were actually able to meet and talk to him, more often than not they became his supporters. But the electorate remained unconvinced by and uneasy with the Romney depicted by the press.

Given the Huckabee derailing in the Iowa caucuses and the rapid pace of the other primaries and caucuses, Romney was never able to completely recover. Again, he had the ability recognize that his strategy had failed and quickly remade himself during the final weeks of the rough-and-tumble contest. Those last weeks made him unexpectedly interesting, with many feeling that he was finally revealing the real Mitt. He gained a larger following and appeared to be on the verge of breaking out and achieving his goal. He may very well have succeeded in winning the Republican nomination, but there was one handicap he could not overcome. Political writer Joe Murray had described it as early as November 2007 as an elephant at every campaign stop and particularly in the polling booths. "This pachyderm, though, is not the long held Republican Party symbol; it is something more subtle, and more damning to the Romney camp. It is his Mormon faith."[92]

Notes

1. Ronald Kessler, "Romney to the Rescue: Mitt Romney's Got the Right Stuff for 2008," NewsMax.com, May 20, 2007, http://archive.newsmax.com/romney/ (accessed July 19, 2007).

2. Ibid.; Hugh Hewitt, *A Mormon in the White House? 10 Things Every American Should Know about Mitt Romney* (Washington, D.C.: Regnery Publishing, 2007), 206; Sridhar Pappu, "The Holy Cow! Candidate," *Atlantic Monthly*, September 2005, 106; Michael Kranish and Michael Paulson, "The Making of Mitt Romney: Centered in Faith, a Family Emerges," *Boston Globe*, June 25, 2007, http://www.boston.com/news/politics/2008/specials/romney/articles/part2_main?mode=PF (accessed June 25, 2007). According to Neil Swidey and Michael Paulson, "Privilege, Tragedy, and a Young Leader," *Boston Globe*, June 24, 2007, http://www.boston.com/news/politics/2008/specials/romney/articles/part1_main?mode=PF (accessed November 14, 2007), Romney was not thrown from the vehicle but was trapped between the steering column and the driver's door. All other sources state that the impact of the crash ejected him from the car.

3. Michael Kranish and Michael Paulson, "Mitt's LDS Roots Run Deep," *Deseret Morning News*, July 2, 2007, http://www.deseretnews.com/article/1,5143 ,680195678,00.html, (accessed July 2, 2007), rpt. from *Boston Globe*, June 25, 2007, http://www.boston.com/news/politics/2008/specials/romney/articles/part2_main/ (accessed June 24, 2008), part two of seven-part series, THE MAKING OF MITT ROMNEY; Preston Nibley, *Stalwarts of Mormonism* (Salt Lake City: Deseret Book, 1954), 173–74.

4. Hewitt, *A Mormon in the White House?* 210.

5. Ibid.

6. This proverbial saying is not exclusive to the Romneys. It was also applied in the same generation to Edwin Woolley, a bishop of legendary stubbornness in Salt Lake City.

7. George and Lenore Romney, quoted in Swidey and Paulson, "Privilege, Tragedy, and a Young Leader."

8. Quoted in David D. Kirkpatrick, "Romney, Searching and Earnest, Set His Path in '60s," *New York Times*, November 15, 2007, http://www.nytimes.com/2007 /11/15/us/politics/15romney.html (accessed November 15, 2007).

9. Quoted in ibid.

10. Ibid.

11. Ibid.; "President H. Duane Anderson," France Paris Mission, http://www
.mission.net/france/paris/presidents.php?prID=4731 (accessed November 12, 2007).
According to this essay, Anderson insisted on returning to France and finishing his
mission because he didn't want the Saints in Pau, whom they were en route to visit,
to blame themselves for his wife's death.

12. Quoted in Swidey and Paulson, "Privilege, Tragedy, and a Young Leader."

13. Karen Tumulty, "What Romney Believes," *Time*, May 10, 2007, http://
www.time.com/time/nation/article/0,8599,1619212,00.html (accessed November
14, 2007).

14. Hewitt, *A Mormon in the White House?* 80–81. Only LDS members in
good standing are issued recommends or permitted to enter LDS temples and participate in the sacred ceremonies.

15. Ibid., 45–46.

16. Robert Gavin and Sacha Pfeiffer, "The Making of Mitt Romney: Reaping
Profit in Study, Sweat," *Boston Globe*, June 26, 2007, http://www.boston.com/
news/politics/2008/specials/romney/articles/part3_main?mode=PF (accessed June
26, 2007). The discussion of Bain Capital that follows is drawn from this source.

17. Ibid.; Hewitt, *A Mormon in the White House?*, 51.

18. Linda Feldmann, "Mitt Romney: Proudly, Quietly Mormon," *Christian
Science Monitor*, August 9, 2007, http://www.csmonitor.com/2007/0809/p01s01
-uspo.html (accessed August 11, 2007).

19. Mitt Romney with Timothy Robinson, *Turnaround: Crisis, Leadership,
and the Olympic Games* (Washington, D.C.: Regnery Publishing, 2004), 12.

20. Swidey and Paulson, "Privilege, Tragedy, and a Young Leader."

21. Tumulty, "What Romney Believes." George Romney also served as president of the LDS Detroit Michigan Stake.

22. Ibid.; Hewitt, *A Mormon in the White House?* 87–88.

23. George Will, "Liberalism Is in Trouble Even in Mass.," *Sunday Capital*,
September 25, 1994, A12.

24. Sara Rimer, "The 1994 Campaign: Massachusetts; 'Perfect Anti-Kennedy'
Opposes the Senator," *New York Times*, October 25, 1994, http://query.nytimes
.com/gst/fullpage.html?res=9C0CEEDD143FF936A15753C1A962958260 (accessed November 13, 2007).

25. Ibid.

26. Mary McGrory, "In the Game of the Father," *Washington Post*, July 17, 1994, http://pqasb.pqarchiver.com/washingtonpost/access/72260886.html (accessed October 10, 2007).

27. Thomas B. Edsall, "These Ads Kept Mitt Romney Out of the Senate," *Huffington Post*, May 20, 2007, http://www.huffingtonpost.com/2007/05/30/these -ads-kept-mitt-romne_n_49954.html (accessed October 8, 2007).

28. "Catholicism, Mormonism Big Part of Senate Race," *Ogden Standard-Examiner*, September 11, 1994.

29. Ibid.; "Priests and Pols: Kennedy Likes Idea of Women in Clergy; LDS Rival Won't Say," *Salt Lake Tribune*, September 8, 1994.

30. Quoted in "Priests and Pols."

31. Sara Rimer, "The 1994 Campaign: Massachusetts; Religion Is Latest Volatile Issue to Ignite Kennedy Contest," *New York Times*, September 29, 1994, http://query.nytimes.com/gst/fullpage.html?res=9B01E0D7113AF93AA1575AC0 A962958260 (accessed October 8, 2007); William F. Buckley, "Kennedy Campaign Uses Religion against Foe," [Syracuse, New York] *Post Standard*, October 4, 1994, A5, for description of the LDS Church and its policies as "arcane"; Jack Anderson and Michael Binstein, "Kennedy Alienates Hatch," *Pacific Stars and Stripes*, November 6, 2007, 17.

32. Rimer, "Religion Is Latest Volatile Issue."

33. Ibid.

34. Ibid.

35. Joseph Sobran, "Kennedy Family Values," *Casa Grande Dispatch*, October 5, 1994, 4. Although Sobran's depiction of Mormons was certainly complimentary, the reality is that many Latter-day Saints, like the general American populace, suffer from weight-related issues and other problems of a sedentary population.

36. Anderson and Binstein, "Kennedy Alienates Hatch."

37. Ibid.; Hewitt, *A Mormon in the White House?* 244.

38. Tagg Romney, quoted in Pappu, "The Holy Cow! Candidate."

39. Scott Horsley, "Loss in '94 Taught Romney to Fight Back," National Public Radio, October 3, 2007, http://www.npr.org/templates/story/story.php?storyId= 14825263 (accessed October 8, 2007). According to Hewitt, *A Mormon in the White House?* 83, media criticism of both Mitt and Ann Romney could be vicious. While Mitt Romney expected it, Ann did not, and it angered her family and friends when the *Boston Globe* did "a hatchet job on her," accusing her of being too good to be true. This accusation implied that her lifestyle and activities were all for show.

As family friend Lynn Shields later explained, "She hadn't had an affair, taken drugs, hadn't gotten drunk and gotten in a car accident. It was like that was the only thing that could make her human was if she'd done some of those things, and I thought how sad that somebody who's lived a pretty good life and certainly done a lot of volunteer work and been very generous in life has been slammed for that." Not all that came out of the 1994 campaign was bad. Romney also learned he could depend upon numerous cash donations from fellow Latter-day Saints eager to see a member of their church succeed politically. During the 1993–94 campaign cycle, according to "Purchasing Power," *Deseret News,* July 9, 1995, B2, Mitt Romney received $95,275 from Utah donors, most of whom were Latter-day Saints.

40. Hewitt, *A Mormon in the White House?* 84–86.

41. Ibid., 67–68, 87; Romney and Robinson, *Turnaround,* 6–7.

42. Romney and Robinson, *Turnaround,* 7.

43. Lewis Rice, "Games Saver," *Harvard Law Bulletin,* Spring 2002, http://www.law.harvard.edu/alumni/bulletin/2002/spring/feature_1-fulltext.html (accessed November 1, 2007).

44. Larry R. Gerlach, "Church and Games: The Mormon Church and the Salt Lake Olympic Winter Games," *Global Nexus: Sixth International Symposium for Olympic Research,* 13, 15–17, 20. A longer version of this article is in *Olympika: The International Journal of Olympic Studies* 11 (2002). See also Romney and Robinson, *Turnaround,* 272–76.

45. Ibid., 377.

46. Rice, "Games Saver."

47. Ibid.; "The 2002 Winter Olympic Games," http://multimedia.olympic.org/pdf/en_report_557.pdf (accessed November 22, 2007).

48. Alexander Davis, "The Man Who Lit Salt Lake's Fire Within: Mitt Romney Presides Over Olympic Turnaround," *Market Watch,* February 8, 2002, http://www.marketwatch.com/news/story/mitt-romney-savior-salt-lake/story.aspx?guid=%7B02D7EC57%2D6270%2D491B%2DB0F5%2DD750BA623503%7D&dist=msr_11 (accessed November 9, 2007); Jeff Call, "The Fire Within," *BYU Magazine,* Winter 2002, http://magazine.byu.edu/g/?act=view&a=843 (accessed November 1, 2007). Romney may not have been the automatic Utah gubernatorial nominee that many pundits supposed. In fact, Romney may very well have been defeated in the nominating convention because the majority of Republican delegates are quite conservative, and the more active rank-and-file Republicans felt concern over Romney's pro-gay stand and especially his pro-choice position, first articulated

during Romney's Senate campaign in 1994. I heard a number of these people comment in late 2001 that Utah did not need someone as "liberal" as Mitt Romney for its governor.

49. Romney, *Turnaround*, 379–82.

50. "Issue: Governor's Race by Date: Jan. 1–April 30, 2002," *Issue Source: Massachusetts Politics and Policy Online,* http://www.issuesource.org/issue.cfm?ID=46&Mode=Background (accessed November 22, 2007); Bob Bernick Jr. and Lisa Riley, "Boston GOP Beseeching Mitt," *Deseret News,* February 22, 2002, http://deseretnews.com/oly/view/0,3949,70001352,00.html (accessed November 1, 2007); Mitch Frank, "Jane Swift Takes One for the Team," *Time,* March 21, 2002, http://www.time.com/time/columnist/frank/article/0,9565,219417,00.html (accessed November 1, 2007).

51. "Issue: Governor's Race by Date: Jan. 1–April 30, 2002"; Davis, "The Man Who Lit Salt Lake's Fire Within."

52. Pam Belluck, "The 2002 Campaign: The Accusations; Tight and Heated Race Rages in Massachusetts," *New York Times,* November 2, 2002, http://query.nytimes.com/gst/fullpage.html?res=9A07EEDA163EF931A35752C1A9649C8B63 (accessed on October 8, 2007); Fred Bayles, "Millionaire Rides Crest of Successful Olympics," *USA Today,* November 6, 2002, http://www.usatoday.com/news/politicselections/2002-11-06-romney_x.htm (accessed October 10, 2007).

53. "Some Election Quotes and Moments of Note throughout Tuesday Evening and Wednesday Morning," *Deseret News,* November 7, 2002, A14; Michael Paulson, "Romney Win Seen as Sign of Acceptance of Mormons," *Boston Globe,* November 9, 2002, rpt. *CESNUR: Center for Studies on New Religions,* http://www.cesnur.org/2002/morm.htm (accessed July 1, 2008).

54. Hewitt, *A Mormon in the White House?* 146; "Mitt Romney," *Light Planet,* http://www.lightplanet.com/mormons/people/mitt_romney.html (accessed November 13, 2007).

55. Hewitt, *A Mormon in the White House?* 146.

56. Quoted in ibid., 110–11.

57. W. James Antle III, "Mitt Romney's Choice," *American Spectator,* February 23, 2005, http://www.spectator.org/dsp_article.asp?art_id=7798 (accessed October 10, 2007). In 1994 Romney claimed to be pro-choice, in part because his mother was pro-choice when she ran for the U.S. Senate in Michigan and also because of a relative's abortion-related death. In 2005, according to Stephanie Ebbert, "Romney Releases Mother's Statement on Abortion Issue," *Boston Globe,* June 28,

2005, Governor Romney's staff released a campaign document from his mother's 1970 campaign showing she had supported abortion rights.

58. Scott Helman, "Romney's '94 Remarks on Same-Sex Marriage Could Haunt Him," *Boston Globe*, December 8, 2006, http://www.boston.com/news/local/articles/2006/12/08/romneys_94_remarks_on_same_sex_marriage_could_haunt_him.html (accessed November 22, 2007).

59. "Mr. Smooth of Massachusetts," *Economist*, July 5, 2007, http://www.economist.com/world/na/displaystory.cfm?story_id=9441455 (accessed June 14, 2008).

60. "New Poll: Romney's Approval Ratings Tanking," WBZTV.com, May 17, 2006, http://www.wbztv.com/local/Mass.Insight.Boston.2.578841.html (accessed June 14, 2007).

61. Weyrich, quoted in Michael Levenson, "Methodical Style Sets Romney Apart from GOP Rivals," *Boston Globe*, November 13, 2007, http://www.boston.com/news/nation/articles/2007/11/13/methodical_style_sets_romney_apart_from_GOP_rivals.html (accessed November 14, 2007).

62. Thomas Burr, "Romney Targets Mormon Magazine Subscribers," *Salt Lake Tribune*, September 11, 2007, http://www.sltrib.com/ci_6863570 (accessed September 13, 2007); "Mitt a Hit in Provo," KSL.com, November 25, 2007, http://www.ksl.com/index.php?nid=481&sid=2213437 (accessed November 26, 2007); Lee Davidson and Bob Bernick Jr., "Mitt Money: Romney's Utah Cash Dwarfs All Others," *Deseret Morning News*, July 17, 2007, http://deseretnews.com/dn/view/0,1249,695192623,00.html (accessed July 17, 2007).

63. Levenson, "Methodical Style Sets Romney Apart."

64. While Bill Richardson, Democrat governor of New Mexico, was a presidential candidate and would have been the first Hispanic American president if elected, by January 2008 he was so far back in the polls that he had no realistic chance of being elected.

65. "Religion and Politics 2008: Sam Brownback," *Pew Forum*, http://www.pewforum.org/religion08/profile.php?CandidateID=7 (accessed May 3, 2007); "Brownback for President," personal email in my possession, (August 13, 2007); Libby Quaid, "Brownback to Withdraw from GOP Race," *Washington Post*, October 18, 2007, http://www.washingtonpost.com/wp-dyn/content/article/2007/10/18/AR2007101800755.html (accessed November 23, 2007).

66. "Religion and Politics 2008: Rudolph Giuliani," *Pew Forum*, http://www.pewforum.org/religion08/profile.php?CandidateID=5 (accessed May 3, 2007).

67. Liz Sidoti, "Guiliani, Wife Each Married Three Times," *Washington Post*, March 23, 2007, http://www.washingtonpost.com/wp-dyn/content/article/2007/03/23/AR2007032301004.html (accessed November 23, 2007); Sheryl Henderson Blunt, "The Guiliani Choice," *Christianity Today*, June 5, 2007, http://www.christianitytoday.com/ct/2007/june/13.20.html (accessed June 5, 2007); and George J. Marlin, "Giuliani's Catholic Problem Won't Go Away," NewsMax.com, November 19, 2007, http://www.newsmax.com/newsfront/catholics_giuliani/2007/11/19/50695.html (accessed November 26, 2007). Other articles discussing Guiliani's potentially problematic social positions are Bishop Thomas J. Obin, "Without a Doubt: My R.S.V.P. to Rudy Guiliani," *Rhode Island Catholic*, May 31, 2007, http://www.thericatholic.com/rudy.html (accessed June 5, 2007), which slammed Guiliani as a hypocrite for his liberal stands on abortion and other moral issues; "Guiliani Questioned about Catholicism," NewsMax.com, August 8, 2007, http://archive.newsmax.com/archives/articles/2007/8/7/202802.shtml (accessed August 8, 2007); Matthew Continetti, "The Vulnerable Frontrunner: Guiliani Versus the Primary Calendar," *Weekly Standard*, September 10, 2007, http://www.weeklystandard.com/Content/Public/Articles/000/000/014/046hecqw.asp (accessed July 1, 2008); Mike Allen, "Guiliani Asks Values Voters to Trust Him," *Politico*, October 20, 2007, http://www.politico.com/news/stories/1007/6463.html (accessed October 22, 2007).

68. "Religion and Politics 2008: Mike Huckabee," *Pew Forum*, http://pewforum.org/religion08/profile.php?CandidateID=10 (accessed September 13, 2007); "Cheery Conservative Huckabee Shakes Up Republican Race," Breitbart.com, November 8, 2007, http://afp.google.com/article/ALeqM5gjyrKXB6YCtu1SasEazhMl8QQuXQ (accessed July 1, 2008); Robert D. Novak, "The False Conservative," *Washington Post*, November 26, 2007, http://www.washingtonpost.com/wp-dyn/content/article/2007/11/25/AR2007112501547_pf.html (accessed November 26, 2007); "Huckabee's Record: Anything But Conservative," NewsMax.com, http://www.archive.newsmax.com/archives/articles/2007/7/2/194431.shtml (accessed July 3, 2007); "Word-of-Mouth Boosts 'Huck' in Iowa Polls," *Washington Times*, November 22, 2007, http://www.washingtontimes.com/article/20071122/NATION/111220067/1001 (accessed November 26, 2007); "Huckabee Shows Amazing Strength," NewsMax.com, October 24, 2007, http://www.newsmax.com/politics/huckabee/2007/10/24/43622.html (accessed October 25, 2007).

69. "Religion and Politics 2008: John McCain," *Pew Forum*, http://pewforum.org/religion08/profile.php?CandidateID=3 (accessed May 3, 2007); "McCain: I'm a

Baptist," NewsMax.com, http://www.newsmax.com/politics/mccain_religion/2007/09/16/33076.html (accessed July 1, 2008).

70. Lisa Riley Roche, "Some LDS in Utah Following McCain," *Deseret Morning News*, July 11, 2007, http://www.deseretnews.com/dn/view/0,1249,685192620,00.html (accessed July 12, 2007).

71. "Religion and Politics 2008: Fred Thompson," *Pew Forum*, http://pewforum.org/religion08/profile.php?CandidateID=11 (accessed September 13, 2007); George Will, "A Rocky Rollout for Thompson," *Washington Post*, September 13, 2007, http://www.washingtonpost.com/wp-dyn/content/article/2007/09/12/AR2007091202025.html (accessed June 26, 2008).

72. Dick Polman, "Thompson's Federalism Draws No 'Amens' from the Religious Right," [Rochester, Minnesota] *Post-Bulletin*, November 12, 2007, http://www.postbulletin.com/newsmanager/templates/localnews_story.asp?z=12&a=315183 (accessed November 23, 2007).

73. "Fred Thompson Was Critical to McCain-Feingold," NewsMax.com, May 29, 2007, http://www.archive.newsmax.com/archives/articles/2007/5/29/133920.shtml (accessed May 30, 2007); Suzanne Struglinski and Lisa Riley Riche, "Actor Heightens GOP Debate Drama," *Deseret Morning News*, June 5, 2007, http://deseretnews.com/dn/view/0,1249,660226839,00.html (accessed June 5, 2007); David D. Kirkpatrick, "As Senator Rose, Lobbying Became Family Affair," *New York Times*, July 2, 2007, http://www.nytimes.com/2007/07/02/politics/02thompson.html (accessed July 2, 2007); "Fred Thompson Was Pro-Choice during 1994 Senate Race," *Daily Kos*, June 2, 2007, http://www.dailykos.com/story/2007/6/2/143215/1521 (accessed July 16, 2007); Dick Morris and Eileen McGann, "Thompson PAC Coddles Son," Townhall.com, July 24, 2007, http://www.dickmorris.com/blog/2007/07/23/thompson-pac-coddles-son (accessed July 26, 2007); Terence P. Jeffrey, "Fred Thompson Rejects GOP's Pro-Life Platform Plank," *Cybercast News Service*, November 5, 2007, http://www.cnsnews.com/ViewPolitics.asp?Page=/Politics/archive/200711/POL20071105c.html (accessed November 6, 2007).

74. Shawn Macomber, "Mighty Mitt Romney," *American Spectator*, March 2006, 22.

75. Ibid.; "Romney Rides High," *Wall Street Journal*, September 25, 2006, http://www.opinionjournal.com/diary/?id=110008991 (accessed October 9, 2006); Andrew Sullivan, "The Mormon Who Might Just Go All the Way," *Sunday Times*, November 26, 2006, http://www.timesonline.co.uk/tol/comment/columnists/andrew_sullivan/article649895.ece (accessed November 27, 2006); "Is Romney Moving on

Up?" *Washington Post*, May 22, 2007, http://www.washingtonpost.com/wp-dyn/content/article/2007/05/21/AR2007052101690.html (accessed May 25, 2007); "Romney Gains Credibility in Early Primary States," *Washington Post*, June 25, 2007, http://www.washingtonpost.com/wp-dyn/content/article/2007/06/24/AR2007062401632.html (accessed June 25, 2007); Marcia Vickers, "The Republicans' Mr. Fix-it," *Fortune*, June 27, 2007, rpt. in CNNMoney.com, July 9, 2007, http://money.cnn.com/magazines/fortune/fortune_archive/2007/07/09/100121803/index.htm (accessed November 24, 2007); Paul Schmitt, "Mitt Romney: The Best Solution to America's Ills," *Daily Illini*, August 21, 2007, http://www.dailyillini.com/news/2007/08/21/ (accessed August 21, 2007).

76. Joe Klein, "Romney's Disappointing Campaign," *Time*, May 31, 2007, http://www.time.com/time/nation/article/0,8599,1626721,00.html (accessed June 1, 2007); "Romney's Convictions," *Wall Street Journal*, February 1, 2008, http://www.online.wsj.com/public/article_print/SB120182471883733637.html (accessed February 1, 2008).

77. Ryan Lizza, "The Mission," *New Yorker*, October 29, 2007, http://www.newyorker.com/reporting/2007/10/29/071029fa_fact_lizza?printable=true (accessed October 29, 2007); Nick Juliano, "Mitt Romney Spent Nearly $2K on Makeup while Governor," *Raw Story*, July 19, 2007, http://www.rawstory.com/news/2007/Mitt_Romney_spent_nearly_2K_on_0719.html (accessed October 8, 2007).

78. Ronald Kessler, "Expert: Hillary Appears Confident," NewsMax.com, November 26, 2007, http://www.newsmax.com/kessler/hillary_body_language/2007/11/26/52180.html (accessed November 26, 2007); "Hot on the Trail: Ask America: The Radar Politics Poll," *Radar* (November 2007): 52. According to Jim Rutenburg, "Romney Favors Hubbard Novel," *New York Times*, April 30, 2007, http://thecaucus.blogs.nytimes.com/2007/04/30/romney-favors-hubbard-novel, (accessed November 27, 2007), Romney appeared insincere when he first said his favorite book was L. Ron Hubbard's *Battlefield Earth* and then changed it to the Bible when people started discussing Scientology as a cult. Other articles discussing the "too good to be true" Mitt Romney include "Mr. Smooth of Massachusetts," *Economist*, June 5, 2007, http://www.economist.com/world/na/displaystory.cfm?story_id=9441455 (accessed July 6, 2007); and Adam C. Smith, "Romney Builds Image as Front-Runner," *St. Petersburg Times*, August 18, 2007, http://www.sptimes.com/2007/08/18/news_pf (accessed August 20, 2007).

79. Elizabeth Holmes, "Romney's Wallet Keeps Him in the Race," *Wall Street Journal*, January 24, 2008, http://online.wsj.com/public/article/SB120113967757

412093.html (accessed January 25, 2008); Suzanne Struglinski, "Mitt Deflects Questions about Faith, Finances," *Deseret Morning News,* January 25, 2008, http:// deseretnews.com/article/content/mobile/0,5223,695247150,00.html (accessed January 25, 2008).

80. "Romney Pledges to Donate Salary If Elected President," *Jerusalem Post,* May 30, 2007, http://www.jpost.com/servlet/Satellite?cid=1180450956277&pagename =JPost%2FJPArticle%2FShowFull (accessed May 30, 2007).

81. "Rebuilding from the Fires of San Diego," The Treasure Box of Friends Blog on MySpace, http://www.treasureboxseries.com/blog2-11-26-2007 .SanDiegoFires.html (accessed March 8, 2008); "Mitt Romney's Stump," http:// www.vincentfam.net/2007-11-14_Mitt_Romneys_stump (accessed March 8, 2008).

82. Michael Scherer, "Can Romney's Inner Geek Win Out?" *Time,* January 27, 2008, http://www.time.com/time/politics/article/0,8599,1707342,00.html (accessed January 29, 2008).

83. Michael D. Shear and Perry Bacon Jr., "Huckabee Wins Iowa's Republican Caucuses," *Washington Post,* January 4, 2008, http://www.washingtonpost.com/ wp-dyn/content/story/2008/01/03/ST2008010304585.html (accessed January 4, 2008); Michael Luo and David D. Kirkpatrick, "At Huckabee Central, Cheers for Evangelical Base," *New York Times,* January 4, 2008, http://www.nytimes.com/ 2008/01/04/us/politics/04repubs.html (accessed January 4, 2008); "Female, Religious Voters Propel Huckabee to Victory in Iowa," CNN.com, January 4, 2009, http://www.cnn.com/2008/POLITICS/01/03/iowa.gop/index.html (accessed January 4, 2008); Thomas Burr, "Romney's Big Investment in Iowa Turns Bitter," *Salt Lake Tribune,* January 3, 2008, http://origin.sltrib.com/ci_7875772 (accessed January 4, 2008).

84. "Resurgent McCain Bests Romney," *Washington Times,* January 9, 2008, http://www.washingtontimes.com/article/20080109/NATION/513619002/1002 (accessed January 9, 2008); Suzanne Struglinski, "Romney Again Settles for Silver, Forges Ahead," *Deseret Morning News,* January 9, 2008, http://www.deseretnews .com/article/1,5143,695242633,00.html (accessed January 9, 2008); Mary Katharine Ham, "Huck, Chuck, and J.C.: Does it work in New Hampshire?" Townhall.com, January 8, 2008, http://www.townhall.com/columnists/MaryKatharineHam/2008/ 01/08/huck,_chuck,_and_jc_does_it_work_in_new_hampshire (accessed January 9, 2008).

85. Ben Johnson, "The Third Comeback Kid," *Front Page Magazine,* January 16, 2008, http://www.frontpagemag.com/ARTICLES/Read.aspx?GUID=AA34B

05F-1A95-44CD-AEE3-1246F3C76629 (accessed January 16, 2008); Michael Levenson, "Romney Gets Big Win in Michigan," *Boston Globe*, January 15, 2008, http://www.boston.com/news/politics/politicalintelligence/2008001/romney_gets_big_1.html (accessed January 16, 2008); Lisa Lerer, "Romney Lets Loose at Victory Celebration," *Politico*, January 16, 2008, http://www.politico.com/news/stories/0108/7925.html (accessed January 16, 2008).

86. Lisa Riley Roche, "Romney Wins Big in Nevada," *Deseret Morning News*, January 20, 2008, http://deseretnews.com/article/content/mobile/0,5223,695245718,00.html (accessed January 22, 2008); see also Lisa Lerer, "Romney Wins Big in Nevada," *Politico*, January 19, 2008, http://www.politico.com/news/stories/0108/7989.html (accessed January 22, 2008); Thomas Burr, "Mormon Support Drives Romney Win in Nevada," *Salt Lake Tribune*, January 19, 2008, http://www.sltrib.com/ci_8020597 (accessed January 22, 2008).

87. "Romney Takes 2% Lead over McCain in Florida, Giuliani Takes Over Third Place Alone," *Real Clear Politics*, January 29, 2008, http://www.realclearpolitics.com/articles/docs/florida-Jan-29-08.html (accessed January 29, 2008); Marc Caputo and Lesly Clark, "Florida Election a Barometer for Country," *Miami Herald*, January 29, 2008, http://www.miamiherald.com/548/v-print/story/397310.html (accessed January 29, 2008); "Analysis: Romney's Attacks Backfired against McCain in Florida" *Salt Lake Tribune*, January 30, 2008, http://www.sltrib.com/ci_8116432?source=rv (accessed January 30, 2008); Melissa Rogers, "Thoughts on and News about Religion's Intersection with Public Affairs," http://melissarogers.typepad.com/melissa_rogers/2008/01/florida-republi.html (accessed February 1, 2008).

88. Bill Schneider, "It Could All Be Over after 'Super Duper Tuesday,'" CNN.com, February 7, 2008, http://www.cnn.com/2007/POLITICS/02/05/schneider.superduper.tuesday/index.html (accessed 14 June 2008); and Chuck Todd, "Will Tsunami Tuesday Be an Afterthought?" MSNBC, May 10, 2008, http://www.msnbc.msn.com/id/18593870 (accessed June 14, 2008).

89. Lisa Riley Roche, "Romney: He Pins Hopes on a Win in California," *Deseret Morning News*, February 5, 2008, http://deseretnews.com/article/content/mobile/0,5223,695250308,00.html (accessed February 5, 2008).

90. "Huckabee Wins All 18 W. Va. Delegates," Breitbart.com, February 5, 2008, http://www.breitbart.com/article.php?id=D8UKBKNG2&show_article=1 (accessed February 5, 2008); Bob Bernick Jr., "Utahns Rally for Romney, Give Obama Edge," *Deseret Morning News*, February 6, 2008, http://deseretnews.com/article/content/mobile/0,5223,695250809,00.html (accessed February 6, 2008); Lisa

Riley Roche and Suzanne Struglinski, "Super Tuesday—GOP: McCain Rolls to a Big Lead in Delegate Tally," *Deseret Morning News*, February 6, 2008, http://deseretnews.com/article/content/mobile/o,5223,695250808,00.html (accessed February 6, 2008); Seema Mehta, "Romney Vows He Will Battle On," *Los Angeles Times*, February 6, 2008, http://www.latimes.com/news/politics/la-na-romney6feb 06,0,5548819.story (accessed February 6, 2008); "McCain Emerges as GOP Leader; Romney Reassesses Campaign," CNN.com, February 6, 2008), http://www.cnn.com/2008/POLITICS/02/06/super.gop (accessed February 6, 2008).

91. "Romney Suspends Presidential Campaign," CNNPolitics.com February 7, 2008, http://www.cnn.com/2008/POLITICS/02/07/romney.campaign (accessed March 8, 2008.

92. Joe Murray, "Is America Ready for a Mormon President?" *Bulletin*, November 13, 2007, http://www.thebulletin.us/site/news.cfm?newsid=19017809&BRD=2737&PAG=461&dept_id=576361&rfi=6 (accessed November 14, 2007). Numerous articles and other publications have mentioned Romney's potentially fatal flaw—his Mormonism. Or, as explained by John Ibbitson, "A Winning Charm and a Knack for Shifting Policies," *Globe and Mail*, November 15, 2007, http://www.theglobeandmail.com/servlet/story/LAC.20071115.MITT15/TPStory/TPInternational (accessed November 15, 2007), Mitt Romney is "a Mormon chameleon."

Chapter 5
The Mormon Question: Left Hook

The speech had been greatly anticipated. Would he explain his Mormonism? Would he apologize for it? Or perhaps defend it? After a continued barrage of questions, insinuations, and outright attacks from the press and critics of the Church of Jesus Christ of Latter-day Saints and months of agonizing over whether even to give a speech, the time had finally come to speak on the subject. A little over one hundred years ago, "Reed Smoot stood on the floor of the U.S. Senate to defend his right to serve there as a member of the Church of Jesus Christ of Latter-day Saints."[1]

During his thirty-minute speech Reed Smoot passionately defended himself and the LDS Church in what historian Michael H. Paulos described as the "JFK speech before JFK gave it." He spoke the day before the Senate voted on whether to allow him to retain his seat, "culminating two years of hearings on his fitness to serve that proved tumultuous and painful for Smoot and for the LDS Church."[2]

Smoot was appointed to the Quorum of Twelve Apostles, the second-ranked authorities of the Mormon Church, in 1900 and was elected to the United States Senate in late 1902. Almost immediately critics of the Church began to protest his election. While the Senate allowed his seating in early 1903, it was provisional, pending hearings by the Committee on Privileges and Elections to determine his fitness to serve in the Senate. The committee began hearings in 1904 that lasted more than two years and ended with a seven-to-five vote for expulsion. Senate floor debate began six months later and finished in January 1907. Its vote, though close, failed of the necessary two-thirds majority, and Smoot went on to a distinguished career of hard-working service that lasted thirty years.[3]

The debate over whether to unseat Smoot, like the committee hearings preceding the full Senate vote, was decidedly more anti-Mormon than anti-Smoot. Furthermore, the committee hearings and floor debate were influenced by outside forces pushing for severe action, not only against Smoot but also, and even particularly, against the Church. "For many years the Protestant Churches and their re-form agencies had combined politically to remove the LDS Church from politics," according to Kathleen Flake, who has written the most thorough analysis of this hearings. Smoot's expulsion from the Senate was seen as a way of accomplishing that goal.[4]

"The Christian lobby's mass mobilization of its most developed weapons of political persuasion against Smoot demonstrates that the evangelicals considered the Utahn to be a serious threat," wrote Ian Shinn, another student of the hearings. "More importantly, by de-claring itself to be the 'voice of the American people,' the Christian lobby drew a clear line as to who was and who was not 'American.'" Some members of the Senate took their cue from the Protestant or-ganizations and press. Some senators argued that, while Smoot had not broken any law, his membership and particularly his leadership in the LDS Church should be considered grounds adequate for re-moval.[5]

In spite of the media attention and heavy campaigning against Smoot, he retained his seat. While his speech in his own defense may have swayed some Senators, the vote was greatly influenced by the outspoken support of President Theodore Roosevelt. Furthermore, he "won over a vast majority of his critics through a consistent dis-play of professional competency and upright character." The public was allowed to see Latter-day Saints as actual American citizens rather than through the biased stereotypes of anti-Mormon litera-ture. According to historian Harvard Heath, Smoot and the LDS Church had won "political legitimacy" with the vote. Many believed that the Mormon question had finally been settled.[6]

The Mormon Question

Despite historical variations on the Mormon question and the extent to which they could participate in American life, the most important part of the Mormon question continues to be: Because Mormons believe in what most Americans see as alien (even non-Christian) doctrines and strange practices, can a Mormon be trusted to preserve, protect, and promote the common good of the United States as president?

In spite of hopeful assumptions that the Mormon question had been settled with the 1907 Senate vote, it has resurfaced at several points in the past century, sometimes in ugly forms. For example, in the 1990s LDS member Pam Roach ran for governor of Washington. She "lost a Republican primary after a telephone campaign led by evangelicals urged voters to reject her because she was not a 'Christian.'"[7] Mitt Romney began his campaign with the blithe assumption that the great majority of Americans "couldn't care less what religion I am." In fact, in an appearance on the *Tonight Show* with Jay Leno, he asserted, "America is ready for people of almost any faith to lead the country." Republican strategist and John McCain supporter Mark McKinnon stated as early as November 2006, "The Mormon issue is way overstated. In the end, it won't be much of an issue." The same article quoted a Romney campaign pollster who said, "We're already down to underwear, the question will wear itself out."[8]

In spite of their predictions that the Mormon issue would soon be forgotten, they were wrong. A poll taken in November 2006 showed that 43 percent of all voters and 53 percent of evangelicals would not vote for a Mormon. In January 2007, another poll showed an encouraging decrease to 37 percent of voters who would not vote for a Mormon. While that dip seemed to promise success on Romney's part, it more likely reflected a different slice of respondents. By May 2007 the number of people saying they would be less likely to support a Mormon for president was still 30 percent. Democratic strategist Susan Estrich correctly pointed out that the actual numbers are probably much higher as people usually do not want to admit their bias.[9]

By the fall of 2007, political pundits and campaign strategists alike were talking about Mitt Romney's Mormon "problem." Hugh Hewitt conceded, "It's a much bigger problem than I thought." Rather than decreasing interest in Mitt's Mormonness, the number of news articles, radio, and television pieces in which it formed a substantial topic increased during 2007. It seemed at times as if the media was pushing the controversy of the Mormon question.[10]

The LDS Church Responds

At first, the LDS Church continued its public relations strategy of silence or, at the most, neutrality when asked about the combination of Mitt Romney's Mormonism and his campaign for the presidency. Since the 1950s, the Church has followed a policy of strict public neutrality in political races. The official position reads: "The Church's mission is to preach the gospel of Jesus Christ, not to elect politicians. The Church of Jesus Christ of Latter-day Saints is neutral in matters of party politics. This applies in all of the many nations in which it is established." Because of this neutrality, no direct or indirect campaigning is allowed on LDS Church property, nor does the Church endorse candidates.[11] Reinforcing this official position, a member of the First Quorum of the Seventy, the third-ranked governing body, stressed in a private interview: "The Church has gone to great lengths to distance itself from Mitt Romney."[12] Thus, while individual Mormons, who may or may not have held leadership positions, may or may not have supported Romney's campaign, the Church as an institution did not.

Nevertheless, the Church's Public Affairs Department soon realized that the interest in Romney and the Church was not going to dissipate. Making matters worse was the high level of anti-Mormon bias in the press and among Americans in general. In many ways, the LDS Church was walking a thin line between not responding assertively enough to counter negative, incorrect press statements and saying too much and appearing to be supporting Romney. Was that line so thin because the Church retained its activity on social issues but stayed neutral on political issues? A misstep would be public relations suicide.[13] Realizing the Church, its image, and doctrines were being defined by its critics, LDS Public Affairs began its own information initiative in the Fall of 2007. Representatives began meeting with various news outlets and the Church established a twenty-hour hot line for political writers and commentators to help get the LDS message out and "dispel myths about Mormon beliefs."[14] The response to these efforts have been mixed. According to LDS Public Affairs spokeswoman Kim Farah, before and during the 2002 Winter Olympics, the LDS Church received visits and calls from numerous journalists; 1,300 journalists visited the Church's media center [in person?] during the actual games. The sports writers were outnumbered by "culture journalists" who had some background knowledge about the Church. In contrast, she observed, most of the journalists who contacted the Church during the Romney campaign "were not as knowledgeable about Mormon history and doctrine." As a result, they tended to focus on the few aspects they did know about, among them the sensational topic of polygamy. She concluded, "There [were] probably more negative than positive articles" as a result of the Romney campaign.[15] An LDS professional journalist corroborated: "The more reporters and pundits know about Mormons . . . the less likely that are to use stereotypes, [and] frame [Mormons] as wacky."[16]

Media Bias

At first glance, given the almost-automatic liberal reflexes of the media, the gulf between America's press and America's religious right makes it seem logical that the media would like anybody the evangelicals hated. On the contrary, Mitt Romney found surprisingly few allies among the media. Some of Mitt Romney's campaign staff accused the media of having an "unhealthy and biased obsession with Romney's religion." Other campaign staffers, however, recognized that curiosity from voters and the media about Romney's Mormonism was natural. The *Boston Globe* published a leaked Romney campaign memo acknowledging that "some view Mormonism as weird and lists ways Romney should defend his faith, from highlighting the way he has lived his life, rather than which Church he attends, to acknowledging theological differences with mainline Christian denominations while refusing to be drawn into an extensive discussion of Mormon doctrine and practices."[17]

Campaign planning and expectations notwithstanding, press attention on Mitt Romney's religion began well before he officially announced his candidacy on February 13, 2007 and has continued to the present. Author and journalist David Bresnahan was already weary of it in May 2006: "Day after day some newspaper somewhere decides to run the same old tired story" about Mitt Romney and Mormonism. A year later, Tim Rutten of the *Los Angeles Times* pulled no punches with his disgust: "'It's been nearly half a century since our political journalism has witnessed anything quite as breathtakingly noxious and offensive as the current attempt to discredit' the former Massachusetts governor for his faith."[18]

Some of these articles were apparently written to discredit not only Romney but also Mormonism. Utah Senator Orrin G. Hatch described these stories as "efforts of smear" and a "business of prejudice against Mormons" while Senator Robert F. Bennett admitted, "There have been more anti-Mormon comments made in the press than I expected."[19] The influential Manchester *Guardian* began its article, headlined "Latter-day President," with a description of visiting LDS Church headquarters in Salt Lake City: "The girls in Temple Square wear long, flowing skirts and uniformly wide smiles. . . . Behind them, steeped in benevolence, too, are white men in dark suits, white shirts and sombre ties. They are elders, keeping the sisters in check. Somehow—unworthily perhaps—you shiver over so much relentless niceness. Somehow, you remember Stepford Wives and the Midwich Cuckoos. But this is Salt Lake City 2007, and there's a bigger question hanging over the temple in the square. Can the next elected leader of the western world be a Mormon?"[20]

Newspaper and magazine articles are written to be sold. In the competitive world of print and electronic news and entertainment, the two are often blurred and information becomes entertainment. This overlap seems particularly true when the media is reporting on religion. In an article titled, "Thank Goodness the Media Will Let

Us Know About the Odd Side of Mormons," Jim Geraghty of *National Review Online* took *Boston Globe* reporter Alex Beam and others to task "for reinforcing the 'Mormons Are Creepy and Weird™' message." He ended his piece: "You know when I want to hear newspaper columnists lament the oddities of the Mormon faith? When they start violent riots over cartoons of Joseph Smith."[21]

Admittedly, Mormonism may seem alien to a majority of the American population. Some LDS beliefs and practices differ markedly from those of other mainstream Christian denominations. But that statement is true of nearly all religions except those so bland and so broad that they *are* the mainstream. Part of religion involves taking what ordinarily seems irrational and accepting it as rational. "The best intellectual argument Romney could use isn't available to him, which is that *all* religions have their odd traditions and beliefs that look highly quirky under close examination," wrote John Dickerson, chief political correspondent for *Slate Magazine*. "Imagine what fun he could have had with the Charismatics, some of whom speak in tongues or drink snake venom."[22]

That simple consideration, however, has not stopped the media from dwelling on, ruminating about, and poking fun at Mormonism, even if reporters are embarrassingly ignorant about what they are discussing. One of the better examples of this phenomenon was Peggy Noonan's attempt at humor when she discussed Fred Thompson's impending declaration as a Republican presidential candidate. In describing a Republican presidential debate, she wrote, "While the other candidates bang away earnestly in a frozen format, Thompson continues to sneak up from the creek and steal their underwear— boxers, briefs and temple garments."[23] Noonan either did not know or did not care how offensive it is to LDS members when others invade their privacy and ridicule their temple garments.

Author/columnist Andrew Sullivan displayed photographs of temple garments and wrote an essay titled, "Mormon Sacred Underwear," commenting, "So Mitt Romney will never have to answer the boxers or briefs question. But will he tell us whether he wears Mormon underwear at all times, including when asleep?"[24] Another writer described temple garments being worn by Mormons "to protect their nether regions from Satan's clutches through special blessings applied directly to the cloth ('They don't say Hanes until Jesus says they say Hanes!')." Many internet sites posted photographs of temple garments, one such display titled, "Mitt Romney's Underwear."[25]

John Dickerson demanded, "If they're talking about your bloomers, it's time to clear a few things up." Mitt Romney, however, ignored questions about whether he wears temple garments, responding only that he would not dignify such an intrusion into his personal life with an answer. One political writer found Romney's position commendable, rebuking, "Does anyone ask Hillary Clinton to describe her underwear?"[26]

The better-informed Dave Wedge of *Boston Herald* explained, "Publishing pictures of the [temple garments] in ridicule is as blasphemous to Mormons as posting pictures of Allah is to Muslims."[27] Although Latter-day Saints might stop short of calling exposure blasphemy, they certainly find it disrespectful. They wear temple garments to symbolize their dedication to the gospel of Jesus Christ, accepted during sacred rites in temples dedicated to worshipping God. The fact that it is underclothing and not outerwear, like orthodox Jewish, Anglican, or Catholic regalia, should be a clear message that they also consider such garments intensely private.

The official website of the LDS Church posted the following statement regarding temple garments:

> Like members of many religious faiths, Latter-day Saints wear religious clothing. But members of other faiths—typically those involved in permanent pastoral ministries or religious services—usually wear religious garments as outer ceremonial vestments or symbols of recognition. In The Church of Jesus Christ of Latter-day Saints, garments are worn beneath street clothing as a personal and private reminder of commitments to God. Garments are considered sacred by Church members and are not regarded as a topic for casual conversation.[28]

The Mormon temple garment was not the only controversial issue brought up by the media. A favorite among media was polygamy (more correctly, polygyny, or multiple wives). The more usual Mormon term is plural marriage. Joseph Smith introduced plural marriage as a circumspect practice limited to a few of his closest associates as part of the general doctrine of a restoration of all things, including the plurality of wives as practiced by Abraham, Isaac, and Jacob in the Old Testament. The practice was publicly announced in 1852 in Utah Territory and openly engaged in for three decades. Then federal legislation against the practice intensified, reflecting the outrage of mainstream Americans who found the practice repugnant, non-Christian, and a threat to the "American home."

The first legislation, passed in 1862 against bigamy, was not enforced, in large part because the Civil War drew energies elsewhere. However, the Edmunds Act (1882) made it easier to arrest, punish, and incarcerate men involved in plural marriage. By the mid-1880s, several hundred Mormon men were serving prison terms for "unlawful cohabitation," which was easier to prove than an illegal marriage. Scores of men (and especially women and their children) went "on the Underground," moving from one town to another and concealing their identities to avoid arrest.[29]

The Edmunds-Tucker Act (1887) disfranchised all women and most Mormon men. It required that all marriages be recorded publicly, required wives to testify against their husbands, and disinherited and illegitimized all children of plural marriages. The act also allowed the federal government to confiscate all LDS Church property above $50,000 and dissolved the Church as a corporate entity.[30]

A few hundred LDS families attempted to escape what they viewed as government persecution by moving to Canada and Mexico. Nevertheless, after a decade of legislation and judicial sentences aimed specifically at crippling the LDS Church and depriving its members of civil rights, Wilford Woodruff, the fourth Church president, announced the withdrawal of official support for new plural marriages in 1890.[31] By that point, journalists and exposé writers had created well-detailed and widely accepted stereotypes: large Mormon harems in which young virgins were seduced and held captive by lecherous old men; armed bands of "Danites" who kept the citizenry in line by murder; and sinister leaders who exercised unlimited power. Although increasingly strict pronouncements by Church leaders further distanced the Church from the practice of polygamy over the next two decades and both the practice of polygamy or even, in some circumstances, belief in it earns quick excommunication, many of these stereotypes have continued to the present. Since the practice is carried on by fundamentalist Mormons who reject the series of official "manifestos" stopping the practice, interest in polygamy remains high among anti-Mormons, internet bloggers, and journalists.[32]

Therefore, when the media discovered that Mitt Romney had polygamous ancestors, it was an irresistible factoid. In August 2006 the *Salt Lake Tribune* asked "Could Ancestors Haunt Romney?" and laid out the historical heritage. (Romney's great-grandfather, Miles Park Romney, had five wives.[33]) An Associated Press article in February 2007 announced, "Romney Family Tree Has Polygamy Branch," and then continued for eighteen paragraphs discussing his polygynous ancestors.[34]

The topic seemed to make Romney uncomfortable. He attempted to deflect it with a joke at the 2005 St. Patrick's Day breakfast in Boston: "I believe marriage should be between a man and a woman . . . and a woman . . . and a woman." More seriously, he admitted to not understanding his ancestors' polygamous marriages. He gave his clearest statement on *60 Minutes* in May 2007: "I have a great-great-grandfather [*sic*]. They were trying to build a generation out there in the desert and so he took additional wives as he was told to do. And I must admit, I can't imagine anything more awful than polygamy."[35]

While Romney's response was obviously intended to quell questions and concerns about the Romney family's polygamous past, neither deflected the articles and irritated some Mormons. One LDS blogger on the Messenger and Advocate wrote: "Nothing more awful than polygamy[,] Mitt? The polygamy practiced by your own ancestors and at one time in your own Church? Apparently those early Mormon prophets, Joseph Smith, Brigham Young, and John Taylor didn't exactly share your viewpoint of polygamy. Neither did some of the ancient prophets of the Old Testament. Of course they weren't running for President (other than Joseph, who never sold his soul to the media for votes)." He added, "Frankly I can't think of anything more awful than a modern Mormon politician saying and doing anything in a media dance for political expediency. It's a cheap shot at what once was considered a very sacred principle in early Mormon history[,] Mitt."[36]

Ironically, the media almost completely ignored the polygamous connections of Democratic presidential candidate Barack Obama. According to a London *Daily Mail* article headlined, "A Drunk and a Bigot—What the U.S. Presidential Hopeful HASN'T Said about His Father," Barack Obama's father, Barack Obama Sr., was polygamously married to three women and the father of at least eight children. He was about to marry a fourth, without having divorced any of his other wives, but was killed in a car accident in Nairobi, Kenya while driving under the influence. An abusive alcoholic, he had already lost his legs in a previous drunk-driving accident. Hussein Obama, a cousin of the presidential candidate, shrugged off his marital arrangements: "You have to remember that his father was an African and in Africa, polygamy is part of life."[37]

Conservatives have not failed to notice the media's apparent double standard about polygamy, whether the subject is Obama or Romney. A website called "Evangelicals for Mitt" posted an article, "Obama's Father a Polygamist." On *News Busters*, Lynn Davidson posted "Double Standards in an AP Article about the Polygamous History of Mitt Romney's Family" in which he commented specifically on the Associated Press's "Family Tree" article: "Since Romney isn't a polygamist himself, and he's disavowed the practice, this information doesn't seem like it would warrant an article." He derided the Associated Press for emphasizing this "non-issue" while not even mentioning Obama's polygamous father.[38]

Romney, who had not expected such a religiously-oriented question in a secular political race, also failed to give a polished and well-prepared answer when the issue of personal revelation came up. In December of 2007, a reporter at WCVB, a Boston television station, asked: "Should God speak to you and ask you to do something that might be in conflict with your duties as president or should he speak to your Prophet who would speak to you—how would you make that decision, how would you handle that?" Romney gave a nervous laugh and responded rather incoherently, "I don't recall God speaking to me. I don't know if he's spoken to anyone since Moses in the bush . . . or perhaps some others."[39]

In 1988 when Pat Robertson was running for president, Tom Brokaw had asked a similar question in a nationally televised interview. Noting that Robertson had claimed to have "God's advice on specific decisions," he referred to him as a television evangelist and then asked, "Do you get His advice on specific political decisions?" Instead of answering the question, Robertson castigated Brokaw for calling him a televangelist. He claimed that he was more than just a televangelist as he ran the fifth largest cable network in America. Robertson also said Brokaw's question demonstrated "religious bigotry."[40]

While these questions are not out of line in determining a religious man's decision-making process, the reporters also communicated a degree of skepticism. Most members of the media seemed able to reconcile and accept both the irrational nature of faith and religiosity and also the Western tradition of rational thinking and analysis, others openly struggle with what they see as a contradiction in these two divergent worldviews. Media personnel in this latter category seem unable to envision a way in which differing views can be complementary, rather than competitive.

Kenneth Woodward, religion editor of *Newsweek*, wrote a thoughtful article, "The Presidency's Mormon Moment," which directly identified Mormonism as Romney's critical problem: "It isn't just evangelical Christians in the Republican base who find Mr. Romney's religion a stumbling block. Among those who identify themselves as liberal, almost half say they would not support a Mormon for president." While this conclusion was hardly new, his reasoning was certainly revealing. Among his assertions essay: "To many Americans, Mormonism is a Church with the soul of a corporation"; "Among the reasons Americans distrust the Mormon Church is Mormon clannishness"; "A good Mormon is a busy Mormon": "Mormons like to hire other Mormons"; "Mormons are perceived to be unusually secretive. . . . This attitude has fed anti-Mormon charges of secret and unholy rites"; and "Any journalist who has covered the Church knows that Mormons speak one way among themselves, another among outsiders."[41]

Hugh Hewitt responded directly to Woodward, asking if "Jew" had been substituted for "Mormon," would the *New York Times* have published Woodward's piece. He then suggested that the title should have been "Protocols of the Elders of Zion."[42]

Another writer who attacked Romney for his Mormonism was Pennsylvania *Patriot-News* correspondent Brett Lieberman. Calling Romney "the Morman [sic] candidate," he announced that Romney would soon be fund-raising in Pennsylvania, "but you'll be hard pressed to see the GOP presidential candidate or his 17 wives." Romney campaign spokesman Kevin Madden quickly complained: "What you did was essentially slander a person and make an offensive remark about someone in reference to their faith." Lieberman shrugged off the complaint, calling his original statement satire and claiming, "That's sort of what we do most every day."[43]

Another example of media bias was Jacob Weisberg's article in *Slate* headlined, "Romney's Religion: A Mormon President? No Way." He opened by asking if it was religious bigotry to not cast a vote for a Mormon and then ended:

> By the same token, I wouldn't vote for someone who truly believed in the founding whoppers of Mormonism. . . . [Joseph Smith] was an obvious con man. Romney has every right to believe in con men, but I want to know if he does, and if so, I don't want him running the country.
>
> One may object that all religious beliefs are irrational—what's the difference between Smith's "seer stone" and the virgin birth or the parting of the Red Sea? But Mormonism is different because it is based on such a transparent and recent fraud. It's Scientology plus 125 years. Perhaps Christianity and Judaism are merely more venerable and poetic versions of the same. But a few eons makes a big difference. The world's greater religions have had time to splinter, moderate, and turn their myths into metaphor. The Church of Latter-day Saints is expanding

rapidly and liberalizing in various ways, but it remains fundamentally an orthodox creed with no visible reform wing.[44]

Christopher Hitchens, perhaps best known for his book, *God Is Not Great: How Religion Poisons Everything*, also authored a *Slate* article titled, "Mitt the Mormon." He first criticized Mitt Romney for his "revolting sanctimony and self-pity" when complaining about anti-Mormon bias. After reminding readers that Romney's family "has been for generations, part of the dynastic leadership of the mad cult invented by the convicted fraud Joseph Smith," Hitchens then stated, "The Mormons claim that their leadership is prophetic and inspired and that its rulings take precedence over any human law. The constitutional implications of this are too obvious to need spelling out, but it would be good to see Romney spell them out all the same."[45]

One of the underlying themes of articles from left-leaning media is a sense of incredulity and contempt for Romney's beliefs and, by extension, those of other Latter-day Saints. Weiberg and Hitchens expressed their lack of respect for the Mormon's founding prophet by dismissing him as a "con-man" and "convicted fraud." Timothy Garton Ash followed the same approach: "My residual problem with Romney being a Mormon is . . . that it seems such a wacky collection of man-made Moronical codswallop. And I do find myself wondering—even if he is a natural conservative, even if Mormonism is, as he puts it, 'the faith of my fathers,' including the most recent father whom he hero-worshipped—how on earth a well-educated man who aspires to lead the most powerful and modern nation in the world can seriously believe this stuff."[46]

One of the most over-the-top attacks against Mitt Romney and his church by liberal members of the media was the diatribe Lawrence O'Donnell launched on the MSNBC show, "The McLaughlin Group." Politically, he calls himself a "practical European socialist" and is known as an "outspoken television political commentator." A former Democratic staffer on two U.S. Senate committees, O'Donnell was a producer and cowriter of NBC's *The West Wing* and has had a recurring guest role as an LDS lawyer on

Big Love.[47] McLaughlin and his invited guests were discussing Mitt Romney's religion speech, delivered three days before on December 6th. In the middle of the discussion, O'Donnell burst out, calling it "the worst political speech in my lifetime." That was just the beginning. For the next three and a half minutes, he attacked Romney and the LDS Church: "This man stood there and said to you, 'This is the faith of my fathers.' And . . . none of these commentators who liked this speech realized that the faith of his fathers is a racist faith. As of 1978, it was an officially racist faith. And for political convenience, in 1978 it switched and it said, 'Okay, black people can be in this Church.'"

Pat Buchanan, one of the other guests, asked O'Donnell, if Romney's Mormonism disqualified him from being president. O'Donnell disregarded the question and continued his tirade: "I'm saying he's got to answer—when he was 30 years old . . . and he firmly believed in the faith of his father that black people are inferior, when did he change his mind? Did the religion have to tell him to change his mind? And when he talks about the faith of his father, how about the faith of his great-grandfather, who had five wives?" O'Donnell didn't stop there. Displaying his ignorance of American and Mormon history, he denounced Joseph Smith as "a lying, fraudulent criminal . . . who was a racist, who was pro-slavery. His religion was completely pro-slavery." He obviously was not aware that Smith campaigned for president on an anti-slavery platform. Virtually out of control, he was "pointing his finger at the camera and other panelists as his tone went from strong to strident to almost hysterical." O'Donnell wound up his outburst: "Romney comes from a religion founded by a criminal who was anti-American, pro-slavery, and a rapist."[48]

Reaction to O'Donnell's attack on Romney and the LDS Church was predictable. Latter-day Saints were angry and offended, not only at O'Donnell's rant but at the apparent calmness with which some of the other guests accepted his denunciations. Scott Pierce of the *Deseret Morning News* announced, "Lawrence O'Donnell is a bigot, pure and simple" and ended his essay with "imagine for a moment that O'Donnell had said this about members of other religions.

He'd never be on TV again." Some Mormons circulated emails encouraging each other to send protests to MSNBC and the McLaughlin Group, but no action appeared to have been taken against O'Donnell except that apparently he has not been asked back as a guest.[49]

Some non-Mormons, in contrast, agreed with O'Donnell. Frank Rich, a columnist for the *New York Times*, seconded O'Donnell's accusation that the LDS Church was "an officially racist faith" until 1978, then commented: "The answer is simple. Mr. Romney didn't fight his Church's institutionalized apartheid, whatever his private misgivings, because that's his character. Though he's trying to sell himself as a leader, he is actually a follower and a panderer, as confirmed by his flip-flops on nearly every issue. . . . It's incredible that Mr. Romney's prejudices get a free pass from so many commentators."[50]

O'Donnell and Rich were not the only members of the media to revive the LDS Church's problematic history regarding blacks as part of a Romney critique. In May 2007, Rev. Al Sharpton, a Pentecostal minister, talk radio host, and former Democratic presidential candidate, while debating Christopher Hitchens, said, "As for the one Mormon running for office, those who really believe in God will defeat him anyways, so don't worry about that; that's a temporary situation." He was immediately criticized and accused of bigotry by people on both sides of the political spectrum.[51]

The Reverend Bob Schenck, an evangelical minister who heads the National Clergy Council, urged Sharpton to apologize because, "while many other Christian groups may have differences with LDS doctrine, to question someone else's sincerity of belief in God is the height of pharisaical arrogance." Romney described Sharpton's statement as "extraordinarily bigoted" and remarked, "I can only, hearing that statement, wonder whether there's not bigotry that still remains in America."[52] Either for political expediency or perhaps because of true umbrage at the LDS Church's past problems regarding race, Sharpton retorted, "I'm the one that belongs to a race that couldn't join the Mormons and I'm the one that's the bigot[?]" He then called on Mitt Romney to explain his views on the LDS Church's position on blacks.[53]

The LDS Church's past prohibition of ordaining black men to the priesthood became an issue during the 2008 presidential campaign, first with Al Sharpton's comments, but mostly because Mitt Romney stated during his nationally televised speech on religion on December 6 , "I saw my father march with Martin Luther King." Alert observers and historians noted that there was no evidence George Romney had marched with Martin Luther King. Furthermore, even if George Romney had marched with King, Mitt could not have seen him do it because he was then in France. Romney responded by saying "It's just a figure of speech" or a way of explaining that his father had been a champion of civil rights.[54]

There is no doubt that George Romney was outspokenly pro-civil rights and did march in support of King and his crusade. In fact, two elderly women came forward and stated that they remembered George Romney marching arm-in-arm with King in Grosse Pointe, Michigan in 1963. Unfortunately, they remembered incorrectly. While George Romney did march for civil rights that day, it was not with King but with other civil rights leaders. Several political pundits commented that it was a shame Mitt Romney embellished the story as his father's unadorned civil rights record was impressive.

Actor-director Robert Redford, who has maintained a residence in Utah for at least three decades and was once married to a Mormon woman, diverged from an interview at the advance screening of his film, *Lions for Lambs*: "[Mormons] are very adept at not being fazed and speaking fluently and gracefully. Why? Because every single male who's a Mormon goes on a mission for two years when they're 19 or 20. They learn how to defect blows and stay on message. No wonder Utah is the place that all these Republican senators go. It's perfect. So when you see Mitt Romney, he's already been practicing how to deflect blows and stay on message. But it's plastic."[56] Chris Hicks of the *Deseret Morning News* found Redford's ignorance embarrassing: "Every single male Mormon goes on a mission? Uh, no. Many do (as do young women), and all are encouraged to go . . . but not all of them go. That's just a simplistic exaggeration for effect." Hicks went on to explain, given Redford's "plastic" comment, "Mormons aren't robots. . . . Mormons are just ordinary people trying to do the best they can. Some succeed incredibly, some fail miserably and most fall somewhere in the middle."[57]

Hugh Hewitt claimed on Fox News's *Hannity & Colmes*, that Mitt Romney was "going to have problem [sic] with anti-Mormon bigots on the left, especially." Rich Lowry of the *New York Post* claimed that "for once, the media aren't so thrilled by a 'first.' . . . Mitt Romney represents the first 'first' that has elicited a lukewarm reaction from the media. Journalists constantly run stories about whether Romney can become the first Mormon president—with an undercurrent suggesting that they'd be just fine if he can't."[58]

Former U.S. Congressman and television talk show host Joe Scarborough claimed: "The press corps, for the most part, there are exceptions, loathe Mitt Romney." That was a belief expressed privately by Romney campaign insiders although they never said so publicly. Going an accusatorial step further, Republican activist Len Munsil wrote in the *Arizona Republic*: "The true religious bigotry in this race is coming from the media." He portrayed the liberal media bias in conspiratorial terms:

> This inappropriate focus [on Mitt Romney's Mormonism] has the potential to divide the Republican Party, which is comprised of numerous interest groups, and people of many different backgrounds and faiths. . . .
>
> Republicans need to understand this—this focus on theology is nothing more than an effort to drive a wedge between an effective political coalition of conservative, pro-family Mormons, Catholics and evangelicals.
>
> We cannot play into the hands of those who disagree with us about these basic principles by dividing over theological doctrines that have nothing to do with public policy.[59]

Whether there has been a concerted effort on the part of the more liberal members of the press to attack and denigrate Mitt Romney and the Mormon Church seems rather improbable. A distaste for conservative religion runs deep—at least back as far as the

Scopes trial of 1925. Nevertheless, the virulent rantings of Timothy Garton Ash, Christopher Hitchens, Lawrence O'Donnell, Robert Redford, and Jacob Weisberg demonstrate a very real anti-Mormon bias that transcends Mitt Romney's campaign of the presidency.

Some of this may be simple anti-religious bigotry. Ash, Hitchens, and Weisberg are openly atheistic. Even so, their anti-Mormon animus appears to go deeper. Perhaps they fear that Romney and the LDS Church would bring too much religiosity into the presidency, nor can it be argued persuasively that George W. Bush's open religiosity has been reassuring to all Americans. On the contrary, to some it has been irrevocably linked to a pattern of poor decisions and ineffective leadership initiative. Britain's *Telegraph* ran an article headlined "If Only Romney Weren't Such a Mormon" and stated, "Suspicion of the Church of Jesus Christ of Latter Day [sic] Saints remains high. Secular voters are inclined to feel 'vague fear of authoritarian power rooted in Salt Lake City.'" Sally Denton, known best for her inadequately researched *American Massacre: The Tragedy at Mountain Meadows*, wrote in an op-ed piece: "In the end, it seems less a candidate's religion that concerns Americans and more an apprehension of fundamentalist fanaticism and a fear that the separation of Church and state is becoming murky. As for Romney and Mormonism, there seems only one legitimate and relevant question: Do you, like the prophet you follow, believe in a theocratic nation state? All the rest is pyrotechnics."[60]

Fear that Latter-day Saints will seize control of the government and force their values onto the general populace could be a result of what Richard Land, president of the Southern Baptist Convntion's Ethics and Religious Liberty Commission, described as the liberal perception that Mormons are "people of faith on steroids." He further commented, "I have known all along that the preponderance of the people who say they wouldn't vote for a Mormon are liberals. And the reason is [that] liberals tend to be leery of people who take faith seriously and who seek to apply it to areas of their lives beyond church and home."[61]

Notes

1. Brooke Adams, "Mormon Apostle Paved the Way for LDS Candidates," *Salt Lake Tribune*, December 8, 2007, http://www.sltrib.com/lds/ci_7664219 (accessed June 18, 2008).

2. Paulos quoted in ibid.

3. Thomas G. Alexander, *Mormonism in Transition: A History of the Latter-day Saints, 1890–1930* (Urbana: University of Illinois Press, 1986), 26. The Committee on Privileges and Elections was a standing committee that oversaw election questions, problems and possible irregularities.

4. Kathleen Flake, *The Politics of American Religious Identity: The Seating of Senator Reed Smoot, Mormon Apostle* (Chapel Hill: University of North Carolina Press, 2003), 15, 50.

5. Ian Shinn, "Scoot-Smoot-Scoot: The Seating Trial of Senator Reed Smoot," *Gaines Junction: Undergraduate Interdisciplinary Journal of History* 3, no. 1 (Spring 2005): 152–53.

6. Rebecca Walsh, "Church Is Harder Hit than Mitt," *Salt Lake Tribune*, May 15, 2007, http://www.sltrib.com/news/ci_5898512 (accessed 18 June 2008); Adams, "Mormon Apostle Paved the Way."

7. "Evangelicals vs. Mitt Romney," *Provo Daily Herald*, November 12, 2006, http://www.heraldextra.com/content/view/199900/3/ (accessed November 13, 2007). For other examples, see Newell G. Bringhurst and Craig L. Foster, *The Mormon Quest for the Presidency* (Independence, Mo.: John Whitmer Books, 2008).

8. Kristina Herndobler, "Romney Says His Faith Isn't a Hindrance," *Salt Lake Tribune*, January 27, 2006, http://www.sltrib.com/nationworld/ci_3442576 (accessed January 27, 2006); "Mitt Romney Discusses His Mormon Faith on 'Tonight Show,'" KSBY, May 3, 2007, http://www.ksby.com/Global/story.asp?S=6462585 (accessed May 3, 2007); Thomas Burr, "GOP Strategists: Impact of Romney's Mormonism Exaggerated," Evangelicals for Mitt, November 30, 2006, http://www.evangelicalsformitt.org/media_items/salt_lake_tribune_gop_strategi.php (accessed July 19, 2008), rpt. from *Salt Lake Tribune*, November 30, 2006. "Underwear" referred to a "Web posting by a Time.com columnist about the Mormon garments."

9. Thomas Burr, "Voting for an LDS Prez Not an Option, 43% Say," *Salt Lake Tribune*, November 21, 2006, http://www.sltrib.com/contents/ci_4698065 (accessed November 27, 2006); Elizabeth Mehren, "A Mormon for President? Voters Balk," *U.S. Times*, July 3, 2006, http://www.ustimes5.com/a_mormon_for_president_

voters_balk.htm (accessed June 28, 2008); Robert Rudy, "Public Views of Presidential Politics and Mormon Faith," *Pew Forum*, May 16, 2007, http://pewforum .org/?DocID=213 (accessed May 22, 2007); Susan Estrich, "The Mormon Question," *Truthdig*, January 8, 2007, http://www.truthdig.com/report/print/ 20070108_susan_estrich_the_mormon_question (accessed November 7, 2007). According to "Many U.S. Adults Are Uncomfortable Voting for a Mormon in the 2008 Presidential Race," PRNewswire, April 12, 2007, http://www.prnewswire.com/ telecommunications/20070411/NYW06011042007-1.html (accessed April 12, 2007), a Harris poll in April showed that given a choice of voting for someone running against a Baptist or someone running against a Mormon, more people would vote for the person running against a Mormon than for the same person if he was running against a Baptist.

10. Jill Lawrence, "Will Mormon Faith Hurt Bid for White House?" *USA Today*, March 12, 2007, http://www.usatoday.com/news/washington/2007-02-12 -romney-cover_x.htm (accessed November 28, 2007).

11. "Political Neutrality," LDS Newsroom, Church of Jesus Christ of Latter-day Saints, http://www.newsroom.lds.org/ldsnewsroom/eng/public-issues/political -neutrality (accessed December 30, 2007). However, the Church reserves the right to take public positions on questions that it deems to be "moral issues."

12. This statement is based on a private interview with a member of the First Quorum of the Seventy.

13. Carrie A. Moore, "Anti-LDS Bias Running High," *Deseret Morning News*, May 12, 2007, http://www.deseretnews.com/dn/view/0,1249,660220022,00.html (accessed May 14, 2007); Thomas Burr, "Mitt's Bid: Church Is Walking a Thin Line," *Salt Lake Tribune*, October 21, 2006, http://www.sltrib.com/ci_4528030 (accessed October 23, 2006).

14. Paul Giblin, "Romney's Candidacy Stirs Interest in Mormons," [Mesa, AZ] *East Valley Tribune*, September 16, 2007, http://redorbit.com/news/technology/ 1067972/romneys_candidacy_stirs_interest_in_mormons_church_bolsters_its_ outreach/index.html (accessed September 17, 2007); Robert Gehrke, "Romney: LDS Representatives Meet with Media Outlets," *Salt Lake Tribune*, October 27, 2007, http://www.sltrib.com/news/ci_4558580 (accessed October 27, 2007); Andrew Glass, "Mormons Heighten Public Relations Efforts," *Politico*, April 9, 2007, http://www.politico.com/news/stories/0407/3449.html (accessed April 10, 2007); and "Two Apostles Visit Editorial Boards to Address Misconceptions," LDS Newsroom, Church of Jesus Christ of Latter-day Saints, November 6, 2007, http://

newsroom.lds.org/ldsnewsroom/v/index.jsp?vgnextoid=f6f89dccfb616110VgnVC
M100000176f620aRCRD&vgnextchannel=9ae411154963d010VgnVCM1000004
e94610aRCRD (accessed November 7, 2007).

15. Craig L. Foster, "Telephone Interview with Kim Farah," November 29, 2007.

16. Joel Campbell, "The Good, the Bad, the Ugly: Finding Balance in Reporting about Mormons," *Editor & Publisher*, December 21, 2007, http://www.mediainfo.com/eandp/columns/shoptalk_display.jsp?vnu_content_id=1003688296 (accessed December 21, 2007).

17. Alex Beam, "A Mormon President? I Don't Think So," *Boston Globe*, March 5, 2007, http://www.boston.com/news/nation/articles/2007/03/05/a_mormon_president_i_dont_think_so (accessed July 10, 2007). See also Roger Simon, "Romney's Religious Riddle," *Politico*, October 18, 2007, http://www.politico.com/news/stories/1007/6421.html (accessed October 18, 2007).

18. David M. Bresnahan, "A Mormon President?" *American Chronicle*, May 4, 2006, http://www.americanchronicle.com/articles/viewArticle.asp?articleID=9009 (accessed May 21, 2007); Tim Rutten, "Fallout from Era of Falwell," *Los Angeles Times*, May 19, 2007, http://articles.latimes.com/2007/05/19/calendar/et-rutten19 (accessed July 19, 2007). According to Ivy J. Seller, "Could Romney's Christianity Really Keep Him from Presidency?" *Human Events* online, May 8, 2006, http://www.humaneventsonline.com/article.php?print=yes&id=14656 (accessed May 9, 2006), "The first thing to remember is that some reporters have nothing original to report, so they regurgitate the same story many others have already written. It's easy to pick on the Mormons, so why not jump on the band wagon?"

19. Hatch, quoted in Stephen Speckman, "Hatch Calls Romney Stories a Smear Tactic," *Deseret News*, October 24, 2006, http://www.deseretnews.com/dn/view/0,1249,650201262,00.html (accessed October 24, 2006). Hatch claimed in the same article to have been "smeared from time to time" by the media. See also *Doug Wright Show*, KSL Radio, January 3, 2008.

20. Peter Preston, "Latter-day President," *Guardian*, August 27, 2007, http://www.guardian.co.uk/print/0,,330634809-103677,00.html (accessed August 29, 2007). The Preston article mentions perceived problems with Latter-day Saint history and doctrine and asks at one point, "Is this a religion or a cult?" The reader is left with no doubt how the reporter feels.

21. Jim Geraghty, "Thank Goodness the Media Will Let Us Know about the Odd Side of Mormons," *National Review Online*, March 5, 2007, http://campaignspot

.nationalreview.com/post/?q=NzlkOWZmNDI3ZWQ0MTQ4N2I3Mjk3MmMzO
WMyODAwOWU (accessed July 10, 2007).

22. John Dickerson, "Time To Talk Mormon, Mitt," *Slate*, November 28, 2006, http://www.slate.com/id/2154566 (accessed November 29, 2006). Donald Kaul, "Religion Doesn't Disqualify a President," *Lake County News-Chronicle*, December 14, 2007, http://www.twoharborsmn.com/articles/index.cfm?id=16256 (accessed December 26, 2007), was even more explicit in his discussion of anti-Mormon bias:

> There seems to be this feeling that Mormonism is more cult than religion and a kooky cult at that. To that I say, let's put it to the test:
>
> Do Mormons drink sacramental wine and pretend they're drinking the blood of their founder? No, Mormons don't drink at all, actually.
>
> Do Mormons, as a matter of ritual, hire a non-medical person to mutilate their baby sons' penises when they're eight days old? I don't believe so.
>
> Do Mormons rush into crowded buildings and blow themselves up in expectation that God will reward them with eternal life in a heaven equipped with 32 virgins per martyr? Never heard of it happening.
>
> All of those things happen in other religions.

Joshua Treviño discussed Mormonism as alien to mainstream America in "Romney, No Rum, & Mormonism," *National Review Online*, July 19, 2007, http://article
.nationalreview.com/?q=OTM4ZWYwYzQzNmI1Y2RkNThhOGZkODA4OD
M3MjI3ZmM (accessed July 19, 2007).

23. Peggy Noonan, "The Man Who Wasn't There," *Wall Street Journal*, May 18, 2007, http://opinionjournal.com/columnists/pnoonan/?id=110010089 (accessed December 26, 2007).

24. Andrew Sullivan, "Mormon Sacred Underwear," *The Atlantic*, November 24, 2006, http://andrewsullivan.theatlantic.com/the_daily_dish/2006/11/mormon_
sacred_u.html (accessed December 7, 2006).

25. Michael Graham, "In a Twist over Knickers: Morality Makes Mitt a Hit with Evangelicals," *Boston Herald*, December 6, 2006, http://www.news.bostonherald
.com/view.bg?articleid=170717&format=text. See also "Mitt Romney's Underwear," http://mittromneysunderwear.com/underwear (accessed December 3, 2007).

26. Dickerson, "Time to Talk Mormon, Mitt"; and Graham, "In a Twist over Knickers."

27. Dave Wedge, "Does Mormon Mitt Have a Prayer?" *Boston Herald*, December 3, 2006, http://news.bostonherald.com/politics/view.bg?articleid=170245&format=text (accessed December 4, 2006).

28. "Temple Garments," LDS Newsroom, http://www.newsroom.lds.org/ldsnewsroom/eng/background-information/temple-garments (accessed December 26, 2007).

29. Brian C. Hales, *Modern Polygamy and Mormon Fundamentalism: The Generations after the Manifesto* (Salt Lake City: Greg Kofford Books, 2006), 35, 41.

30. Ibid., 41.

31. Ibid., 51–55.

32. Craig L. Foster, *Penny Tracts and Polemics: A Critical Analysis of Anti-Mormon Pamphleteering in Great Britain, 1837–1860* (Salt Lake City: Greg Kofford Books, 2002), 166–70, 174–75; Craig L. Foster, "Old Themes and Stereotypes Never Die: The Unchanging Ways of Anti-Mormons," *FAIR*, 2003, http://www.fairlds.org/FAIR_Conferences/2003_Unchanging_Ways_of_Anti-Mormons.html (accessed November 8, 2007).

33. Thomas Burr, "Could Ancestors Haunt Romney?" *Salt Lake Tribune*, August 21, 2006, http://www.sltrib.com/ci_4212788 (June 28, 2008). The article, discussing Romney's "polygamous family tree," mentions that two of Romney's great-great-grandfathers had ten wives each.

34. Jennifer Dobner and Glen Johnson, "Romney Family Tree has Polygamy Branch," Breitbart.com, February 24, 2007, http://www.breitbart.com/article.php?id=D8NGC8IO0&show_article=1 (accessed July 18, 2007).

35. Adam Reilly, "Take My Wives . . . Please!," *Slate*, April 26, 2006, http://www.slate.com/id/2140539/ (accessed April 27, 2006); and "Mitt Romney Wants to Re-Tool Washington," *60 Minutes*, May 13, 2007, http://www.cbsnews.com/stories/2007/05/10/60minutes/main2787426.shtml (accessed: June 14 2008). See also "Romney Troubled by Mormonism's Polygamous Past," *Washington Post*, May 10, 2007, http://www.washingtonpost.com/wp-dyn/content/article/2007/05/10/AR2007051001877_p (accessed May 14, 2007). According to Jennifer Dobner and Glen Johnson, "Romney Family Tree Has Polygamy Branch," *CBS News*, February 24, 2007, http://www.cbsnews.com/stories/2007/02/24/ap/politics/mainD8NGC8IO0.shtml (accessed May 14, 2007), Romney had earlier described polygamy as "bizarre."

36. Guy Murray, "Mitt Romney Caves on Polygamy," *Messenger and Advocate*, May 11, 2007, http://messengerandadvocate.wordpress.com/2007/05/11/mitt%20romney%20caves%20on%20polygamy/ (accessed July 16, 2007).

37. Sharon Churcher, "A Drunk and a Bigot—What the U.S. Presidential Hopeful HASN'T Said about His Father . . . ," *Daily Mail*, January 27, 2007, http:// www.dailymail.co.uk/pages/live/articles/news/news.html?in_article_id=431908&in _page_id=1770 (accessed July 7, 2007).

38. "Obama's Father a Polygamist," *Evangelicals for Mitt*, March 1, 2007, http://www.evangelicalsformitt.org/front_page/obamas_father_a_polygamist.php (accessed July 9, 2007); Lynn Davidson, "Double Standards in an AP Article about the Polygamous History of Mitt Romney's Family," *News Busters: Exposing and Combating Liberal Media Bias*, February 26, 2007, http://newsbusters.org/node/ 11053 (accessed July 9, 2007).

39. Chris Vanocur, "Romney's Statement on Prophets May Contradict LDS Doctrine," *ABC 4 News*, December 21, 2007, http://www.abc4.com/news/local/ story.aspx?content_id=ff03ab09-a1bf-423d-8d0b-ed018d03bf31&rss=20 (accessed December 21, 2007).

40. Calvin Skaggs, *With God on Our Side: George W. Bush and the Rise of the Religious Right in America*, TV documentary (Brooklyn, N.Y.: Icarus Films, 2004). According to the Internet Movie Database, http://www.imdb.com/title/ tt0431468/trivia (accessed July 1, 2008), Channel 4 in the United Kingdom broadcast this documentary the night before the U.S. presidential election in 2004.

41. Kenneth Woodward, "The Presidency's Mormon Moment," *New York Times*, April 9, 2007, http://www.nytimes.com/2007/04/09/opinion/09woodward .html (accessed July 30, 2007).

42. Ibid.; Hugh Hewitt, "To Many Americans, Mormonism Is a Church with the Soul of a Corporation," Townhall.com, April 9, 2007, http://hughhewitt.townhall.com /blog/g/05304605-c01a-4eb1-a13f-10d07c03e166 (accessed July 30, 2007). Although Mark Davis is a conservative Texas talk show host, his article, "Romney Can't Ignore Questions about Mormonism," *Real Clear Politics*, August 20, 2007, http://www.real clearpolitics.com/articles/2007/08/a_religious_time_bomb_only_rom.html (accessed August 21, 2007), is a good example of the incredulity expressed on both sides of the political spectrum: "But most Americans have not examined what Mormons believe, and when they do, some of them are going to recoil. It is a lot to swallow, from the prophet status afforded a young farmer named Joseph Smith to the scriptures he supposedly transcribed from golden plates whose location was revealed to him by an angel."

43. "DC Notebook: News Blogger's 'Satire' Equates Romney with Polygamist," *Salt Lake Tribune*, October 28, 2007, http://www.sltrib.com/news/ci_7302839 (accessed October 29, 2007).

44. Jacob Weisberg, "Romney's Religion: A Mormon President? No Way," *Slate*, December 20, 2007, http://www.slate.com/id/2155902/ (accessed December 27, 2007). While a number of Latter-day Saints considered Weisberg's piece anti-Mormon, John Schroeder, "When Does Opposition Descend into Bigotry?" Article VI Blog, January 16, 2007, http://www.article6blog.com/2007/01/16/when-does-opposition-descend-into-bigotry (accessed December 6, 2007), felt that it was "not so much anti-Mormon bigotry as it was anti-religious screed."

45. Christopher Hitchens, "Mitt the Mormon: Why Romney Needs to Talk about His Faith," *Slate*, November 26, 2007, http://www.slate.com/id/2178568 (accessed November 27, 2007). Howard Kurtz, "Romney and Religion," *Washington Post*, November 28, 2007, http://www.washingtonpost.com (accessed November 29, 2007), acknowledged Hitchens's desire to have Romney explain everything, including whether he wears temple garments. He was concerned, however, about how far the media would go in personal matters. "I would agree it's fair game to ask Romney about the Church's past racial practices. But the danger is that we in the media won't stop there, or even with said underwear, in making Mormonism an issue."

46. Timothy Garton Ash, "Could You Vote for a Man Who Abides by Moronish Wisdom?" *Guardian*, December 27, 2007, http://www.guardian.co.uk/commentisfree/story/0,,2232363,00.html (accessed December 28, 2007). Ash is an author and columnist, as well as a Fellow at St. Anthony's College, Oxford, and a Senior Fellow of the Hoover Institute at Stanford University. In spite of his scholarly background, Ash's comments are disturbingly personal and insulting. Unfortunately, his essay occurs practically at the same level of personal attack as Matt Taibi, "Mitt Romney: The Huckster," *Rolling Stone*, October 19, 2007, http://www.rollingstone.com/politics/story/1983679/mitt_romney_the_huckster (accessed December 3, 2007). For example, this article descends to the following level: "The most common thing you hear from voters after a Romney event is how impressed they are with his demeanor and delivery, his obvious vitality, by the fact that he looks like he could do this twenty-four hours a day and twice on Sunday, taking off only twenty-six minutes once a week to make monogamous, missionary-position love to his baby-factory wife."

47. "Lawrence O'Donnell," Harry Walker Agency, http://www.harrywalker.com/speakers_template_printer.cfm?Spea_ID=353 (accessed December 12, 2007); Scott D. Pierce, "Punditt Bashes Mitt, Mormons," *Deseret Morning News*, December 14, 2007, http://www.deseretnews.com/article/content/mobile/0,5223,695235563,00.html (accessed December 17, 2007); Bill Steigerwald, "A Liberal Who Loves

Markets: 'The West Wing's' Lawrence O'Donnell," Cagle Cartoons Subscription Download Site, November 11, 2005, http://caglecartoons.com/column.asp ?columnID=%7B3C798B88-CC34-4D12-865C-B7E91A29F0CE%7D (accessed December 27, 2007).

48. Pierce, "Pundit bashes Mitt, Mormons"; Jason Linkins, "Lawrence O'Donnell Loses His Ever-Loving Mind on McLaughlin," *Huffington Post*, December 9, 2007, http://www.huffingtonpost.com/2007/12/09/lawrence-odonnell-loses-_n_ 75987.html (accessed December 11, 2007); *The McLaughlin Group*, December 8–9, 2207, official transcript, http://www.mclaughlin.com/library/transcript.asp?id= 629 (accessed December 11, 2007). According to Mark Finkelstein, "Larry O'Donnell's Latest Rant: Mormonism 'Demented, Ridiculous,'" *News Busters*, December 9, 2007, http://www.newsbusters.org/node/17692 (accessed December 10, 2007), O'Donnell was "infamous for his in-your-face rant at John O'Neill of the Swiftboat Veterans."

49. Pierce, "Pundit Bashes Mitt, Mormons"; Todd Weiler, email to Weiler family et al., December 17, 2007, copy in my possession.

50. Frank Rich, "Latter-Day Republicans vs. the Church of Oprah," *New York Times*, December 16, 2007, http://www.nytimes.com/2007/12/16/opinion/16rich .html (accessed December 17, 2007).

51. "Sharpton Denies Questioning Romney's Faith," NewsMax.com, May 8, 2007, http://archive.newsmax.com/archives/ic/2007/5/8/211850.shtml (accessed July 19, 2008); "Romney Says Sharpton's Dig Could Be Considered Bigoted," NewsMax.com, May 9, 2007, http://archive.newsmax.com/archives/ic/2007/5/9/ 142040.shtml (accessed May 10, 2007); Lisa Riley Roche, "Catholics and Evangelicals Leap to Romney's Defense," *Deseret Morning News*, May 10, 2007, http://www .deseretnews.com/dn/print/1,1442,660219285,00.html (accessed May 10, 2007).

52. Roche, "Catholics and Evangelicals Leap."

53. Ibid. According to Peggy Fletcher Stack, "Sharpton Broadcasts from Salt Lake City, Says He Respects Mormons as Christians," *Salt Lake Tribune*, May 21, 2007, http://www.sltrib.com/ci_5947994 (accessed May 22, 2007), Sharpton later apologized for his remarks and, at the Church's invitation, visited Salt Lake City. He met with LDS Church officials, toured the Church's Welfare Square with its humanitarian center (which collects and distributes clothes, food, and medical supplies around the world), visited the spacious Conference Center, and toured the world-famous Family History Library. He told reporters, "Whatever differences I have with their denomination or religion had nothing to do with my respect of their faith."

54. Steve Benen, "Mitt Romney, Martin Luther King, and the Final Word," *Carpetbagger Report*, December 23, 2007, http://www.thecarpetbaggerreport.com/archives/14020.html (accessed December 28, 2007).

55. Mike Allen, "Witnesses Recall Romney-MLK March," *Politico*, December 21, 2007, http://www.politico.com/news/stories/1207/7524.html (accessed December 21, 2007); *Hannity & Colmes*, Fox News, December 20, 2007. Pat Buchanan said on *Hardball*, MSNBC, December 21, 2007, that there was plenty of evidence Romney had marched in support of civil rights. Mark Halprin, *The Live Desk with Martha McCallum*, Fox News, December 21, 2007, lamented Romney's "series of misstatements." He explained that Romney's "father was a great champion of civil rights" and Mitt Romney did not need to word it as he had.

56. "Redford Wants 'Lion' to Provoke Debate," *Washington Times*, November 8, 2007, http://washingtontimes.com/apps/pbcs.dll/article?AID=/20071108/ENTERTAINMENT/111080103/1001 (accessed November 9, 2007).

57. Chris Hicks, "Redford Shows Little Class with LDS Comment," *Deseret Morning News*, November 30, 2007, http://www.deseretnews.com/article/content/mobile/0,5223,695231780,00.html (accessed November 30, 2007). Unidentified writer, "Robert Redford, Aging Pretty Boy, Assesses Mormons," *National Review Online*, November 13, 2007, http://campaignspot.nationalreview.com/post/?q=MDE5NzkwMTdkNmI0YjY4YTIxMmZiMDQ1YTM2MTgyNWM (accessed November 14, 2007), took issue with Redford's statement that "Utah is where all these Republican senators go." *National Review Online* responded with "Yes, all *two* of them." The article then went on to say, "As usual, it's acceptable to make derisive remarks about Mormonism that would never be tolerated about other faiths."

58. "Hewitt Baselessly Claimed Romney Is 'Going to Have Problem with Anti-Mormon Bigots on the Left, Especially,'" *Media Matters for America*, http://www.mediamatters.org/items/ptintable/200703130012 (accessed November 28, 2007); Rich Lowry, "Mauling Mitt for Mormonism," *New York Post*, May 15, 2007, http://www.nypost.com/seven/05152007/postopinion/opedcolumnists/mauling_mitt_for_mormonism_opedcolumnists_rich_lowry.htm (accessed May 15, 2007).

59. Len Munsil, "Spotlight on Religion Works to Fracture Republican Coalitions," *Arizona Republic*, December 18, 2007, http://www.azcentral.com/arizonarepublic/opinions/articles/1218munsil18.html (accessed December 19, 2007).

60. Alex Spillius, "If Only Romney Weren't Such a Mormon," *Telegraph*, June 13, 2007, http://www.telegraph.co.uk/opinion/main.jhtml?xml=/opinion/2007/06/

13/do1305.xml (accessed June 13, 2007); Sally Denton, "Romney's Cross to Bear," *Los Angeles Times*, June 10, 2007, articles.latimes.com/2007/jun/10/opinion/op -denton10 (accessed June 12, 2008).

61. Ronald Kessler, "Liberals See Mormons as People of Faith on Steroids," NewsMax.com, June 13, 2007, http://archive.newsmax.com/archives/articles/2007/ 6/13/135928.shtml (accessed June 14, 2007). Land also said that it is a myth that liberals are "sweet, loving, and tolerant." Instead, "liberals do not tolerate people who disagree with them. And, of course, the one group they are least tolerant of is people who believe in moral absolutes."

Chapter 6

The Mormon Question: Right Cross

Early in the 2008 presidential election cycle, Richard Land, president of the Southern Baptist Convntion's Ethics and Religious Liberty Commission suggested that most of the anti-Mormon bias would come from the left. Although liberal disdain for Romney was considerable, the strongest negative reaction came from the right, including the media. As early as February 2007, *Media Matters for America*, a "progressive research and information center" which monitors conservative news outlets, accused Fox News of whitewashing evangelical hostility to Romney's Mormonism. According to *Media Matters*, Fox News had "largely avoided discussion of evangelical hostility to Mormonism and featured guests who have blamed the media and liberals for attacks on Romney's faith." For example, on Fox News's *Special Report*, guest commentator Fred Barnes said the anti-Mormonism was not "bigotry on the part of conservatives." Also, during coverage of the New Hampshire primary, Fox News showed a news clip from the anti-Mormon website, www.josephlied.org.[1]

However, from my perspective, reporting the 2008 election demonstrated less of a bias against the LDS Church than a bias for evangelicals. An example, during the reporting of the Iowa caucuses on January 3, 2008, was the issue of whether the evangelical vote had gone to Mike Huckabee because of the religious right's anti-Mormon sentiment. Bill Kristol, editor of the *Weekly Standard*, scoffed at the idea, said he had found no evidence of anti-Mormon sentiment in Iowa, and suggested that Romney had lost because of his flip-flopping. Carl Cameron, who traveled with the various

Republican campaigns, commented repeatedly through the evening
about how much Romney had spent and about his personal wealth.
At one point, he smirked, Romney was "supposed to be the big man"
who swept the first states. In contrast, Huckabee's win was "a won-
derful example of Huckabee connecting with the heartland." He
completely ignored the religious issue.[2]

During the New Hampshire primary, political analyst Juan
Williams commented that Romney's Mormonism had hurt him even
in New Hampshire. Bill Kristol immediately said, "You don't know
that." Williams opened his mouth to respond, but Kristol cut him
off: "You can't prove that." He then changed the subject. Whether the
downplaying of evangelical antipathy toward Romney and
Mormonism was a Fox News policy or whether it was the sentiment
of a few people on that network is unknown. What is known is that
the religious right is an important portion of Fox News's viewing audience, which Fox would be foolish to offend or alienate.[3]

The Religious Right

Joe Murray of the *Bulletin* wrote, "There always seems to be an
elephant waiting for [Mitt Romney] in the room during his campaign stops. This pachyderm is not the long held Republican symbol;
it is something more subtle, and more damning to the Romney camp.
It is his Mormon faith." As with the media and those on the left of
the political spectrum, those on the right have problems with Mitt
Romney's Mormonism.[4]

Bradley University religion professor Robert Fuller suggested
that "the Mormon issue will be a formidable obstacle" for Mitt
Romney because "there is an unspoken, tremendous rejection of the
Mormon religion" on both the right and left. In fact, while 43 percent of Americans in one poll said they would not vote for a
Mormon, 53 percent of evangelicals said they wouldn't. The figure
was significant and was part of the reason a South Carolina Assembly
of God pastor said Mitt Romney's faith "might make a [negative]
difference in the [GOP] primary, but not in a general election."[5]

The primaries are the most important elections at the beginning of a presidential campaign, and with more than 50 percent of evangelicals—a significant portion of the Republican base—refusing to vote for a Mormon, Romney's candidacy faced a formidable obstacle. Robert D. Novak warned in April 2006 that, while the U.S. Constitution prohibits a religious test for public office, "prominent, respectable Evangelical Christians had told me [Novak], not for quotation, that millions of their co-religionists cannot and will not vote for Romney for President solely because he is a member of The Church of Jesus Christ of Latter-day Saints." In a column in October 2007, Novak he stated that, wherever he traveled, Romney's "religious preference is cited everywhere as the source of opposition to his candidacy."[6]

Recognizing potential problems with the religious right, Mitt Romney met with fifteen prominent evangelicals and fundamentalists at his home near Boston in the fall of 2006. Invitations to forty-five were extended through Mark DeMoss, a Duluth-based public relations consultant who specializes in Christian ministries and whose clients include both Billy and Franklin Graham. The informal meeting was reportedly productive. DeMoss explained "The response was pretty interesting, because I knew there were some very strong feelings doctrinally about Mormonism. As it turned out, it appeared not to be a big issue." Romney felt reassured that religious right voters would be open to his candidacy.[7]

Unfortunately for Romney, there still were and are millions of Americans who won't vote for a Mormon. Despite the fact that Mormons are, according to one newspaper writer, "very much part of the American fabric" and "mainstream . . . in everything but their theology and their squeaky-clean, quirky Utah culture," they are still viewed with fear and suspicion by a large percentage of the population.[8]

Indeed, it seems to all come back to the Mormon question: Can a Latter-day Saint be trusted to hold high office? "The subtext to evangelicals' objections . . . is that a Mormon candidate is not worthy of the public's trust. Only a 'genuine' Christian should have the levers of power, many of them argue." Conservative columnist Craig

Chamberlain explained, "Anti-Mormonism is the last respectable bigotry in the United States."[9]

Christian or Not Christian

Evangelicals, especially Southern Baptists, both for and against Mitt Romney's candidacy, had warned him to not try to describe himself as a Christian. "I told him, you cannot equate Mormonism with Christianity; you cannot say, 'I am a Christian just like you,'" said Representative Bob Inglis of South Carolina, which was the first Southern state to hold its primary, in January 2008. "If he does that, every Baptist preacher in the South is going to have to go to the pulpit on Sunday and explain the differences."[10]

Richard Land observed, "When he [Romney] goes around and says Jesus Christ is my Lord and savior, he ticks off at least half the evangelicals. He's picking a fight he's going to lose." Instead, Land has suggested that he looks at the LDS Church "as another faith in the same sense that I would look upon Islam as another faith. I think the fairest and most charitable way to define Mormonism would be to call it the fourth Abrahamic religion—Judaism being first, Christianity being the second, Islam being the third, and Mormonism being the fourth. And Joseph Smith would play the same character in Mormonism that Muhammad plays in Islam."[11] Most evangelicals have absorbed the idea that Mormons are not Christian. Mary Doren, a Des Moines stay-at-home mom, was quoted as saying, "I'm a Christian. I don't think a Mormon or a Catholic is a Christian." Not only do they consider Mormons as not Christian, but many also "consider the church to be a mongrel sect."[12]

That attitude has been reflected over the years in LDS-evangelical interaction. For example, in 2004, "Mormons were barred from conducting services during National Day of Prayer ceremonies by the group's task force chairwoman," Shirley Dobson, whose husband, James C. Dobson, is founder and chair of the conservative Focus on the Family. Senator Robert F. Bennett (R-UT) remembered that, when he chaired the National Prayer Breakfast, some people expressed surprise that a Mormon would be allowed to conduct it since the prayer breakfast "had always been so Christian."[13] Because evangelicals and fundamentalists believe that the LDS Church is not "a Biblical-based, Judeo-Christian religion," indeed, nothing more than a cult, many have drawn the conclusion they could not vote for a Mormon candidate. Another Iowa evangelical explained that she wanted a president who "would be able to pray to the God of the Bible and He would be able to hear his prayers." She wondered if Romney's prayers "even get through."[14]

Other religious leaders were even more outspoken in asserting that the LDS Church is nothing more than a non-Christian cult. Pastor Ted Haggard, then president of the National Association of Evangelicals, stated that evangelicals were appalled at some Mormon doctrines, particularly their belief in the Book of Mormon: "We evangelicals view Mormons as a Christian cult group. A cult group is a group that claims exclusive revelation. And typically, it's hard to get out of these cult groups. And so Mormonism qualifies as that." Haggard's credibility was considerably tarnished less than a month later when he admitted in his church that he was a "deceiver and liar" and that he had been "sexually immoral" with a man over a three-year period. He was forced to resign his various ecclesiastical positions.[15]

Haggard, however, was not the only ecclesiastical or political leader to equate Mormonism with a cult. In Marion, Iowa, city councilman Craig Adamson sent out an email: "If 'you think religion, especially Christianity, is being marginalized by ACLU and other organizations' then 'you would be piling on' if you vote for Mitt Romney because 'Mormonism is a cult. In case I didn't type clearly enough . . . Mormonism is a cult.'" He continued, "'Based on my knowledge of Mormonism, I would not trust him as my president as he might be fooled into believing most anything. How could he possibly negotiate with Islamic radicals? He might believe Muslims and Mormons are the same, just like [he] tries to pass off Mormons as Christians."[16]

Adamson's comments, however, were mild compared to the public excoriations of the Reverend Bill Keller, who had earlier served nearly three years in a federal prison for an insider-trading scam but now managed the website LivePrayer.com. Known as the "Dr. Phil of prayer" and "the next big thing in mass media religion," "he claims to operate the largest interactive Christian Website, to send his emails to 2.4 million people, to receive 40,000 emails per day, and to receive over $2 million last year in donations." On May 11, Keller issued a warning through his *Daily Devotionals* that a vote Romney would be "a vote for Satan." Keller called Mormonism a cult and its founder Joseph Smith a "murdering polygamist pedophile. Romney getting elected president will ultimately lead millions of souls to the eternal flames of hell!!!" He then added that "having Romney as President is no different than having a Muslim or Scientologist as President."[17] A month later, hosting his television show "Live Prayer TV," he titled the program, "Mr. Romney, show me your underwear!" and wore LDS temple garments over his clothing. During the show he condemned Mormonism as "a satanic cult," announced that "Mormons are people who have been inspired by Satan—literally," warned repeatedly that Mormons are liars and if challenged on their beliefs, "they will flat out lie to you." As for Romney, "Mr. Romney, like all members of his satanic cult, is a liar. A liar!"[18]

In response to accusations the LDS Church is a cult and is not Christian, Kim Farah, a spokeswoman from LDS Public Affairs, did not quibble: "The fact that we are Christians is non-negotiable." Elder Jeffrey R. Holland of the Quorum of the Twelve, second-ranked governing body in the LDS Church, announced in the October 2007 general conference, "Even as we invite one and all to examine closely the marvel of it, there is one thing we would not like anyone to wonder about it—that is whether or not we are Christians."[19]

Near the year's end, the LDS Church issued a statement that began: "There is a spiritual maturity demonstrated by those who can accept religious common ground with others and also respectfully acknowledge differences." Without reference to the Romney campaign, the press release continued: "It is bewildering to a Mormon to hear or read that some others feel that she or he is not a Christian. To a Mormon, any person who worships, loves and honestly tries to live by the teachings of Jesus Christ, as the Son of God and Savior of Mankind, is a fellow Christian. Theological differences unquestionably exist, but genuine, reverent love for and sincere striving to emulate the Savior qualify any person to call her- or himself a Christian."[20]

The Rev. Robert Jeffress, who had previously instructed his congregation at First Baptist Church of Dallas to vote for "a Christian," not for Romney, responded to Mormon Christian claims. On the powerfully engaging and thought-provoking documentary, *Article VI*, he explained that it was hypocritical of Mormons to admit there are differences between Mormonism and Christianity and then "to get upset" when Mormons are told they're not Christian.[21]

The Fear of Legitimizing Mormonism

Those from the religious right not only continue to doubt that Latter-day Saints are Christian, but view them as a very real threat. In fact, there appeared to be deep concern on the religious right that a Romney presidency would legitimize the LDS Church. Robert L. Millet, a professor of religious education at Brigham Young University, explained, "The far right fears that gaining the presidency would mean the grand legitimization of Mormonism as a Christian religion, and they don't want to see that happen."[22]

The fear of a Mormon presidency was verified by R. Philip Roberts, president of Midwestern Baptist Theological Seminary and coauthor of *Mormonism Unmasked* (1998), who wrote, "if you're a Christian, DON'T vote for Mitt Romney. Unless he repents from Mormonism and repudiates the Mormon Church, his Presidency can't help but endorse the Mormon church as a legitimate Christian faith and embolden others to follow him on the wide road that leads to destruction. (Certainly the Mormon church will use a Mormon President as proof of their legitimacy.) For the sake of the lost, don't put a Mormon in the White House. It's the loving thing too."[23]

On another occasion, Roberts said that a Mormon presidency would, "in essence, 'give every LDS missionary the calling card of legitimacy anywhere in the world.'" Televangelist Bill Keller, on another program of his Florida-based "Live Prayer TV," said, "If Romney was elected president, it would give mainstream credibility and acceptance to the Mormon cult and lead millions of people into

Mormon for President
Brian Fairrington

Brian Fairrington, "Mormon For President," Cagle Cartoons, February 9, 2007.

that cult." James Walker, president of the Watchman Fellowship, said, "My main concern with a Romney presidency is the hundreds of thousands of new converts that would be brought into the Mormon church." He also saw a Mormon in the White House as providing "instant credibility." Shawn McCraney, an ex-Mormon and now a born-again evangelical, admitted that he felt Mitt Romney would do a good job as president but that Christians should still vote against him because his election would legitimize Mormonism.[24]

Sheep Stealing and Poaching Converts

One of the major reasons that evangelicals, Southern Baptists in particular, fear allowing any more legitimacy to the LDS Church is because, as Richard Land explained, "There's a special tension with Mormonism, because probably two of the more aggressive evangelistic faiths in America are Southern Baptists and Mormons."[25]

This reputation of getting converts from each other, or, as some call it, stealing sheep or poaching converts, may explain some of the intense animosity, mostly on the part of the evangelicals but certainly not exclusive to them. As already discussed, evangelicals and Latter-day Saints have traditionally been antagonistic toward each other. Missionary work has been a part of the Latter-day Saint tradition since before the Church was established in 1830. In the deep South, Mormon proselytizing was marked by hostility that did not stop short of beatings and even murder. With the phrase, "every member a missionary" during the 1960s, an even greater emphasis was placed on missionary work. It coincided with an era when "fundamentalist Christians, including Baptists, Pentecostals and others, began a similar push."[26]

The difference between Latter-day Saints and the more evangelistic Protestant organizations is that the latter claim to "evangelize" rather than "proselytize." In other words, according to some scholars, there is an unwritten rule among Protestant denominations that they may evangelize (meaning take the message of Jesus Christ to non-Christians) but not proselytize (meaning attempting to attach people who are already Christians to their particular denomination). Because LDS missionaries go to all people, including other Christians, Southern Baptists, and other evangelists consider them proselytizing rather than evangelizing.[27]

Louis C. Midgley, an outspoken defender of Mormonism, suggested that this rule against trying to convert other Christians is why Southern Baptists are so adamant that Mormons are not Christians, "even very low voltage Christians." If they recognized Mormons as Christians, "their efforts to attack [Mormonism] would violate their own rule against sheep stealing."[28] Thus, the two groups continue to be rivals in the soul-saving contest.

"Religious fundamentalists traditionally fear potential rivals," observed one commentator. In fact, in the past, "some church-run colleges in the South were more receptive to Jews than Catholics on the faculties. That's because their daughters were much less likely to marry a Jew or convert to Judaism; Catholicism was more of a threat." The same reasoning extends to politics. Richard Land ex-

Pat Bagley, "Mormon Vote," *Salt Lake Tribune,* January 8, 2007.

plained that "most Southern Baptists had absolutely no problem with an observant Jew running for vice president. The difference [between Judaism and Mormonism] is that Judaism is not an actively evangelistic faith."[29]

There appears to be good reason for this animosity or fear of Mormons among the Southern Baptists. Richard Land stated in November 2007, "There are now more Mormons that used to be Southern Baptist than any other denomination."[30] In April 1988, the Arizona *Latter-day Sentinel* announced, "A recent study by the Southern Baptists revealed that an average of 282 members of their church join the LDS church every week. Coincidentally, the aveage [*sic*] Southern Baptist congregation has 283 members, which means the Baptists lose 52 congregations each year to Mormons."[31] LDS Church spokesperson Kim Farah acknowledged that the Church is accused of "poaching" Southern Baptists. She explained that while the Church does not keep statistics on new converts' prior religious affiliation, internal studies confirmed "significant growth" in the Southern states where the Baptist Church is most prevalent.[32]

Because of LDS missionary success among Southern Baptists and other evangelical denominations, these other denominations have produced movies, tracts, books, as well as lectures, classes, and seminars "to inoculate [evangelicals] against . . . Mormon missionaries." Furthermore, various ministries have evangelized Mormons and other visitors to LDS meetings and events by handing out literature, protesting, and verbally jousting with them.[33]

The Southern Baptist Convention even went so far in its religious war against the LDS Church as to hold its annual convention in Salt Lake City in 1998. Three thousand Southern Baptists, who had been prepared beforehand with literature and courses portraying Mormonism as a non-Christian cult, went door to door in an effort to evangelize Mormons. At the actual convention were press packets that included the video, *The Mormon Puzzle*, and the book, *Mormonism Unmasked*. There were also numerous vendor exhibits supplying a plethora of anti-Mormon material. The convention was opened with a minister saying they were meeting in the "headquarters of a counterfeit Christianity."[34]

In spite of the media build-up before the Salt Lake City convention, the large amount of anti-Mormon literature, and the army of Southern Baptists who converged on Salt Lake, there was very little actual confrontation between the two denominations. Over the years that has not always been the case. At times, the contests have been intense, with evangelicals and fundamentalists usually being the more aggressive.

The Christian Right vs. Latter-day Saints

Confrontations have ranged from simply passing out literature critical of Mormon history and doctrine to physically abusive encounters. Twice a year the LDS Church holds a two-day general conference in which Church leaders address the members. Although most of the membership around the world gathers in local stake centers for satellite transmissions of the sessions, those who attend in person at the 21,000-seat Conference Center must run a gauntlet of protestors who hand them printed matter accompanied by a barrage of verbal abuse.

As part of their "Christian witness," the evangelical demonstrators tell the Mormon faithful that they are going to hell for following a false prophet and that they are evil people who should come to the real Jesus. Some have called women "Mormon whores," a term also hurled at newly married brides still in their wedding gowns exiting the Salt Lake Temple. Holding the dubious distinction of "most obnoxious" are the Street Preachers, a group not affiliated with the Southern Baptist Convention. They wave large placards reading, for example, "L=Liars, D=Deceivers, S=Seducers" and "Mormonism is worse than child molesting homosexuals."[35]

In 2003, in a particularly offensive display, the Street Preachers wrapped temple garments around their necks, wiping their noses on them. One preacher wiped his backside with the garments as if they were toilet paper and then threw them on the ground and stamped on them. Angered at such blatant disrespect for sacred clothing, two Mormon men pushed the Street Preachers and grabbed the garments away. Both Mormon men were arrested for assault by Salt Lake City police and fined.[37] However, no other violence was reported.

Similar unfortunate confrontations have occurred across the country at other temples and Mormon pageants. Evangelicals have also sponsored a steady stream of seminars and publications critical of the LDS Church, inevitably resulting in heightened dislike and distrust between the two religious groups. Their acrimonious relationship has not gone unnoticed by the press and, in fact, at times seems to have been coaxed along by news reporters hungry for a good story. This was particularly the case with the 2008 presidential race, as a number of stories highlighting evangelical dislike for Mormonism appeared in print and electronic form. This rancor was also exploited by the various campaigns.

Some political pundits commented that the 2008 election might end up being the dirtiest one on record. While that may be an exaggeration, by February 5, 2008, when "Super Tuesday" saw state primaries simultaneously in twenty-four states, both Democrats and Republicans had witnessed a number of political dirty tricks. Some on the Republican side dealt with aspects of the Mormon question, apparently with the goal of scaring evangelicals away from voting for Mitt Romney.

Anti-Mormon websites and publications by evangelicals, ex-Mormons, and other critics of the LDS Church gave warnings against voting for Romney. In December 2007 the *Baptist Press* published a series of articles on Mormonism while the Reverend James R. Spencer published an essay against Romney on his Maze Ministry website. Professional anti-Mormons like Ed Decker of Saints Alive in Jesus and Rocky Hulse of the Christian's Visitors Center published books about the Romney run for the presidency. Tricia Erickson, a former Mormon who left the LDS Church in her teens, "launched a media blitz designed to discredit Mitt Romney based on his religion." She has also advertised herself as a lecturer on Mormonism and brainwashing.[38]

Conspiracy Theories: The Mormon Plot for Political Domination

Among the arguments used to dissuade potential evangelical voters were the traditional accusations that Mormonism is a non-Christian cult and focus on such sensationalized aspects as its polygamous history, temple garments, strange doctrines, and other sensational accusations. Perhaps the most lurid anti-Mormon accusation used against Mitt Romney during the first part of the 2008 presidential campaign was the supposed Mormon plot to take over the American government with the ultimate goal of world domination.

While some secularists expressed concern that a Romney presidency would be too religious and that Mitt Romney's religiosity would influence his decisions, those on the Christian right claimed that a Romney presidency would be controlled by Mormon leaders in Salt Lake City. Evangelicals expressed concern that "Mormon requirements for eternal life" would make Romney "more accountable to [his] prophet than the U.S. Constitution." In other words, he would get his "marching orders from his 'living prophet'" rather than the American people.[39]

One evangelical arguing anonymously against a Mormon presidency announced that "Jesus is an Anti-Mormon" because He warned against false apostles. His weblog entry concluded: "Don't vote for Mitt Romney. His Mormon cult, complete with 12 'apostles' (AND a 'living prophet') is just too goofy. (And creepy.) Unless you've come out of Mormonism yourself or live in a Mormon enclave, you really can't know how Mormons think. There's no predicting what Mitt Romney will do as President, except to know he's bound to do what his church leadership tells him to do. Go ahead. Be a bigot like Jesus. Don't put a Mormon in the White House."[40]

Ed Decker, an ex-Mormon who has made a lucrative living since the 1970s with his anti-Mormon lectures and literature, advertised his 2008 book, *My Kingdom Come: The Mormon Quest for Godhood*, in which he called Mormonism the "American Islam." He disclosed what he said were Mormon plans to make America "a Mormon theocracy" in which Mitt Romney would "lead the way as both U.S. President and LDS high priest." He warned his readers "You need to read it now before it is too late."[41]

Michael Moody, a Las Vegas resident and former "Nevada coordinator of Republicans for Kerry," claimed to be a seventh-generation Mormon as well as having "long-time personal ties to his one-time college fraternity brother, Mitt Romney." This rather vague and tenuous connection was Moody's claim to expertise, which he felt justified his book *Mitt—Set Our People Free!* published in 2008 by Revelation Press. The press release announcing the publication of the book trumpeted, "Like Toto in Oz, this book tears away the curtain and reveals the truth behind the Mormon Church and its beliefs about the U.S. presidency." During the press conference, Moody "mocked his former religion (in very nasty terms)" and called it "the great American cult."[42]

Also predicting that America was "in dire straits," was the website, "Freedom Defense Advocates" headed by John Boyd, a resident of Lynchburg, Virginia, headquarters of Jerry Falwell's now-disbanded Moral Majority and his Liberty University. Boyd warned, "Your God-given freedoms will be lost and replaced by an evil government plotting to force its Satanic doctrines upon the American people." The evil, of course, was Mormonism, which was described as "a rehashed version of Islam." Boyd also sent letters to Florida voters, referring them to the website and asking for a donation.[43]

One of the most colorful and outlandish accusations of a Mormon conspiracy to take over America and ultimately the world was a story that has been around since at least the early 1980s and re-published in 2007 as a response to the Romney campaign. According to stories published by at least two former Mormons turned anti-Mormon, the Washington D.C. LDS Temple, located in Kensington, Maryland, north of the District of Columbia, has "an exact replica of the Oval Office of the White House." From this mock Oval Office "the prophet could run the nation just as easily as he could from the White House itself."[44]

In an effort to quash rumors of an insidious Mormon plot to take over the government, as well as to allay fears that he would follow orders from Salt Lake City, Mitt Romney announced on CBS's "Face the Nation" program, "No president could possibly take orders or even input from religious leaders telling him what to do. My church wouldn't endeavor to tell me what to do on an issue, and I wouldn't listen to them on an issue that related to our nation."[45]

An editorial that appeared in *National Review* came to Romney's defense: "Distinctively Mormon views on salvation will not affect, and have not affected Romney's conduct in office. But at the same time he should make it clear that Mormon values will have a large effect—and that these values are widely shared." Tom Minnery, the political director of Focus on the Family, added fairly that Romney hadn't turned "the governor's mansion in Massachusetts into a Mormon temple."[46]

In an interesting twist, an article in the *New York Times* in 1998 had pointed out that the country's highest elected officials were all Southern Baptists: from President Bill Clinton and Vice-President Al Gore down to the House Minority Leader Richard Gephardt. Richard Land was quoted saying, "We're no longer out in the cold. We're on the inside now. We don't have to explain to Bill Clinton and Al Gore how important Southern Baptists are to the political life of this nation. We had to explain it to George Bush." A conservative Baptist news site commented editorially on this article, "I would rather have a 'secular' George Bush in office that [*sic*] a 'saved' Southern Baptist if they 'all' turn out like Carter, (Mormons are Christian advocate[s]) and Clinton (Sodomite advocate) [*sic*]."[47]

Notes

1. "Fox News Whitewashes Evangelical Hostility to Romney's Faith," *Media Matters for America*, February 27, 2007, http://www.mediamatters.org/items/printable/200702280002 (accessed January 11, 2008); email to fairapol@lists.fairlds.org, February 11, 2008, copy in my possession.

2. My notes on "Special Report on the Iowa Caucus Night," Fox News, January 3, 2007. Cameron appeared to have taken a personal dislike to Romney, making reference to Romney's wealth in a number of reports over a long period of time. Romney's wealth continued to be a hot topic for Fox News commentators who repeatedly attributed Romney's staying in the campaign to his personal fortune. Rarely did they mention that, up through mid-January 2008, Romney had also brought in more money through campaign donations than any other Republican candidate. For example, Fox News heralded the fact that John McCain's campaign raised $7 million during January 2008 but ignored the even more impressive fact that Romney's campaign raised $5 million in a single day in January.

3. My notes, "Special Report on the New Hampshire Primary," Fox News, January 8, 2008. Bill Kristol, *Geraldo at Large*, Fox News, January 20, 2008, explained that McCain was the candidate with the momentum because he was the only one to win two primaries. Actually, Romney had by then won the Michigan primary, won caucuses in both Nevada and Wyoming, and had the most delegates. Since Romney's withdrawal from the presidential race, most of the commentators on Fox News appear to be outspokenly positive about a possible McCain-Romney ticket.

4. Joe Murray, "Is America Ready for a Mormon President?" *Bulletin*, November 13, 2007, http://www.thebulletin.us/site/news.cfm?newsid=19017809&BRD=2737&PAG=461&dept_id=576361&rfi=6 (accessed November 14, 2007).

5. Fuller, quoted in Michael Miller, "Mitt Romney Has Turned Many Eyes to the LDS," *Daily Journal*, August 16, 2007, http://www.daily-journal.com/archives/dj/display.php?id=401150 (accessed August 20, 2007); Thomas Burr, "Voting for an

LDS Prez Not an Option, 43% Say," *Salt Lake Tribune*, November 21, 2007, http://www.sltrib.com/ci_4698065 (accessed November 27, 2006); Carolyn Click, "Will Evangelicals Support a Mormon?" *State*, September 2, 2007, http://www .thestate.com/news/v-print/story/161753.html (accessed September 4, 2007).

6. Robert D. Novak, "Robert Novak: Romney's Candidacy May Face an Unfair Religious Test," *Union Leader*, April 26, 2006, http://www.unionleader.com/default .aspx?storyDate=2006-04-27 (accessed April 27, 2007); Robert Novak, "Romney Can't Ignore Religious Bias," *Chicago Sun-Times*, October 4, 2007, http://www .suntimes.com/news/novak/587704,CST-EDT-novak04.article (accessed October 8, 2007).

7. "Mitt Romney, and Whether a Mormon Can Win the Hearts of Southern Baptists, Methodists," *Atlanta Journal-Constitution*, November 27, 2006, http:// www.ajc.com/metro/content/shared-blogs/ajc/politicalinsider/entries/2006/11/27/ mitt_romney_and_whether_a_morm.html (accessed November 29, 2006). Among the fifteen were Richard Land, president of the Southern Baptist Convention Ethics and Religious Liberty Commission; Franklin Graham, president and CEO of Billy Graham Evangelistic Association; Jerry Falwell, former leader of the now-defunct Moral Majority; Gary Bauer, former GOP presidential candidate and leader of the group American Values; Jay Sekulow, leader of the American Center for Law and Justice; Richard Lee, pastor of First Redeemer Baptist Church of Cumming, Georgia; Wendy Wright, president of Concerned Women for America; Paula White, co-pastor of the massive Church Without Walls in Tampa, Florida; Lou Sheldon, of the Traditional Values Coalition.

8. Barry Cleveland, "Time to Set Aside One More Prejudice," *Carmi Times*, November 8, 2007, http://www.carmitimes.com/articles/2007/11/08/news/news3.prt (accessed November 9, 2007).

9. "Evangelicals vs. Mitt Romney," *Daily Herald*, November 12, 2006, http:// www.heraldextra.com/content/view/199900/3 (accessed November 13, 2006).

10. Hans Nichols and Christopher Stern, "Romney Shouldn't Equate Mormons, Christians, Evangelicals Say," Bloomberg.com, October 30, 2008, http:// www.bloomberg.com/apps/news?pid=20601070&sid=aU_vOirVlXhY (accessed November 1 2007).

11. Hans Nichols and Christopher Stern, "Evangelicals Bristle over Mitt's Faith," *Deseret Morning News*, October 30, 2007, http://www.deseretnews.com/ article/mobile/0,5223,695223044,00.html (accessed October 31, 2007); David Van Biema, "What Is Mormonism? A Baptist Answer," *Time*, October 24, 2007, http://

www.time.com/time/nation/article/0,8599,1675308,00.html (accessed October 29, 2007). Land's comparisons of Joseph Smith and the LDS Church to Muhammad and Islam is not by happenstance. This misconception has been a part of anti-Mormon literature since the earliest days. See Craig L. Foster, *Penny Tracts and Polemics: A Critical Analysis of Anti-Mormon Pamphleteering in Great Britain, 1837–1860* (Salt Lake City: Greg Kofford Books, 2002); Craig L. Foster, "Old Themes and Stereotypes Never Die: The Unchanging Ways of Anti-Mormons," FAIR Conference, 2003, http://www.fairlds.org/FAIR_Conferences/2003_Unchanging_Ways_of_Anti-Mormons.html (accessed July 16, 2008); Craig L. Foster, "Victorian Pornographic Imagery in Anti-Mormon Literature," *Journal of Mormon History* 19 (Spring 1993): 130–32; and J. Spencer Fluhman, "An 'American Mahomet': Joseph Smith, Muhammad, and the Problem of Prophets in Antebellum America," *Journal of Mormon History* 35, no. 3 (Summer 2008): [in press].

12. Doran, as quoted in Barbara Bradley Hagerty, "Romney Faces Uphill Battle for Evangelical Voters," National Public Radio, July 9, 2007, http://www.npr.org/templates/story/story.php?storyId=11762390 (accessed July 9, 2007). While Mormonism is one of the main targets of evangelical animosity, it certainly is not the only one. Catholicism has traditionally borne a series of verbal and print attacks. For example, as late as 2001 a flurry of letters to the editor of the *Kingsport Times-News* debated whether Catholics and Mormons are Christians. "Catholics and Mormons Unwelcome in Sullivan County, Tennessee," http://www.sullivan-county.com/nf0/fundienazis/cath_attacked.htm (accessed May 21, 2007). Columnist Andrew Greeley, "Faith Should Play a Minor Role in Politics," *Times Union*, January 4, 2008, http://timesunion.com/AspStories/story.asp?storyID=652336 (accessed January 4, 2008), wrote: "I'm a Catholic. You got a problem with that? I'm a Christian too. . . . We've been Christians since the beginning. The claim of the evangelicals to a monopoly on the term is little more than a century old. It excludes Mormons, secularists and Catholics. We don't like being excluded and we might just begin to make trouble about it. We invented Christianity, guys, and your claim to sole rights is historical nonsense—and bigotry too."

13. "O'Reilly Asserted Secular Progressives Think 'Mitt Romney Is a Dangerous Mormon,' But Polls Show Conservatives More Reluctant to Vote for a Mormon," *Media Matters for America*, January 9, 2008, http://mediamatters.org/items/200801100001 (accessed July 7, 2008); "Interview with Senator Robert F. Bennett," *The Doug Wright Show*, KSL Radio, January 3, 2008.

14. Bronsislaus B. Kush, "Mormons Can Face Resistance," *Worcester Telegram & Gazette News*, October 7, 2007, http://www.telegram.com/article/20071007/NEWS/710070505 (accessed October 8, 2007); Linda Wertheimer, "Romney Faces Questions over Faith in S. Carolina," National Public Radio, November 15, 2007, http://www.npr.org/templates/story/story.php?storyId=16315111 (accessed November 15, 2007); Michael Luo, "In Iowa, Mormon Issue Is Benefiting Huckabee," *New York Times*, November 28, 2007, http://www.nytimes.com/2007/11/28/us/politics/28repubs.html (accessed November 28, 2007).

15. Elizabeth Mehren, "Romney's 2008 Bid Faces Issue of Faith," *Los Angeles Times*, October 10, 2006, http://www.latimes.com/news/nationworld/nation/la-na-mitt10oct10,1,6805742.story?coll=la-headlines-nation (accessed October 10, 2007); Dennis Prager, "Is Ted Haggard a Hypocrite?" *World Net Daily*, November 7, 2006, http://www.worldnetdaily.com/news/article.asp?ARTICLE_ID=52816 (accessed January 31, 2007); "Church Forces Out Haggard for 'Sexually Immoral Conduct,'" CNN.com, November 4, 2006, http://www.cnn.com/2006/US/11/03/haggard.allegations/index.html (accessed January 31, 2007).

16. "Iowa City Councilman calls Mormonism a Cult," ABC News, December 13, 2007, http://www.boxxet.com/60_Minutes/ABC_NEWS_Jake_Tapper_Iowa_City_Councilman_Calls_Mormonism_a_Cult.1e79ki.d (accessed December 17, 2007).

17. LivePrayer.com homepage, http://www.liveprayer.com/index.cfm (accessed December 31, 2007); "Message from the President," *FAIR Journal*, July 2007, http://www.fairlds.org/FAIR_Journal/FJ200707.html (accessed January 31, 2007); "Televangelist Bill Keller Calls Mormonism and Islam 'False Religions,'" *Jews on First!* June 23, 2007, http://www.jewsonfirst.org/07c/keller.html (accessed December 31, 2007). For Keller's prison record, see Alexandra Alter, "TV Preacher Aims at the Multitudes," *Miami Herald*, May 28, 2006, http://www.liveprayer.com/press/mh.htm (accessed March 12, 2008). The Americans United for Separation of Church and State, according to "Group Sics IRS on Mormon Critic," *World Net Daily*, April 17, 2008, http://www.wnd.com/index.php?fa=PAGE.printable&pageId=41892 (accessed April 17, 2008), made a formal written request that Keller's ministry be reviewed for possible violations of federal tax law. Keller responded, "Let them come after me for making a spiritual statement about Mitt Romney."

18. "Televangelist Bill Keller Calls Mormonism and Islam 'False Religions,'" *Jews on First!*; "Message from the President," *FAIR Journal*. Keller later claimed victimhood for the negative fallout. In "The Fallout from Taking On Romney, the Mormons and Other Evangelical Leaders," Live Prayer, November 27, 2007, http://

www.liveprayer.com/ddarchive3.cfm?id=3136 (accessed February 21, 2008), he wrote, "Even though I expected it, what made me saddest of all were the brutal attacks by those who identified themselves as Christians."

19. Nichols and Stern, "Evangelicals Bristle over Mitt's Faith"; "Teachings Worry Some Conservatives," *Fort Worth Star-Telegram*, December 4, 2007, http://www.star-telegram.com/national_news/story/339912.html (accessed December 4, 2007); and "Real Differences, Real Similarities and Biblical Christianity," LDS Newsroom, http://newsroom.lds.org/ldsnewsroom/eng/commentary/real-differences-real-similarities-and-biblical-christianity (accessed October 16, 2007). Comments among the rank and file members of the LDS Church are perhaps even more revealing regarding about whether Latter-day Saints are Christian. I heard one Mormon say, "I can't believe how arrogant some of them are to question if we're Christian or not. I may not agree with Baptists, Catholics or Methodists, but I take it at face value they're Christian. Who am I to question their hearts and decide on my own if they're Christian? I'll leave that to God to decide."

20. "Peace on Earth, Goodwill to All Men—Not Just Those Who Share My Beliefs," LDS Newsroom, December 21, 2007, http://newsroom.lds.org/ldsnewsroom/eng/commentary/peace-on-earth-goodwill-to-all-men-not-just-those-who-share-my-beliefs (accessed January 2, 2008).

21. Bryan Hall and Jack Donaldson, *Article VI: Faith. Politics. America*, documentary film, Living Biography Media and Wiley Rhodes Productions in association with Outside Eyes Film, 2008.

22. Julia Duin, "Evangelicals Key to Romney Run," *Washington Times*, September 11, 2006, http://www.washingtontimes.com/news/2006/sep/10/20060910-115756-6222r (accessed September 12, 2006).

23. Rachel Waligorski, "Romney 'Unlikely' Choice of Evangelicals," *Baptist Press*, June 21, 2007, http://www.bpnews.net/BPnews.asp?ID=25946 (accessed January 2, 2008); Carrie Sheffield, "Evangelicals against Mitt," *American Spectator*, January 3, 2008, http://www.spectator.org/dsp_article.asp?art_id=12514 (accessed January 3, 2008); Frank Pastore, "Christian Angst over a Romney Presidency," Townhall.com, December 18, 2007, http://www.townhall.com/columnists/FrankPastore/2007/12/18/christian_angst_over_a_romney_presidency (accessed December 19, 2007).

24. Waligorski, "Romney 'Unlikely' Choice of Evangelicals"; Paul Chesser, "Prejudiced for Eternity," *American Spectator*, November 1, 2007, http://www.spectator.org/dsp_article.asp?art_id=12251 (accessed November 6, 2007); Craig L.

Foster, Shawn McCraney, et al., "Panel Discussing Mormonism and the U.S. Presidency at a Screening of Adam Christing, *A Mormon President* (La Mirada, Calif.: Creek Park Pictures, 2008)," December 12, 2007.

25. Howard Berkes, "Faith Could Be Hurdle in Romney's White House Bid," National Public Radio, June 19, 2007, http://www.npr.org/templates/story/story.php ?storyId=7260620 (accessed June 19, 2007).

26. Thomas B. Edsall, "Will Anti-Mormon Sentiment Cost Romney GOP Nomination?" *Huffington Post*, June 7, 2007, http://www.huffingtonpost.com/2007 /06/07/thomas-b-edsall-will-ant_n_51232.html (accessed July 27, 2007). So deep is the evangelical dislike for Latter-day Saints that in 2000 the Festival of Faith, "celebrating a common faith in Christ," would not allow Latter-day Saints to participate. While forty Christian denominations and five hundred congregations were represented, "hard-line evangelical faiths insisted the [LDS] church be excluded or they themselves would not attend," according to Lawn Griffiths, "Christian Fest Snubs Mormons: Hard-Liners Would Not Attend Event with Latter-day Saints," *East Valley Tribune/Mesa Tribune*, January 31, 2000, http://www.mazeministry.com/ mormonism/mormons_evangelicals/mesa.htm (accessed December 12, 2007). Unfortunately, such uncomfortable confrontations are not uncommon.

27. Louis Midgley, Letter to FAIR Apologetics List, December 24, 2007, copy in my possession.

28. Ibid.

29. Land, quoted in Albert R. Hunt, "The Race for President: Is It a Matter of Faith?" *International Herald Tribune*, July 22, 2007, http://www.iht.com/articles/ 2007/07/22/america/letter.php (accessed November 28, 2007); Berkes, "Faith Could Be Hurdle in Romney's White House Bid."

30. Richard Land, quoted in "Baptists Cool to Mitt because Mormons Keep Luring Away Their Congregation?" Hot Air, November 20, 2007, http://hotair.com/ archives/2007/11/20/baptists-cool-to-mitt-because-mormons-keep-luring-away -their-congregation/ (accessed June 14, 2008).

31. Ed Stoddard, "Romney a Tough Sell for Many U.S. Christians," *Washington Post*, November 20, 2007, http://www.washingtonpost.com/wp-dyn/content /article/2007/11/20/AR2007112002302.html (accessed November 26, 2007); *Latter-day Sentinel*, April 2, 1988, as quoted in Rick Branch, "Stealing Pastors and Converting Their People," *Watchman Expositor* 6, no. 8 (1989), http://www.watchman.org/lds /stealing.htm (accessed January 4, 2008).

32. Craig L. Foster, "Telephone Interview with Kim Farah," November 29, 2007.

33. Stoddard, "Romney a Tough Sell for Many U.S. Christians."

34. Neil J. Young, "Southern Baptists vs. the Mormons," *Slate*, December 19, 2007, http://www.slate.com/id/2180391 (accessed January 5, 2008).

35. Scott Gordon, "Message from the President," *FAIR Journal*, July 2007, http://www.fairlds.org/FAIR_Journal/FJ200707.html (accessed July 19, 2008); "Main Street Plaza Opened to Opinion," BYU News Net, April 7, 2003, http://newsnet.byu.edu/story.cfm/43695 (accessed March 13, 2007). "Utah Street Preacher Lonnie Pursifull," *Edifying Spectacle*, April 22, 2004, http://edifyingspectacle.org /archives/gullibility/religious_intolerance/utah_street_preacher_lonn.php (accessed March 13, 2007). One preacher verbally abused a group of twelve- and thirteen-year-old girls who were helping plant flowers on the plaza, yelling, "I would rather be gay than fornicate with you." The Street Preachers' Fellowship, according to its website, http://www.streetpreachersfellowship.com (accessed March 13, 2007), is a worldwide organization that preaches at numerous places and events, including the Super Bowl, Mardi Gras (which the Street Preachers' website refers to as "the annual Catholic whoremongers' riot"), and the NOW parade in Washington, D.C. (which the Street Preachers' website refers to as the parade of the "National Organization of Wackos, Witches & Whores").

36. Brady Snyder, "Conference Clashes Result in 2 Arrests," *Deseret News*, October 6, 2003, http://www.rickross.com/reference/mormon/mormon122.html (accessed June 14, 2008).

37. "In Our View: Protesters Went Past Free Speech," *Provo Daily Herald*, October 12, 2003, http://www.heraldextra.com/content/view/74577/150/ (accessed July 19, 2008); Doug Robinson, "Provo Man Is Hero, Not a Criminal," *Deseret Morning News*, October 14, 2003; Bob Lonsberry, "How about Tolerance for All?" FAIR.org, October 7, 2003, http://www.fairlds.org/Anti-Mormons/How_About_ Tolerance_For_All.html (accessed July 7, 2008). Even evangelical ministers felt that the Street Preachers had gone too far and were inciting a riot. About two weeks after the arrests, two dozen evangelical Christian clergy gathered in front of the Conference Center and expressed disapproval of the Street Preachers' words and actions. "Alliance Condemns 'Boorish' Behavior," *Salt Lake Tribune*, October 18, 2003; Peggy Fletcher Stack, "Salt Lake City Clergy Call for Civility toward LDS," *Salt Lake Tribune*, October 22, 2003, http://www.sltrib.com/2003/Oct/10222003/ utah/104229.asp (accessed October 24, 2003). During the following April General Conference, Standing Together Ministries announced they would have people on sidewalks outside the Conference Center "not to protest or protest against the pro-

testers, but to express 'love and kindness to whoever passes' by." Brady Snyder, "Evangelicals to Join Crowds on Sidewalks," *Deseret Morning News*, April 1, 2004.

38. Rachel Waligorski, "Romney 'Unlikely' Choice of Evangelicals"; Lawn Griffiths, "Christian Fest Snubs Mormons"; "Anti-Mormon Advertiser Running Romney Ads on Google," ClickZ, December 18, 2007, http://post.blog .searchenginestrategies.com/cgi-bin/mt/mt-tb.cgi/12800 (accessed January 2, 2008; Chris Faulkner, "Nauvoo Man Authors Book about Mormonism," *Fort Madison Daily Democrat*, December 10, 2007, http://www.dailydem.com/articles/2007/12/ 07/news/news2.txt (accessed December 11, 2007); Sheffield, "Evangelicals against Mitt"; "Tricia Erickson," Renaissance Women, http://www.rwnetwork.net/Profiles .php?id=22 (accessed January 5, 2007). Erickson, who has been a Hollywood casting director, was then head of a modeling agency that represented well-known women like Fawn Hall and Donna Rice. She is now a crisis management expert and speaks professionally on Islam, Mormonism, Wal-Mart, Michael Jackson, scandals, adultery, and divorce, among other subjects.

39. William K. Poston Jr., letter to editor, "Mormonism May Be 'Legitimate,' But It Differs from Christianity," *Des Moines Register*, November 25, 2007, https:// www.desmoinesregister.com/apps/pbcs.dll/article?AID=/20071125/OPINION04/71 (accessed November 25, 2007); Waligorski, "Romney 'Unlikely' Choice of Evangelicals."

40. "Jesus on Mitt Romney's False Apostles," Romney for President. NOT!, a blog on Townhall.com, July 14, 2007, http://romneyforpresident.townhall.com/ 2007/07 (accessed July 7, 2008). The site's address is deliberately misleading to attract Romney supporters who are then subjected to anti-Romney and anti-Mormon messages.

41. "The TRUTH about Mitt Romney and the Mormon Agenda for the USA," Mormon Agenda, http://mormonagenda.com/newsletters/nov-dec2007/nov-dec2007 .htm (accessed December 13, 2007).

42. "Revelation Press Publishes Blockbuster Exposé: Mitt—Set Our People Free," Reuters, January 7, 2008, http://www.reuters.com/article/pressRelease/ idUS173077+07-Jan-2008+PRN20080107 (accessed January 8, 2008). Apparently, the press was unimpressed with both the author and the news conference. Mary Ann Akers, "Lapsed Mormon Unloads on Mitt Romney," *Washington Post*, January 7, 2008, http://blog.washingtonpost.com/sleuth/2008/01/former_classmate_and_ lapsed_mo.html (accessed January 8, 2008), described the press conference and book as "dirty tricks." James Joyner, "New Book Reveals Romney . . . a Mormon," *Outside*

the *Beltway*, January 7, 2008, http://www.outsidethebeltway.com/archives/2008/01/
new_book_reveals_romney_a_mormon (accessed January 8, 2008), commented on
both the author and press, "These people are clearly buffoons."

43. "Freedom Defense Advocates," http://www.exposemittromney.com (accessed January 2, 2008); Thomas Burr, "Letter Claims LDS Conspiracy," *Salt Lake
Tribune*, January 1, 2008, http://www.sltrib.com/news/ci_7855506 (accessed
January 2, 2008).

44. William P. Schnoebelen, "Mitt Romney and the Mormon Plan for
America," http://www.withoneaccord.org/store/Romney.html (accessed December
18, 2007); Daniel C. Peterson, "A Modern Malleus maleficarum," *FARMS Review*
Vol. 3 (1989), http://farms.byu.edu/display.php?table=review&id=72 (accessed
January 6, 2008); Daniel C. Peterson, "P. T. Barnum Redidivus," Lightplanet.com
http://www.lightplanet.com/response/decker-handbook.htm (accessed January 6,
2008); "The Mormon Conspiracy within the Church," http://www.mormonconspiracy
.com/mormon.html (accessed December 19, 2007). Rev. Bill Keller, "An Evil Tool of
Satan Masquerading as a Godly Grandfather Is Burning in Hell," Live Prayer,
January 29, 2008, http://liveprayer.com/ddarchive3.cfm?id=3207 (accessed February
21, 2008), commented about the supposed Oval Office replica in the Washington
D.C. Temple but described it only as "a special room . . . that has been prepared and
in place for over 30 years, which will be the seat of power of the Mormon-led government which will supplant our current government." Keller probably realized that
his reading audience would scoff at the idea of an actual Oval Office replica in the
temple so he left out that detail.

45. Nicholas Johnston, "Romney Won't 'Take Orders' from Church," *Deseret
Morning News*, October 22, 2007, http://deseretnews.com/article/1,5143,695220737
,00.html (accessed October 22, 2007).

46. "Romney's Religion," *National Review Online*, November 16, 2007, http://
article.nationalreview.com/?q=MGQ4YmM4Y2U3Yjc3MzYzNDQwYzk3YTVjM
TI5YTkwNzg= (accessed November 19, 2007); Nichols and Stern, "Evangelicals
Bristle over Mitt's Faith."

47. Laurie Goodstein, "The Nation: Look Who's Leading the Country," *New
York Times*, June 14, 1998, http://query.nytimes.com/gst/fullpage.html?res=9904
E2D61F3AF937A25755C0A96E958260 (accessed January 6, 2007); "Government
Run by Southern Baptists?" *Christian News & Reviews*, May–June 1998, http://
cnview.com/news_service/cnv_may_1998.htm#Government%20Run%20By%20
Southern%20Baptists? (accessed January 5, 2008).

Chapter 7
The Mormon Question: Low Blow

In spite of Mitt Romney's attempts to assuage evangelical fears and misgivings, his reception by the Religious Right was cool at best. Other evangelicals used political dirty tricks and publicly waged a campaign to discourage their fellow religionists from supporting Romney, including one who broadcast a proposed Romney campaign slogan, "Send him to the White House before he goes to hell." A day before the Iowa straw poll, a flyer was passed out stating, "we strongly believe that Jesus Christ, if he were alive in the flesh in this time and voted, would NEVER vote for Mitt Romney under any circumstances." A week before the presidential primary debate in South Carolina a tract titled, "Mormons in Contemporary American Society: A Politically Dangerous Religion?" was mailed to Republican voters. In the tract, Joseph Smith was called the "Mohammed of the West."[1]

Other political dirty tricks played on religious mistrust. In the middle of November 2007, voters in both Iowa and New Hampshire received phone calls criticizing Mitt Romney and Mormonism. The apparent push-polls discussed Romney's "flip-flops," then described Mormonism as a cult and discussed the Book of Mormon and Mormon doctrines. The same phone calls also praised John McCain, thus giving the impression that McCain had authorized the phone calls.[2] The reaction from both the Romney and McCain campaigns was quick and strong. Mitt Romney called the phone calls "un-American" while John McCain angrily denied ordering the phone calls and demanded an investigation to get to the bottom of who had really ordered and paid for the calls.

The New Hampshire attorney general's office began an investigation of what one political commentator called "cowardly gutter politics."[3] The investigation, which continued into January 2008, turned up the bizarre revelation that the calls had come from a Utah firm called Western Wats. Further muddying the waters was the fact that the Lindorf family, original owners of Western Wats, were Romney's friends and donors to the campaign. Rumors started to spread on the internet that the calls had been either set up by Romney or his associates or could have been orchestrated by the LDS Church to see if Romney's Mormonism was going to be an issue among voters. The Romney campaign vehemently denied these accusations, and the Lindorf family informed the press that they had sold the company in 2006. Furthermore, the New Hampshire attorney general's office found that, while Western Wats had performed the calling, Moore-Information, a Portland, Oregon, company, had acted as middleman and hired the Utah company.[4]

While the investigation continued, fingers pointed in different directions. Among the suspects was Mike Huckabee and his campaign, because a group supporting Huckabee did push-polling in early December. The Huckabee campaign immediately denied any connection. The phone calls attacked Rudy Guiliani, John McCain, and Fred Thomson but ignored Mitt Romney. That omission, however, was probably designed to throw suspicion on an innocent party much as the earlier push-polls had attempted to implicate John McCain.[5]

Another political dirty trick focusing on Romney's religion was Christmas cards sent to many South Carolina Republicans, supposedly from the Romney family. The card contained passages that underscored differences between Mormon beliefs "and those of denominations that are prevalent in South Carolina." On the back of the card was a photograph of an LDS temple with the caption, "Paid for by the Boston Massachusetts Temple." The South Carolina Republican Party chairman, Katon Dawson, promised to report the mailings to the FBI's Elections Fraud Division, and the Romney campaign called the cards and similar tactics "gutterball politics."[6]

Campaign Dirty Tricks

While some of these political dirty tricks might have been the work of independent groups, most, if not all, were probably inspired and perhaps even acted out by campaign operatives. Dirty tricks are, unfortunately, often a part of political campaigns, especially presidential campaigns. They had practically become a hallmark of Richard Nixon's campaign, leading to the Watergate break-in that eventually brought down his presidency. During the 2008 presidential campaign, accusations flew back and forth between the various candidates, and virtually none escaped unscathed.

For example, Mitt Romney's campaign was accused of creating an anti-Fred Thompson website called "Phoney Fred." The day before the Iowa caucuses, according to the Huckabee campaign, Romney supporters had called Huckabee's supporters, giving them incorrect caucus locations. The Romney campaign denied those charges, but the Huckabee campaign remained unconvinced. In South Carolina, Huckabee workers warned that Romney's political consulting firm had a history of dirty election tactics and to look out for other deceptions.[7]

However, most of the unethical practices flowed in one direction and focused on Romney's Mormonism. They ranged from the subtle and simplistic to the more complex and hard-hitting. For example, in South Carolina, what one British newspaper called "the foulest swamp of electoral dirty tricks in America," the Romney campaign was plagued by phone calls, emails, and regular mailings. One political operative commented, "Without question, the dirtiest campaigners in South Carolina are the ones who represent the family-values candidates. No question about it. They're going after the hymn-book vote, but the methods are satanic."[8]

The anti-Romney dirty tricks began early. An online mass mailing "cautioned of the 'dark secrets' of Mitt Romney's Mormonism." Paper mailings went out of literature critical to both Romney and Mormonism, including an anonymous, eight-page letter explaining why Mormonism was politically dangerous.[9]

The aim in political dirty tricks is to hurt the rival candidate without having anything bounce back negatively on the candidate originating the attacks. Anonymity is the best way to avoid potential negative publicity. During the 2008 election, the origin of some political attacks and dirty tricks remained unknown while others didn't. When discovered, some candidates quickly apologized and tried to put the event behind them while others did not.

For example, when one of Sam Brownback's campaign workers sent out an email raising the Mormon question and suggesting that Romney was not a real Christian, Brownback apologized, explained that candidates should not be subjected to a "religious test," and instructed that people working on his campaign should not "have this discussion." He insisted that his campaign was about policy issues, not theological questions and religious beliefs. He then personally apologized to Mitt Romney, who graciously accepted. Previous to the apology, Romney had not been as gracious. In fact, he had specifically pointed out that Brownback had "run a uniformly negative campaign, distorted the truth and been mean-spirited."[10]

By the summer of 2007, most of the campaigns were using "whispers and innuendo," hoping to cause doubts among voters. Steffen Schmidt, a political science professor at Iowa State University, said, "Without saying it overtly, all of [Romney's] adversaries are sort of dropping hints. 'Well, do you really want to have a Mormon?' There is an effort to make it an issue."[11]

In June 2007, Chad Workman, chairman in Warren County, Iowa, for the McCain campaign, questioned whether Mormons were Christian and then cited an article "charging [that] the Mormon church helps fund Hamas militants and compar[ing] the church's treatment of women to the Taliban." One Republican activist present when Workman made his comments summed up Workman's argument this way: "The fundamental flaw of Mitt Romney . . . was that he was Mormon, not because he thinks this way or that way on one issue."[12]

Workman wasn't the only member of McCain's campaign to attack Romney's religion. In 2006, Chuck Larson, a former Iowa GOP chairman and one of McCain's top Iowa advisors, called the LDS

Church a "cult." In South Carolina, McCain operatives handed out literature questioning whether a Mormon could win the presidency. While the McCain campaign offered a blanket apology for the various attacks, John McCain, unlike Sam Brownback, refused to apologize personally to Mitt Romney, which was not surprising in light of McCain's intense dislike of Romney. In public forums McCain could barely conceal his loathing for Romney, but his posture toward Romney went beyond simple churlishness to openly questioning Romney's character. While discussing Romney on one occasion, McCain replied insultingly, "Never get into a wrestling match with a pig. You both get dirty, and the pig likes it."[13]

Romney, however, appeared oblivious to McCain's antipathy toward him. When questioned about McCain's refusal to apologize personally, Romney said, "[McCain] can do whatever he feels is the right thing. There's no need for me to suggest how people respond to things that go on in the campaign." The closest McCain came to personally apologizing was when an anti-Mormon comment was generated a little closer to home. In a November 2007 interview on MSNBC, McCain's ninety-five-year-old mother, Roberta McCain, responded to a question about Romney's success with the 2002 Olympics by retorting, "He's a Mormon and the Mormons of Salt Lake City had caused that scandal." John McCain, smiling during the interview, interposed that his mother's views did not represent his own. He later commented, "Mormons are great people and the fact that Mitt Romney is a Mormon should play no role whatsoever in people's decision."[14]

While John McCain and other candidates may have broached the Mormon question, Mike Huckabee became the first presidential candidate to drop "the Mormon Bomb on Mitt." According to commentators, he used religion "as [a] hammer to attack Mitt Romney," and the Republican presidential race became "a proxy religious war" or "holy war" between Huckabee and the evangelicals and Romney's Mormonism.[15]

Mike Huckabee, a former Baptist minister and governor of Arkansas who attributed his surprising rise in the 2007 polls to "Divine providence," campaigned as a "Christian leader." In an obvious swipe at Romney's faith and the evangelical perception that the LDS Church is not Christian, Huckabee played a TV advertisement in Iowa in which he said, "Faith doesn't just influence me. It really defines me." He ended the commercial by telling the viewing audience, "Let us never sacrifice our principles for anybody's politics. Not now, not ever."[16]

Recognizing his potential appeal to evangelical voters and understanding how to work the network of churches, Mike Huckabee used the "highly decentralized" evangelical community to his advantage. He regularly addressed congregations during Sunday services, insisting that he wasn't campaigning, just preaching the word of God. Of course, the facts that he visited the church, had the local pastor personally endorse him, and then admonished the congregation to vote for someone with their religious values, certainly helped his numbers.[17]

Huckabee was the only Republican presidential candidate to specifically reach out to evangelical pastors and attempt to organize their assistance. In Iowa, he held private meetings with pastors; several hundred attended a single meeting. In the early primary states, the Huckabee campaign also held conferences that were free for pastors, including meals and hotel rooms. Tim LaHaye, author of the apocalyptic *Left Behind* series, Rick Scarborough, and other high-profile evangelicals sent letters, made phone calls, and helped in other ways. Beverly LaHaye used the email list maintained by Concerned Women for America to encourage people to attend conferences to learn more about Mike Huckabee. Tim LaHaye claimed, "People will follow us from the pew into the voting booth."[18] Gary Glenn, president of the American Family Association of Michigan, sent out a memorandum explaining what steps to take and who to contact to get out the vote for Huckabee. The memo spelled out what churches and pastors could legally do in their campaign efforts and then specifically listed who not to contact under the heading of "Which churches should we leave alone?" He wrote, "According to a *Detroit News* poll, Romney leads by a wide margin among Catholics and, obviously, Mormons."[19]

While Mike Huckabee was popular among some evangelical pastors, he failed to get the backing of many big-name evangelicals such as Richard Land of the Southern Baptist Convention. On more than one occasion, he complained bitterly that Land and other leaders had not supported him because they "make electability their criterion. But I am a true soldier for the cause. If my own abandon me on the battlefield, it will have a chilling effect."[20] Mike Huckabee's consternation and criticism about what he saw as a lack of support from evangelical leaders did not end with his eventual withdrawal from the presidential campaign. "There were leaders of the conservative movement that, had they stood with me early, I think the outcome would have been different," Huckabee groused to reporters in April 2008. He later carped, about some evangelical leaders, "When it gets to their own political realm, they think more secularly than even the secular people."[21]

Despite Huckabee's lack of appeal among some leaders, he certainly was attractive to pastors and evangelical congregations, partly because he had once been an ordained minister. He placed great emphasis on his religion and his training. The biographical campaign material stated that he earned a BA at Ouachita Baptist University and an MA in theology at Southwestern Baptist Theological Seminary. He then served as a Baptist minister (1980–92) and was the president of the Arkansas Baptist State Convention (1989–91). Huckabee mentioned more than once that he was "the only guy [running for president] with a theology degree." Unfortunately, that was not true. While Huckabee had forty-six credit hours, including three years' study of New Testament Greek, toward an M.A. at Southwestern Theological Seminary, he had dropped out of school to work for James Robison, "who bought him his first decent wardrobe and showed him how to use television." He later tried to explain, "my degree was actually in religion."[22]

Nevertheless, Mike Huckabee is known for having a friendly personality, quick wit, self-deprecating humor, and being a very engaging preacher/speaker. As an ordained Southern Baptist minister, he combined campaigning with preaching to congregations in Iowa, New Hampshire, South Carolina, and other campaign states. He explained to the *Baptist Press*, "I think I've had far more opportunities because of my position as a governor and now as a candidate for president to share my faith." Plus, such "sharing" allowed fellow evangelicals to get to know him better.[23]

In spite of the slight exaggeration regarding his theological training, Mike Huckabee had a successful religious career, working first with a televangelist and then as a pastor in two different churches. These opportunities gave him experience working with and understanding television as well as speaking and performing in public. He learned how to create a public persona of joviality and likability that sets people at ease, allows him to work with them—and also work them.

Public persona notwithstanding, Mike Huckabee could also be tough with a pragmatic, no-nonsense attitude. As governor of Arkansas, he was described as being "at war with much of his party." He even referred to his Republican opponents as "Shi'ites." Huckabee used this same approach in the presidential race as he cultivated his public image of "Mr. Nice" while underscoring the concern of evangelicals and other conservative voters about Mitt Romney's faith, hoping they would shift their votes Huckabee's way.[24]

One of Huckabee's aides even admitted that this was their approach. Romney's Mormonism "is definitely a factor in the race. . . . To a lot of people, [Mormonism] is a strange religion that they don't understand." As Howard Kurtz wrote, "This is a twofer: The aide gets to demean not just Romney but also an entire religion." That approach did no go unnoticed by political observers. Charles Krauthammer complained: "Huckabee has exploited Romney's Mormonism with an egregious subtlety" and "highly paraded [his] evangelical Christianity." George F. Will wrote, "Although Huckabee is considered affable, two subliminal but clear enough premises of his Iowa attack on Mitt Romney are unpleasant: That almost 6 million American Mormons who consider themselves Christian are mistaken about that. And—55 million non-Christian Americans should take note—America must have a Christian president."[25]

This was not the first time Mike Huckabee's campaign and his supporters had used religion as a hammer for political gain, nor was

Mitt Romney the only anvil. Shortly before the Iowa straw poll, Sam Brownback castigated Huckabee for not condemning an email sent by Pastor Tim Rude to a number of Iowa evangelicals asking them to reconsider their support for Brownback, a Catholic, and to encourage supporting Huckabee because he was "one of us" (an evangelical). Rude later issued a "sort of" apology, but the Huckabee campaign did not since Rude was not an official member of the campaign.[26] Brownback's campaign commented that Rude's statement was "an admission that he offended people, but it is certainly not an apology or recognition of the bigoted substance of his remarks." In other words, Rude apparently regretted that the email had become public knowledge rather than its anti-Catholic tone. Nor did Brownback supporters find persuasive Rude's explanation that "all I was trying to say is that Protestants should vote for Protestants."[27] They particularly resented Huckabee's failure to condemn Rude's email for its anti-Catholic rhetoric nor did he denounce the campaign tactic of playing the religion card. They believed the lack of condemnation encouraged what they called an "anti-Catholic whisper campaign." A Huckabee spokesperson angrily fired back, "It's time for Sam Brownback to stop whining and start showing some of the Christian character he seems to always find lacking in others." In short, the Huckabee campaign simply washed its hands of the issue.[28]

Interestingly enough, the Huckabee campaign used the same tactic on Mitt Romney and his religion. On a website titled "Quilter for Huckabee," Carole Schutter, the co-screenwriter and author of the embarrassingly inaccurate and inept movie and book, *September Dawn* (about the Mountain Meadows Massacre), wrote a long, rambling post accusing Mormons of not being Christian and encouraging readers to visit anti-Mormon internet sites. She also stated: "I'm amazed that evangelicals prefer to support someone who has changed his mind as Governor of Massachusetts and now changes his mind again as Presidential candidate. Money and the unbelievable power and organization of the LDS church . . . backs Romney." The Huckabee campaign ignored a request to repudiate this post's inaccurate and derogatory language.[29]

Furthermore, the Huckabee campaign allowed comments attacking the LDS Church to remain on the blog site of the official campaign webpage. These messages were posted by supporters. Obviously, the campaign workers could not help what people wrote, but they certainly could have removed offensive messages. They did not. Among the messages attacking the LDS Church and its members were: "As evangelicals, we cannot stand for this Mormon garbage to get into office. . . . I'm for God's vote, Huckabee '08." Another wrote concerning voting for a Mormon, "we might as well elect a witch." And yet another wrote that someone should "completely expose the strange beliefs of the Mormon cult."[30]

Radio talk show host Doug Wright believed that Mike Huckabee was encouraging "in an underhanded way" the anti-Mormon rhetoric present before the Iowa caucuses. By allowing "hate speech" to remain on the campaign website, Huckabee was encouraging bigotry. "It's the insidious attacks, the winks and nods" that bothered Wright, who broadcast from Iowa for several days before the caucuses.[31]

An example of Huckabee's using innuendo to plant seeds of distrust came in an interview with a *New York Times* reporter when he asked "in an innocent voice, . . . 'don't Mormons believe that Jesus and the devil are brothers?'" This question came uninvited and immediately following an exchange in which Huckabee had been asked "if he considered Mormonism a cult or a religion. He answered, 'I think it's a religion. I really don't know much about it.'" Mitt Romney angrily replied, "I think attacking someone's religion is really going too far. It's just not the American way, and I think people will reject that."[32]

Huckabee's question and Romney's response were featured in media coverage globally, with both positive and negative reactions. Huckabee apologized in person to Romney, but some felt he had done the damage purposely, and his apology was too little, too late. Others, however, came to his defense. Huckabee supporter Star Parker wrote that his apology said "more about the graciousness of Huckabee than any alleged transgression," and Bob Burney stated that Mormons should tell the truth about their theology. In other words, Mormons should explain what they really believe about Jesus Christ and Satan rather than public explanations.[33]

The LDS Church issued an official statement explaining that, like other Christians, they believe "Jesus is the divine Son of God." The statement continued, "As the Apostle Paul wrote, God is the Father of all. That means that all beings were created by God and are His spirit children. Christ, however, was the only begotten in the flesh, and we worship Him as the Son of God and the Savior of mankind." The statement did not specifically mention Satan, but its description of God creating "all beings" would include Satan, who rebelled against God and was cast out of heaven. Critics of Mormonism, especially evangelicals, have used the "brothers" argument as a twisted example of Mormonism's alien theology, and Huckabee would have been completely familiar with the ways in which it distorted Mormon beliefs—hence, the reason for the strong, angry reaction from Romney and other Mormons.[34]

Although some Huckabee supporters protested that he really was asking an honest question, this defense was disingenuous. As a Southern Baptist minister, Huckabee not only was fully aware of "counter-cult" literature (which included information on the LDS Church) but would probably have attended lectures, seminars, and classes about Mormonism. Furthermore, he had keynoted the 1998 Southern Baptist Convention in Salt Lake City. Since the convention's theme was to fight against Mormonism, the free literature handed out to the press and speakers included R. Philip Roberts's book, *Mormonism Unmasked: Confronting the Contradictions between Mormon Beliefs and True Christianity*. This book discusses the concept that God is the father and creator of all beings, including Lucifer. Furthermore, its publisher was also the publisher of Huckabee's book. Thus, despite protestations that Huckabee was honestly ignorant, he was clearly well aware of this standard anti-Mormon ploy.[35]

Claims of innocence notwithstanding, even non-Mormons recognized the underlying bigotry of the question, describing it as "weasely" and "sleazy." Hugh Hewitt called it a "below the belt hit on Mormons," while George F. Will compared the question to examples

Brian Fairrington, "Romney and the Evangelicals," Cagle Cartoons, October 12, 2007.

of early anti-Semitism and denounced Huckabee's question as a repudiation of Reaganism. Former U.S. Senator Jim Talent saw it as "an attempt to stir up anti-Mormon prejudice." Even Huckabee's apology was met with skepticism as an example of "nonapology apologies." It had served only to focus the "strong prejudice among many fundamentalist Christians against Mormonism," especially in Iowa.[36]

What bothered both Mormons and non-Mormons was that Huckabee was using religion to attack his opponent and further his own political ambitions. One outspoken writer complained of "the sleazy and underhanded way [Huckabee was] demagogically using his religion specifically against Mitt Romney." He was especially offended by Huckabee's "knowing and purposeful manipulation of his Christian faith to use as a weapon against a fellow Christian, purely for his own political gain." Huckabee had "repeatedly and carefully, with unmistakably malice aforethought, borne false witness against Mormons and purposefully stoked anti-Mormon bigotry" to get more votes. Another writer complained that "Huckabee has ridden Christ's coattails all the way to first place in the Iowa polls and second place nationally by deftly exploiting anti-Mormon prejudice."[37]

They clearly saw the ethical contamination of using religion for political ends.

Latter-day Saints responded with a mixture of anger and frustration. Ken Jennings, the all-time winner on *Jeopardy*, denounced it in a scathing op-ed piece: "The truth, Huck, is that Mormons believe that God is the Father of all, which does, I guess, in some sense make Jesus and Satan brothers. And by the same logic, we also believe that Moses and Orville Redenbacher and Attila the Hun and Neil Diamond are brothers. Happy now?" Perhaps two of the more poignant responses came from two radio and television talk-show hosts who had joined the LDS Church as adults. Bob Lonsberry, who had been a contributing Huckabee supporter until the Jesus and Satan blow-up, explained how he had grown up in the Baptist Church and had learned to sing, "They'll Know We Are Christians by Our Love," then commented, "It's a pretty poor thing when, if you can't beat a man on the issues, you try to beat him with his religion. It is ungentlemanly, it is un-American and, if that old song was right, it's un-Christian."[38]

Conservative talk-show host Glenn Beck came face to face with Mike Huckabee at an airport and, in a private meeting, discussed the issue. In the course of their conversation, Beck gave a brief explanation of the persecutions and forced exodus of the Mormons and related his own conversion story. As he did so, tears filled his eyes. He later commented that Huckabee did tell him he was sorry. But there was something that bothered Beck. "We were knee to knee. Not once did this pastor reach out and put a hand on my shoulder or on my knee and say, I am so sorry, Glenn. He did say those words and I accepted those words, but as I told him in the end, by their fruits ye shall know them."[39]

Mike Huckabee's disdain for Mitt Romney as a candidate and also for Romney's Mormonism was obvious during the early primaries and caucuses. On several occasions when complimenting the other Republican candidates, he pointedly ignored Romney. When Romney's campaign complained about Huckabee's self-advertisements as the "Christian leader," Huckabee smiled and commented, "If there are inferences, there's a saying we have in the South, 'If you throw a rock across the fence, it's the hit dog that hollers.'" Doug Wright was irritated by Huckabee's subtle anti-Mormonism: "If Governor Huckabee sees Romney's religion as a problem then be up front about it. Be a man. Be a Christian."[40]

Some conservatives complained that Huckabee's tactics were dividing the party. Shortly before the Michigan primary, Congressman Pete Hoekstra was troubled by two campaign aspects that he traced to Huckabee. The first was that his office received phone calls from folks "furious" that he would support a Mormon. The second was that Hoekstra saw the Huckabee campaign as "a divisive vessel of religious and class warfare."[41]

On numerous occasions, Huckabee or his staff made snide comments about Romney's wealth and social position, displaying an embarrassing streak of jealousy and class envy. Even Huckabee's campaign literature included references to Romney's wealth. But more troubling than Huckabee's obsession with the Romney campaign finances was his encouragement of religious bigotry. Rob Bishop, a Utah Congressman and Latter-day Saint, commented that he didn't think Mike Huckabee personally was actually a bigot but that "Huckabee exploited the issue" to his political benefit. Conservative columnist Kathryn Jean Lopez took Huckabee to task because "he had been presented with a real opportunity to bring people together, to take the media obsession off of how religious evangelicals cannot tolerate a Mormon president. But instead of rising to the occasion, Huckabee [made] things worse."[42]

For his part, Mike Huckabee complained he was being unfairly smeared for his comments about Mormons, then decried what he felt was undue interest in his own religious background. He claimed to have been attacked for being a Southern Baptist: "There seems to be a great deal more attention on—really an intense scrutiny on—the details of my faith, than there is on anybody else's, including Mitt Romney's." Shortly after Romney's religion speech, Huckabee said, "I think I've probably been asked far more questions about my faith than Mitt Romney's been asked about his. Maybe I ought to be doing the 'God speech' out there." Then he quipped, "I might even include an altar call and an offering with mine."[43]

Mitt Romney and the Mormon Question

Huckabee's claim that he received more scrutiny about being Southern Baptist than Mitt Romney received about Mormonism is, based on internet searches and a *Pew Forum* report, much exaggerated. "More than one-third (35%) of all religion-related campaign stories [between January 2007 and April 2008] focused on [Mitt] Romney, a Mormon. . . . His chief competitor for the evangelical vote, Huckabee, was the focus of only 4% of all religion-related stories." Furthermore, the difference between Huckabee and Romney was that Huckabee purposefully played up his religion, then reacted with frustration when news reporters pressed him on his ministerial background and aspects of Southern Baptist doctrine. Romney, on the other hand, repeatedly tried to downplay his religion and established a purposeful policy of not discussing it in any detail.[44]

This policy was established for two reasons. First, Romney felt that, while his presidency should certainly reflect core religious values, those values were universal in religion and did not depend on Mormonism's specific theology. The second—and probably more realistic—reason is that he and his advisors were "well aware of the animosity among many Americans toward the LDS Church and its adherents."[45] Detailed discussions that focused on Mormonism's differences from other Christian religions would only intensify that animosity. Despite this policy, however, Romney never tried to distance himself from his Mormonism, consistently affirming his adherence to and appreciation of its principles and stressing that it was a long and valued tradition in his family. (In contrast, Arizona Senator Mo Udall, running against Jimmy Carter for the Democratic nomination in 1976, had consistently positioned himself as someone who had been an inactive Mormon since his youth and a nonbeliever in some of its tenets and policies.[46]) Romney was aware of the subtle prodding of interviewers about the depth of his attachment to Mormonism and commented in June 2007 that he believed some political pundits were "hoping" he would "distance himself from the church to help him politically." He asserted unequivocally, "That's not going to happen."[47]

Perhaps the question kept coming up because Romney was obviously working hard to use language familiar to evangelicals. He talked publicly about his favorite evangelical author and alluded to reading the Gideon Bible. He frequently mentioned how his values were like those of other Christian faiths, which observers saw as an attempt to "signal his kinship with evangelical Christians."[48]

Reinforcing voter unease was Romney's record of changing opinion on social issues like abortion. Accusations of flip-flopping were underscored by his refusal to answer questions about his religion. Throughout the early part of the campaign, columnist Paul Campos reported, Romney was "at least six times more likely to be described as a flip-flopper" than other Republican candidates, even though John McCain's record of flip-flopping was much worse than Romney's.[49] Another observer, Dan Bartlett, a former White House advisor, suggested that the "flip-flop" label may have actually been covering up the real problem—Romney's Mormonism. "People are not going to step out and say, 'I have a problem with Romney because he's Mormon.' What they're going to say is he's a flip-flopper." A study conducted by scholars at Vanderbilt University and Claremont Graduate University found that 26 percent of those who accused Romney of flip-flopping also indicated that Mormonism, not flip-flopping, was their real problem with Romney. This pattern was especially strong among evangelicals.[50]

At times, Romney's evasiveness about Mormon doctrine and lack of detailed defense bothered fellow members. More than a few complained that he had "done a poor job explaining his religion." Others were frustrated when he seemed embarrassed about Mormon doctrines. One outspoken member wrote in an internet blog, "Dude, Mitt, stop being embarrassed about being a Mormon!" Many, however, realized that it was an unwinnable fight. No matter what Romney said, it still wouldn't be right for some critics. As Steven L. Mayfield, long a documentation collector on Mormon subjects, wryly commented, the LDS Church is "the church of the damned if you do and damned if you don't."[51]

The Speech

Like Reed Smoot more than a century earlier, Mitt Romney's religion speech was much anticipated and discussed by the press, pundits, and voters, even before he had officially announced his candidacy. The longer Romney put off making the speech, the more restive some became. Deciding whether to make such a speech and, if so, exactly what it should say, was fraught with complications.[52] Romney had ambivalent feelings about giving such a speech in the first place. Debate among his campaign staff and advisors compounded the tension. In October 2007, after months of sidestepping queries, Romney gave an inkling of the behind-the-scenes debate: "I have some folks who think I should do it soon, some say later, some say never, some say right away. I'll make the decision."[53]

Romney's hand was probably forced by Mike Huckabee's playing the religion card in Iowa, Romney's serious drop in poll numbers, and public pressure from other prominent Republicans. Among them was Senator Orrin G. Hatch, who publicly declared on November 27, 2007, that Romney needed to give a speech to put people's fears of Mormonism to rest. Utah pollster Dan Jones succinctly explained, "What [Romney has] to do is stop the bleeding. He's been going down. They think it's mainly about misunderstandings of the LDS faith."[54] On December 2, 2007, an upbeat Mitt Romney finally announced that he would give the much-anticipated speech. His announcement of the title, " Faith in America," and the approach he would take, his "views on religious liberty," were an attempt to shape it toward philosophy, rather than theology. (For the full text of the speech, see Appendix A.)

The fact that Romney could be forced into giving the speech in the first place was an indication that Romney had already lost at least some control over his campaign. Talk show host Sean Hannity, acknowledging that Romney "ha[d] to give the speech," lamented: "He has been . . . the victim of a very vicious, nasty campaign by people that are attacking religion and using religion as a wedge." Frank Pignanelli, a Catholic Democrat who served ten years in the Utah House of Representatives, wrote, "It is a filthy outrage that this speech needed to occur. For a man of Mitt Romney's exemplary life to have to defend his faith in 21st-century America is a disgrace and a blemish to our entire country." Regrets were also voiced from the conservative side. Dr. Tony Campolo, president of the Evangelical Association for the Promotion of Education, said he was sorry that it was evangelicals who had been questioning whether Mitt Romney was a good American, while even Rush Limbaugh acknowledged that Romney gave the speech because he had "been relentlessly attacked as something less than a true American."[55]

Political insiders and commentators alike agreed that the speech would be risky as Romney would have to walk a fine line of explaining just enough to allay fears but not enough to crystallize amorphous fears of Mormonism. Several pundits recognized the dilemma and predicted that, no matter how Romney explained Mormon doctrine, some would be offended and turn away from him at the polls.[56] Romney himself recognized not only the impossibility of pleasing everyone but also the danger that probably no explanation would succeed in laying the Mormon question definitively to rest. Privately, he referred to the Mormon issue as his "comma problem" because journalists always followed his name "by a comma, the words 'a Mormon,' and another comma." He observed, "If I give a speech about Mormonism, I'll never get beyond the comma problem."[57]

Romney delivered his "Faith in America" speech December 6 at the George H. W. Bush Presidential Library in Houston, Texas. As promised by the title, it focused on the role of religion in modern America, and he showed his awareness of his multiple audiences by the balance he struck between affirmation and autonomy. By declaring his faith in the divinity of Jesus Christ, he tried to allay the concerns of fundamentalist and evangelical Christians. Then he promised that, as president, he would "serve no one religion, no one group, no one cause, and no one interest." He announced that "freedom requires religion just as religion requires freedom," declaring, "we welcome our nation's symphony of faith."[58]

Romney's speech was considered a watershed event and immediate reaction was positive. Chris Matthews said, "I heard greatness," while Joe Scarborough said Romney "hit this thing out of the park."

James Dobson of Focus on the Family called the speech "a magnificent reminder of the role religious faith must play in government and public policy."[59] Even more significantly, the speech was discussed in print and on radio and television for days after.

Critics from both ends of the political spectrum also weighed in. On the left, some complained that Romney had ignored the feelings of atheists and other nonbelievers. Christopher Hitchens called it a "windy, worthless speech." Kenneth Woodward carped that it "was hardly a speech for the ages" and saw it as "a political speech in the narrowest sense, aimed at reassuring evangelical primary voters, especially in Iowa, who are wary of his Mormon faith."[60] This statement was perceptive. Parts of Romney's speech were obviously aimed at the evangelical audience, but few evangelical activists and pastors felt that it erased their fears of a Mormon president. Ultimately, Mitt Romney did not receive the hoped-for bounce in the polls nor the acceptance among evangelicals that he had worked so hard to accomplish. The uncomfortable relationship between Mitt Romney and evangelical voters continued into the early primaries, and "Romney himself acknowledged that, had he been a Baptist, for example, he may not have lost the Iowa caucuses—a devastating setback to his early surge strategy."[61]

Repercussions

In the course of the 2008 presidential race, religion played a greater role than in previous presidential races. Politically and religiously charged imagery and words were used as weapons, with ordinarily innocuous terms like "Christian leader," "religious right," "Muslim," "evangelical," "values voter," and "Mormon" being used to attack and hurt. While the religion issue impacted the campaigns of candidates like Barack Obama, Sam Brownback, and Mike Huckabee, the Mormon question loomed larger than the rest. As a result, accusations of bigotry and narrow-mindedness volleyed back and forth, and emotions ratcheted up.

Some evangelicals, both Romney supporters and nonsupporters, were uncomfortable with, even embarrassed by, the more heated rhetoric and blatant examples of anti-Mormonism. Throughout the tumultuous, often bitter, history of the interaction between the Latter-day Saints and the evangelicals, some on both sides have been take-no-prisoners warriors while others have expressed dismay at the mutual antipathy. For example, in 2004 Richard Mouw, president of Fuller Theological Seminary, spoke at an ecumenical event in the Salt Lake Tabernacle. He acknowledged that "friendship has not come easily between our communities" because both sides had "tended to marginalize and simplify the others' beliefs." Then, in the words of one observer, he offered "a stunningly candid apology" to Latter-day Saints by admitting that evangelicals "have often misrepresented the faith and beliefs of Latter-day Saints. . . . Let me state it clearly. We evangelicals have sinned against you."[62]

Others, however, reacted defensively, even angrily to accusations that they manifested bigotry. Paul Edwards, an evangelical pastor, wrote dismissively: "The teachings of the Mormon Church are aberrant on fronts too numerous to mention." He charged: "Romney's strategy for defending against legitimate questions about his Mormon faith is to cry 'bigotry.'" These "accusations of bigotry germinated in the blogosphere and spread like a virus though media, both old and new." Frank Pastore explained that Christians must always choose the moral over the legal and then asked, "Is this bigotry or is it voting as a Bible-believing Christian?" He then explained, "I'm a Christian-American-Conservative-Republican—in that order. I support Christianity first and foremost, everything else flows from that."[63]

Phoenix talk show host Andrew Tallman offered an equally passionate but more thought-provoking essay about Mormonism and bigotry. "I care about a candidate's religion. It's not the only thing I care about, but, still, I care about it. And I'm about fed up with people telling me I'm a bigot and un-American because I happen to have a different idea of what matters in my decision for whom to vote than they do. . . . If I did in fact believe that a candidate's religion were evil, would you really be so audacious as to tell me that I'm not allowed to consider that when I enter the voting booth?" Tallman pointed out that, even though it is illegal to require a religious test for office, it is not illegal for an individual to consider a candidate's religion. To insist on excluding individual judgments about a candidate's religion would be reverse bigotry.[64]

These evangelical arguments typify the underlying dilemma: Do Americans have the right to vote as they wish, even if it involves what others believe to be bigotry, or will they be shamed or otherwise compelled to vote against their wishes? Like Pastore and Edwards, other evangelicals refused to be shamed or coerced into disregarding the Mormon connection, allowing that to override whatever their positive judgement of Romney's qualifications might have been.

On the Mormon side, the negative, sometimes visceral, reaction against not only Romney, but more specifically his religion, left many Latter-day Saints reeling with shock, frustration, and anger. They were surprised at "the level of intensity and sometimes flat out animosity." Mormons thought they had been accepted by mainstream America, especially after the positive press surrounding the 2002 Salt Lake Olympics. As the Romney campaign demonstrated, "anti-Mormonism in American society is anything but dead."[65] "I don't think that any of us had any idea how much anti-Mormon stuff was out there . . . the equivalent of anti-Semitism," Mormon sociologist Armand Mauss commented. *Salt Lake Tribune* editorial writer Rebecca Walsh agreed, even with the comparison: "Romney's defeat has peeled back the layers of a lingering religious bigotry as virulent as anti-Semitism and closeted racism." Former Utah House Minority Leader Frank Pignanelli, a non-Mormon, complained, "The Republican primaries demonstrated that many Southern evangelicals view Mormons as subhuman and unfit for the presidency."[66]

The Church of Jesus Christ of Latter-day Saints issued a statement that it would "increase its efforts to ensure that the public better understands its beliefs and the values it represents." Some Church members claimed Mormons were treated as "neither a mainstream church nor mainstream citizens." One member, speaking in a church meeting about the bigotry brought to light as a result of Romney's presidential bid, described his reaction. "As people have made harsh statements, some of the statements have been mean-spirited and ugly and I've thought, man, I'd like to get that guy in a dark alley. Then I realized, I can't be like them. I need to be like the Savior and have charity in my heart for all men and show love even to those who hate me."[67]

The response of Republican Latter-day Saints who had worked and voted for Republicans of other Christian faiths, including Southern Baptists and other evangelicals, reflected not only surprise but also frustration and anger. A Utah editorial writer commented shortly after Mitt Romney suspended his race on February 7, 2008, "It was surprising to [Latter-day Saints] that fundamentalist Christians found it acceptable political strategy to undermine Romney's campaign by attacking his LDS faith. This despite the fact that Utah has been one of the most reliably Republican strongholds in the nation and preferred George W. Bush by larger margins in the two past elections than any other state."[68]

In December 2006, Justin Webb of BBC Radio stated that Mitt Romney would "present the Republican Party . . . with a dilemma. . . . Put simply, are the Mormons too strange for prime-time? Or, put another way, is the Republican Party too bigoted to select a Mormon as its presidential candidate?" A little over a year later, it appeared that, while Republicans talked of a "big tent," that tent seemed to have become "a revival tent" and Latter-day Saints were on the outside looking in. Over a hundred years after Reed Smoot's hearings, the Mormon question was still haunting the Latter-day Saints.[69]

A January 2008 meeting of the Utah Republican Party's state central committee brought the faithful together to conduct party business. It also afforded them the opportunity to discuss the presidential election and complain about the obvious anti-Mormon bias in light of Utah's strong Republican support. The discussion involved both Mormons and non-Mormons. Several said that if Mike Huckabee won the nomination, they would not vote for him "because of his anti-Mormonism."[70] These state central committee members were not alone in their intention to avoid Huckabee. During a discussion on an LDS-oriented email list, one person wrote, "My hunch is that Huck, if nominated, will not carry Utah." Another responded with, "Not only will he not carry Utah, the GOP will probably also lose Nevada, Idaho, Arizona, Colorado, and Wyoming." Another participant agreed. "Huckabee is the only Republican that could get the Mountain west LDS Republicans to vote Democratic."[71]

Whether a Huckabee nomination would have caused a large number of Republican Latter-day Saints to vote Democratic is certainly debatable, but the question became moot after Huckabee dropped out of the race in early March 2008. Nevertheless, Mormon hurt and anger over how Romney and Mormonism had been treated was palpable, and that anger extended beyond just Huckabee. After it became obvious that John McCain was going to be the Republican nominee, Kirk Jowers, head of the University of Utah's Hinckley Institute of Politics, said, "In Utah you could hear the wailing and gnashing of teeth." In a poll taken shortly after Mitt Romney suspended his campaign in February 2008, "only 30% of Utahns said they would vote for McCain."[72] As a religion news writer put it, "A churchgoing, clean-living, non-cussing, doesn't-even-drink-coffee Mormon could hardly be any worse for this country than a warmongering Methodist or a Southern Baptist with a hyperactive libido." Alan Wolfe, director of the Boisi Center for Religion and American Public Life at Boston College, underlined the irony: "As long as the Republican Party is primarily a party with an evangelical base, I don't see how any Mormon could do any better than Romney."[73]

The anti-Mormon animus in the 2008 presidential race was more than mere religious bigotry. It went to the very foundation of the country and the importance and efficacy of Article VI of the U.S. Constitution. And at that Constitutional foundation is a dream long held and long fought over from the battlefields to the pulpits and pews in American history—freedom. In this case, not only physical and political freedom, but also religious freedom where Americans are able to express their religious beliefs without fear of persecution and, on a higher level, where there is respect for other people's religious beliefs, even if they are contrary to one's own personal beliefs. As John F. Kennedy so eloquently explained in his own religious speech almost fifty yeas ago, he hoped for a nation where "no religious body seeks to impose its will directly or indirectly upon the general populace or the public acts of its officials; and where religious liberty is so indivisible that an act against one church is treated as an act against all."[74]

Notes

1. "The Corner," *National Review Online*, July 19, 2007, http://corner
.nationalreview.com/post/?q=NWY1ODc4Yjc1MWE4ZjFiNjBiNDZlYWZlOG
NmYjJiZDE= (accessed September 5, 2007); Lisa Wangeness, "At Straw Poll,
Group Attacks Romney on Mormonism," *Boston Globe*, August 11, 2007, http://
www.boston.com/news/politics/politicalintelligence/2007/08/group_attacks_r.html
(accessed August 15, 2007; Jason Spencer, "Critics Target Romney's Mormonism,"
Go Upstate, May 11, 2007, http://www.goupstate.com/article/20070511/NEWS/
705110310/-1/LIFE (accessed May 11, 2007). Evangelicals also put pressure on pastors and other evangelical leaders who publicly supported Romney. Pastor Don
Wilton, former president of the South Carolina Baptist Convention, retracted his
endorsement of Romney, saying it was a personal error, after coming under public attack by other evangelicals. "Baptist Pastor Retracts Endorsement of Romney," Fox
News, October 23, 2007, http://www.foxnews.com/story/0,2933,304576,00.html
(accessed October 24, 2007).

2. Jonathan Martin, "Anti-Romney, Anti-Mormon Calls Being Made in Iowa,"
Politico, November 15, 2007, http://www.politico.com/blogs/jonathanmartin/1107/
AntiRomney_antiMormon_calls_being_made_inIowa.html (accessed November
16, 2007); "NH, Iowa Voters Get Anti-Romney Calls," Newsmax.com, November
15, 2007, http://newsmax.com/insidecover/romney_push_polling/2007/11/15/
49899.html (accessed November 16, 2007); Thomas Burr, "Calls to Voters Target
Romney's LDS Faith," *Salt Lake Tribune*, November 17, 2007, http://www.sltrib
.com/ci_7488526 (accessed November 19, 2007); Sarah Baxter, "Mormon Smears
Turn Republican Race Sour," *Sunday Times*, November 18, 2007, http://www
.timesonline.co.uk/tol/world/us_and_americas/article2891073 (accessed November
26, 2007).

3. Douglas MacKinnon, "Cowardly Gutter Politics," Townhall.com, November
19, 2007, http://www.townhall.com/columnists/DouglasMacKinnon/2007/11/19/
cowardly_gutter_politics (accessed November 26, 2007); Fred Lucas, "New
Hampshire AG Probes 'Push Poll' Attack on Romney," CNSNews.com, November
16, 2007, http://www.cnsnews.com/ViewPolitics.asp?Page=/Politics/archive/200711
/POL20071116c.html (accessed November 26, 2007); Philip Elliott, "Romney,
McCain Attack Anti-Mormon 'Push Polls,'" *Deseret Morning News*, November 17,
2007, http://deseretnews.com/article/content/mobile/0,5223,695228483,00.html
(accessed November 19, 2007; Doug G. Ware, "Who Is Behind the Anti-Romney

Mormon-Bashing Calls?" January 3, 2008, http://www.kutv.com/news/local/story
.aspx?content_id=492da40f-ca4a-417a-909b-3614f8e59a56 (accessed January 4, 2008).
   4. "Romney's Western Wats connection," *Free Republic*, November 16, 2007,
http://www.freerepublic.com/focus/f-news/1927022/posts (accessed November 19,
2007); "Romney Is Friends with Western Wats family," http://www.eye08.com/
2007/11/16/romneys-friends-with-western-wats-family (accessed November 19,
2007); Thomas Burr, "Orem Firm Denies 'Direct' Ties to Mitt," *Salt Lake Tribune*,
November 20, 2007, http://www.sltrib.com/news/ci_7512821 (accessed November
26, 2007); Laura Hancock, "Utah Firm Hired to Smear Romney?" *Deseret Morning
News*, November 24, 2007, http://www.deseretnews.com/article/content/mobile/
0,5223,695230357,00.html (accessed November 26, 2007); Doug G. Ware, "Who Is
behind the Anti-Romney Mormon-Bashing Calls?"; Copy of the transcript of the
Moore-Information phone survey in my possession.
   5. Jonathan Martin, "Apparent Pro-Huckabee Third-Party Group Floods Iowa
with Negative Calls," *Politico*, December 3, 2007, http://www.politico.com/blogs/
jonathanmartin/1207/Apparent_proHuckabee_thirdparty_group_floods_Iowa_with
_negative_calls.html (accessed January 9, 2008).
   6. Jim Davenport, "Bogus S.C. Card Cites Mormon Passages," *Seattle Times*,
December 29, 2007, http://seattletimes.nwsource.com/html/politics/2004098860_
apromneycard29.html (accessed January 2, 2008); Thomas Burr, "Iowa Primary
Smackdown: Mitt Miffed by 'Personal' Attacks on Mormon Faith," *Salt Lake Tribune*, December 31, 2007, http://www.sltrib.com/ci_7846405 (accessed January 2,
2008).
   7. "Anti-Thompson Site Connects to Romney Camp," *Washington Post*, September 10, 2007, http://blog.washingtonpost.com/the-trail/2007/09/10/antithompson
_site_connects_to.html (accessed December 6, 2007); "The Political Wire:
Candidates Make Last-Minute Caucus Appeals," Fox News, January 3, 2008, http://
youdecide08.foxnews.com/2008/01/03/the-political-wire-thompson-denies-plans
-to-drop-out (accessed January 4, 2008); Murfee Faulk, "Got Dirt?" *Metro Spirit*,
January 17, 2008, http://www.metrospirit.com/index.php?cat=11011007070439984
&ShowArticle_ID=11011601081107349 (accessed January 19, 2008).
   8. Tim Reid, "Snarls, Smears and Innuendo for Hillary Clinton as Attack Dogs
Get Ready for the Fray," *Times*, November 22, 2007, http://www.timesonline.co.uk
/tol/news/world/us_and_americas/article2917646 (accessed November 27, 2007);
Michael Brendan Dougherty, "Steeple Chase: Capturing South Carolina's Crucial

'Hymn-Book Vote' Requires the Right Balance of Religiosity and Ruthlessness," *American Conservative*, January 14, 2008, 22.

9. Reid, "Snarls, Smears, and Innuendo for Hillary Clinton"; Michael Isikoff et al., "The Dirty War Moves South," *Newsweek*, January 12, 2008, http://www .newsweek.com/id/91664 (accessed January 15, 2008); Michael Scherer, "Dirt Starts Flying in South Carolina," *Time*, January 13, 2008, http://www.time.com/time/ politics/article/0,8599,1703221,00.html (accessed January 14, 2008); Leslie Wayne, "In South Carolina, the Campaign Mud Arrived before Santa," *New York Times*, January 17, 2008, http://www.nytimes.com/2008/01/17/us/politics/17attack.html (accessed January 17, 2008).

10. Ibid.; O. Kay Henderson, "Brownback Apologizing to Romney for Aide's Email Message on Mormonism," *Radio Iowa*, June 18, 2007, http://www.radioiowa .com/gestalt/go.cfm?objectid=404AEDF6-BA32-34FE-09E66865638E6E30 (accessed January 10, 2008); Mike Glover, "Romney Weighing Speech on Religion," *Guardian*, July 26, 2007, http://www.guardian.co.uk/worldlatest/story/0,,-6807329 ,00.html (accessed July 27, 2007).

11. Jens Manuel Krogstad, "Will Americans Elect a Mormon President?" *WCF Courier*, August 19, 2007, http://www.wcfcourier.com/articles/2007/08/19/news/ metro/c6d05a768a86acc48625733c000f8a1e.txt (accessed July 7, 2008).

12. Jens Manuel Krogstad, "Will Americans Elect a Mormon President?"; Scott Helman, "Rival Camps Take Aim at Romney's Religion," *Boston Globe*, June 21, 2007, http://www.boston.com/news/nation/articles/2007/06/21/rival_camps_take_ aim_at_romneys_religion (accessed January 10, 2008).

13. Krogstad, "Will Americans Elect a Mormon President?"; "McCain Representative Engages in Extreme Mormon-Bashing," *Practical Reasoning*, June 23, 2007, http://practicalreasoning.org/2007/06/23/mccain-representative-engages -in-extreme-mormon-bashing (accessed January 10, 2008); Michael Luo, "Romney Leads in Ill Will Among G.O.P. Candidates," *New York Times*, January 24, 2008, http://www.nytimes.com/2008/01/24/us/politics/24romney.html?ei=5065&en=db4 7c187783bc922&ex=1201755600&partner=MYWAY (accessed January 24, 2008).

14. Luo, "Romney Leads in Ill Will Among G.O.P. Candidates"; Brock Vergakas, "Romney: Repeated Campaign Attacks on Mormon Religion Troubling," *Seattle Times*, June 23, 2007, http://seattletimes.nwsource.com/html/nationworld/ 2003760023_webromneyreligion23.html (accessed June 26, 2007); Thomas Burr, "McCain's Mom Slams Romney," *Salt Lake Tribune*, November 10, 2007, http:// www.sltrib.com/ci_7422560 (accessed November 12, 2007); "McCain's Mom Says

Mormons to Blame on Olympics Scandal," (November 9, 2007), http://www.ksl .com/?nid=148&sid=2125338 (accessed November 9, 2007). The idea of McCain personally apologizing appears to have been unrealistic. According to Lorraine Woellert with Paula Dwyer, "Searching for the Real McCain," *Business Week*, November 22, 1999, http://www.businessweek.com/1999/99_47/b3656117.htm (accessed July 8, 2008), McCain is known in the Senate for freely using foul language, for being "brooding, obsessed," bad tempered, and for having "a vicious streak." Rich Tucker, "Red-Faced for a Reason," Townhall.com, April 25, 2008, http://www .townhall.com/Columnists/RichTucker/2008/04/25/red-faced_for_a_reason (accessed April 28, 2008), addressed McCain's reputation of having an anger problem. Tucker quotes Senator Bob Kerrey's comment: McCain's "anger always has a purpose."

15. Rich Galen, "Religion Politics," Townhall.com, November 28, 2007, http:// www.townhall.com/news/business/2007/11/28/bankers_plead_guilty_in_enron_case (accessed November 30, 2007); John Nichols, "'Champions for Christ' Crusade Puts Huckabee on Top in Iowa," *Nation*, November 30, 2007, http://www.thenation .com/blogs/campaignmatters?bid=45&pid=255641 (accessed December 6, 2007); Patrick J. Buchanan, "The Mitt-Mike Religious War," Townhall.com, December 11, 2007, http://www.townhall.com/columnists/PatrickJBuchanan/2007/12/11/the_ mitt-mike_religious_war (accessed December 11, 2007); Carl Campanile, "Huck Plays Coy on Romney's Mormon Faith," *New York Post*, December 5, 2007, http:// www.nypost.com/seven/12052007/news/nationalnews/add_in_cult_to_gop_injury_ 293634.htm (accessed December 6, 2007).

16. Mark Karlin, "Mike Huckabee Says God Is Pushing His Poll Numbers Up," BuzzFlash.com, December 1, 2007, http://www.buzzflash.com/articles/node /3825 (accessed January 15, 2008); "Evangelicals for Huckabee," *State*, December 16, 2007, http://www.thestate.com/local/v-print/story/259149.html (accessed December 19, 2007); Liz Sidoti, "Romney Fights Back in Iowa, N.H.," *Washington Post*, December 1, 2007, http://www.washingtonpost.com/wp-dyn/content/article /2007/12/01/AR2007120100588 (accessed December 3, 2007). A video of Huckabee shows him at an evangelical gathering, describing the source of his rapid rise in poll numbers to the same source that fed 5,000 with two fishes and five loaves of bread. Ted Olson, "Huckabee on Why His Poll Numbers Are Surging," *Christianity Today*, December 7, 2007, http://blog.christianitytoday.com/ctliveblog/archives/2007/12/ huckabee_on_why.html (accessed July 8, 2008).

17. Wayne Slater, "Invisible Force Helping Mike Huckabee," *Dallas Morning News*, December 24, 2007, http://www.dallasnews.com/sharedcontent/dws/dn/

religion/stories/122407dntexhuckabee.2b8de7b.html (accessed January 3, 2008); Libby Quaid, "Huckabee Eschews Politics for Preaching," *My Way News,* January 13, 2008, http://www.apnews.myway.com/article/20080114/D8U5AF180.html (accessed January 14, 2008); Julie Farby, "Huckabee Hopes to Shore Up Support among Evangelicals in South Carolina," *All Headline News,* January 14, 2008, http://www.allheadlinenews.com/articles/7009710724 (accessed January 14, 2008); Michael Foust, "Election 08: Huckabee Pauses Campaign to Preach Salvation at South Carolina Church," *Baptist Press,* January 14, 2008, http://www.bpnews.net/printerfriendly.asp?ID=27184 (accessed January 15, 2008); "Huckabee Supporters Get Warning Letters," NewsMax.com, January 2, 2008, http://www.newsmax.com/politics/Iowa_Caucus_Shaping_NH_Po/2008/01/03/61392.html (accessed January 3, 2008). According to Michael Scherer, "More on Letters to Pro-Huckabee Pastors," *Time,* January 3, 2008, http://thepage.time.com/more-on-threatening-letters-to-pro-huckabee-pastor (accessed January 3, 2008), some Iowa pastors supporting Mike Huckabee received letters warning that they could endanger their tax-exempt status if they actively campaigned in their churches.

18. "Huckabee Won't Give Views on Mormonism," Newsmax.com, December 4, 2007, http://www.newsmax.com/insidecover/huckabee_religion/2007/12/04/54408.html?s=al&promo_code=3EA4-1 (accessed December 5, 2007); "'Patriot Pastors' . . . for Huckabee?" *Right Wing Watch,* November 30, 2007, http://www.rightwingwatch.org/2007/11/patriot_pastors_2.html (accessed November 17, 2008); David D. Kirkpatrick, "Evangelical Help for Huckabee," *New York Times,* November 19, 2007, http://thecaucus.blogs.nytimes.com/2007/11/19/evangelical-help-for-huckabee (accessed January 21, 2008); Scherer, "More on Letters to Pro-Huckabee Pastors."

19. Gary Glenn, "How to Win Michigan for Huckabee!" January 6, 2008, reproduced online at *Politico,* http://www.politico.com/static/PPM43_080110_mich_huckabee.html (accessed July 22, 2008).

20. Zev Chafets, "The Huckabee Factor," *New York Times,* December 12, 2007, http://www.nytimes.com/2007/12/12/magazine/16huckabee.html?pagewanted=1&_r=1 (accessed December 15, 2007).

21. "Huckabee Blames Evangelical Leaders for Failed Bid," Insider report from Newsmax.com, April 20, 2008, http://news.newsmax.com/?Z6CRXHfF2bie5g29F7WeB3QKkXbktJR1Z (accessed April 20, 2008).

22. "Religion and Politics 2008: Mike Huckabee," *Pew Forum,* http://www.org/religion08/profile.php?CandidateID=10 (accessed September 13, 2007);

"Huckabee's Theology Answer to CBN Causing Stir," CBN News.com, December 14, 2007, http://www.cbn.com/cbnnews/287527 (accessed December 17, 2007); "Huckabee's Theology Degree? Now Says Ain't Necessarily So," WorldNetDaily, December 14, 2007, http://www.worldnetdaily.com/news/article.asp?ARTICLE_ID=59222 (accessed January 11, 2008).

23. "Huckabee: Jesus Still Important," Newsmax.com, November 6, 2007, http://www.newsmax.com/insidecover/huckabee_campaign/2007/11/06/47099.html?s=al&promo_code=3C81-1 (accessed November 7, 2007); Jared Strong, "Huckabee Takes Break to Preach," Des Moines Register, July 2, 2007, http://desmoinesregister.com/apps/pbcs.dll/article?AID=/20070702/NEWS09/707020317/1001/NEWS& template=printart (accessed July 2, 2007); Perry Bacon Jr., "Huckabee Steps Back into the Pulpit at Evangelical Church in N.H.," Washington Post, January 7, 2008, http://www.washingtonpost.com/wp-dyn/content/article/200801/06/AR 2008010602261_pf.html (accessed January 8, 2008); Chafets, "The Huckabee Factor."

24. "Huckabee Alienates GOP in Arkansas," Washington Times, January 24, 2008, http://www.washingtontimes.com/apps/pbcs.dll/article?AID=/20080124/ NATION/8463148/1001 (accessed January 25, 2008); Gabriel Sherman, "Bad Huck," New Republic, December 31, 2007, 11–12.

25. Howard Kurtz, "The Hit-Job Mentality," Washington Post, December 17, 2007, http://www.washingtonpost.com/wp-dyn/content/article/2007/12/17/AR 2007121700389_pf.html (accessed December 18, 2007); Charles Krauthammer, "Huck's Unholy Dance," National Review, December 7, 2007, http://article.nationalreview.com/?q=Nzk4MmY2N2I5NGEzOTk4ZWNkYzU2ZWY0Njk5N WRkNjI (accessed December 10, 2007); George F. Will, "The Affable but Subliminally Unpleasant Mike Huckabee," Seattle Post-Intelligencer, November 30, 2007, http://seattlepi.nwsource.com/opinion/341631_willonline02.html (accessed December 4, 2007).

26. Nathan Black, "Brownback Campaign Again Calls Huckabee to Denounce 'Anti-Catholic' Slur," Christian Post, August 2, 2007, http://www.christianpost.com /article/20070802/brownback-campaign-again-calls-huckabee-to-denounce-anti -catholic-slur.htm (accessed January 12, 2008).

27. Psycheout (username), "More on the Brownback/Huckabee Brawl," Blogs 4 Brownback, August 3, 2007, http://blogs4brownback.wordpress.com/2007/08/03/ more-on-the-brownbackhuckabee-brawl/ (accessed January 12, 2007).

28. Ibid.

29. Carole Schutter, "A Heartfelt Letter to America from the Co-Author of *September Dawn*," Quilter for Huckabee, October 23, 2007, http://quilterforhuckabee .blogspot.com/2007/10/heartfelt-letter-to-america-from-author.html (accessed October 24, 2007). I contacted the Huckabee campaign by email, included the text of Shutter's blog post, and asked whether the campaign agreed with the message and, if not, whether campaign personnel would request its removal. I never received an answer.

30. Thomas Burr, "Despite Apology, Huckabee's Website Hosts Comments Critical of Romney's Mormonism," *Salt Lake Tribune*, January 2, 2008, http://www .sltrib.com/ci_7861166 (accessed January 2, 2008); my notes taken from *Doug Wright Show*, KSL-Radio, January 3, 2008.

31. *Doug Wright Show*, January 3, 2008.

32. Lisa Riley Roche, "Romney Says Voters to Reject Attacks on Faith," *Deseret Morning News*, December 13, 2007, http://www.deseretnews.com/article /content/mobile/0,5223,695235608,00.html (accessed December 17, 2007); Kathleen Parker, "He's Not Satan, He's My Brother," Townhall.com, December 14, 2007, http://www.townhall.com/columnists/KathleenParker/2007/12/14/hes_not_ satan,_hes_my_brother (accessed December 17, 2007); Libby Quaid, "Huckabee Asks if Mormons Believe Jesus, Devil Are Brothers," *Time*, December 11, 2007, http://www.time.com/time/printout/0,8816,1693659,00.html (accessed December 12, 2007); Joanne Kenen, "Huckabee Questions Tenet of Romney's Mormon Faith," *Washington Post*, December 12, 2007, http://www.washingtonpost.com/wp-dyn/ content/article/2007/12/12/AR200712120083 (accessed December 17, 2007).

33. Star Parker, "Religion and Political Discourse," Townhall.com, December 17, 2007, http://www.townhall.com/columnists/StarParker/2007/12/17/religion_ and_political_discourse (accessed December 18, 2007); Bob Burney, "Mormons: A Plea for Candid Truth Telling," Townhall.com, December 19, 2007, http://www .townhall.com/Columnists/BobBurney/2007/12/19/mormons_a_plea_for_candid _truth_telling (accessed December 21, 2007). Burney, according to his Townhall biography, graduated from Bob Jones University in 1970 and was ordained to the ministry in 1971. He is a radio talk show host and, in 2000, he founded a ministry called Crosspower Ministries.

34. "Answering Media Questions about Jesus and Satan," LDS Newsroom, December 12, 2007, http://newsroom.lds.org/ldsnewsroom/eng/commentary/ answering-media-questions-about-jesus-and-satan (accessed December 17, 2007).

35. "New Revelations about Huckabee and Mormonism," Newsmax.com email, December 23, 2007; Matt Lewis, "My Man Mitt: Huckabee Spoke at 'Anti-

Mormon' Convention," Townhall.com, December 10, 2007, http://www.townhall
.com/blog/g/bd79f9f6-bce1-4e18-a0d9-d534d26e1c6b (accessed December 11,
2007); Dennis Clayson, "Huckabee Fails Test to Be Next Leader," *Courier*, December 30, 2007, http://www.wcfcourier.com/articles/2008/01/03/columnists/clayson
/0ef473cc0d8895f9862573bf005945b9.txt (accessed January 2, 2008); R. Philip
Roberts, *Mormonism Unmasked: Confronting the Contradictions between
Mormon Beliefs and True Christianity* (Nashville, Tenn.: Broadman & Holdman,
1998), 66. Roberts has published a number of articles critical of the LDS Church.

36. Daniel Radosh, "Don't Baptists Believe?" *Huffington Post*, December 14,
2007, http://www.huffingtonpost.com/daniel-radosh/dont-baptists-believe_b_
76806.html (accessed December 17, 2007); Hugh Hewitt, "Mike Huckabee's Low
Blow," Townhall.com, December 13, 2007, http://www.townhall.com/columnists
/HughHewitt/2007/12/13/mike_huckabees_low_blow (accessed December 17,
2007); George F. Will, "The '70s Hit Parade," *Washington Post*, December 20,
2007, http://www.washingtonpost.com/wp-dyn/content/article/2007/12/19/AR
2007121901854.html (accessed December 20, 2007); Toby Harnden, "Mike
Huckabee Apologises for Mormon 'Smear,'" *Telegraph*, December 17, 2007, http://
www.telegraph.co.uk/news/main.jhtml?xml=/news/2007/12/13/wuspols213.xml
(accessed December 17, 2007); Katherine Q. Seelye, "Apologies from the Heart (of
Darkness?)," *New York Times*, December 14, 2007, http://www.nytimes.com/2007
/12/14/us/politics/14clinton.html (accessed December 17, 2007).

37. Al Barger, "Mitt Romney Makes a Better Christian Than Mike Huckabee,"
Blog Critics Magazine, December 17, 2007, http://blogcritics.org/archives/2007/12
/17/070607.php (accessed December 7, 2007); "Christ's Candidate? Huck, Mitt
Play God Games," *Union Leader*, December 12, 2007, http://www.unionleader.com
/article.aspx?headline=Christ's+candidate%3F+Huck%2C+Mitt+play+God+game&
articleId=256e4953-660a-41ea-a21e-851063e450b9 (accessed April 6, 2008).
Barger was especially offended by Huckabee's comparing himself and his campaign
to Jesus's miraculous feeding the multitudes. He wrote, "That shows a real lack of
Christian humility, to put it mildly. Indeed, that he's so willing to vainly invoke his
Lord and Savior in his own crass little political campaign is grounds for me to begin
doubting the sincerity of his beliefs right there."

38. Ken Jennings, "Politicians & Pundits, Please Stop Slandering My Mormon
Faith," *New York Daily News*, December 19, 2007, http://www.nydailynews.com/
opinions/2007/12/19/2007-12-19_politicians__pundits_please_stop_slander.html
(accessed December 19, 2007); Bob Lonsberry, "Is Huckabee a Religious Bigot?"

December 12, 2007, http://www.lonsberry.com/writings.cfm?story=2282&go=4 (accessed December 17, 2007). Bob Lonsberry, "I'm Voting for Mitt," *Free Republic*, January 22, 2008, http://freerepublic.info/focus/f-news/1957956/posts (accessed January 22, 2008), took umbrage at what he believed to be 'Huckabee's use of religion to win votes: "He has prostituted his religion, seeming to actively promote Christian ties for personal political gain, and cunningly using religious bigotry against at least one opponent. He is too clever by half and it comes off looking not just cunning, but sinister."

39. Glenn Beck, "Glenn Meets Huck Face to Face," December 14, 2007, http://www.glennbeck.com/news/12142007a.shtml (accessed December 18, 2007). Regarding the painful history of Mormon persecution, one internet blogger called it "a campaign of ethnic cleansing . . . which drove members of the LDS church and its members [*sic*] from three states and finally to Utah." See also Christopher Rich, "GOP Campaign Workers Target Romney's Religion," NPR News Blog, June 21, 2007, http://www.npr.org/blogs/news/2007/06/gop_campaign_workers_target_ro .html (accessed April 5, 2008).

40. Harnden, "Mike Huckabee Apologises for Mormon 'Smear'"; *Doug Wright Show*, January 3, 2008.

41. Kathryn Jean Lopez, "Mike Huckabee Divides Republicans," Townhall.com, December 14, 2007, http://www.townhall.com/columnists/KathrynJeanLopez/2007 /12/14/mike_huckabee_divides_republicans (accessed December 17, 2007); Kathryn Jean Lopez, "Identifying a Problem," *National Review*, January 14, 2008, http://article.nationalreview.com/?q=MzdhMjEyOWU0Yzc1NTA3Y2NiYWJjYT IzOTAwY2NhYjM (accessed January 15, 2008).

42. "Huckabee Plays the Woe-Is-Me-Card," Newsmax.com, December 20, 2007, http://www.newsmax.com/politics/huckabee_woe_is_me/2007/12/20/58770 .html (accessed December 20, 2007); Mike Huckabee to Dear Friend, dated January 2008, copy of letter and Huckabee for President, Inc., donation materials in my possession; Craig L. Foster, "Interview with Congressman Rob Bishop," January 12, 2008, unpublished; Lopez, "Mike Huckabee Divides Republicans."

43. Joseph Curl, "Romney Puts Faith in Christian Past," *Washington Times*, November 28, 2007, http://www.washingtontimes.com/apps/pbcs.dll/article?AID =/20071128/NATION/111280064/1001 (accessed November 28, 2007); Thomas Burr, "Huckabee Scolds Those Who Say He Has Alienated Mormons," *Salt Lake Tribune*, February 13, 2008, http://www.sltrib.com/news/ci_8246955 (accessed February 14, 2008); Mark Silva, "Huckabee Says His Faith Is Drawing Greater Scrutiny," *Swamp*, November 28, 2007, http://www.swamppolitics.com/news/politics

/blog/2007/12/huckabee_says_his_faith_is_dra.html (accessed November 28, 2007); Ieva M. Augstums, "Huckabee Declines Theology Discussion," *Washington Post*, December 7, 2007, http://www.washingtonpost.com/wp-dyn/content/article/2007/12/07/AR2007120700942.html (accessed December 7, 2007). According to the Center for Media and Public Affairs, "Election Study Finds Media Hit Hillary Hardest; Obama, Huckabee Fare Best; FOX Is Most Balanced (not a typo)," December 21, 2007, http://www.cmpa.com/releases/07_12_21_Election_Study.pdf (accessed January 24, 2008), Romney's religion was the fourth most heavily covered election/candidate-related issue during the last quarter of 2007.

44. "Running on Faith: Study Finds Media Coverage of Religion in Primary Campaign Rivaled that of Race and Gender Combined," *Pew Forum*, p. 2., July 10, 2008, http://pewforum.org/docs/?DocID=312 (accessed July 14, 2008). "In 2007, 5% of the religion-related campaign coverage was on [Barack] Obama. From March through April 2008, when the Wright controversy hit its peak in the news media . . . he became the lead newsmaker in 55% of the religion-focused campaign stories."

45. Jonathan Turley, "When Religion Becomes Fair Game," *USA Today*, November 19, 2007, http://www.blogs.usatoday.com/oped/2007/11/when-religion-b.html (accessed November 19, 2007).

46. See Newell G. Bringhurst and Craig L. Foster, *The Mormon Quest for the Presidency* (Independence, Mo.: John Whitmer Books, 2008), chap. 3.

47. "Romney Professes Pride in Mormon Faith Despite Questions," *Boston Globe*, May 17, 2007, http://www.boston.com/news/local/massachusetts/articles/2007/05/16/romney_professes_pride_in_mormon_faith_despite_questions (accessed May 18, 2007); *Face the Nation*, transcript, CBS News, October 21, 2007, http://www.cbsnews.com/htdocs/pdf/face_102107.pdf (accessed July 22, 2008); Suzanne Struglinski, "Romney Defends His Faith as 10 Hopefuls Vie at Debate," *Deseret News*, June 6, 2007, http://www.deseretnews.com/dn/print/ 1,1442,660227212,00.html (accessed June 6, 2007).

48. Struglinski, "Romney Defends His Faith as 10 Hopefuls Vie at Debate"; Michael Luo, "Gingerly, Romney Seeks Ties to Christian Right," *New York Times*, October 16, 2007, http://www.nytimes.com/2007/10/16/us/politics/16romney.html (accessed October 16, 2007).

49. Paul F. Campos, "The Media's Love Affair with McCain," Scripps Howard News Service, January 22, 2008, http://www.shns.com/shns/g_index2.cfm?action=detail&pk=CAMPOS-01-22-08 (accessed January 23, 2008).

50. "Angry Mitt: I'm More than Mormon," *Boston Herald*, October 15, 2007, http://news.bostonherald.com/news/national/politics/view.bg?articleid=1038172 (accessed October 16, 2007); "Vanderbilt Poll Explains Why Romney's Flip-Flopper Label Sticks; Political Scientist Says Anti-Mormon Bias Finds Cover," Vanderbilt News Network, January 22, 2008, http://www.vanderbilt.edu/news/releases/2008/ 1/18/vanderbilt-poll-explains-why-romneys-flip-flopper-label-sticks-political -scientist-says-anti-mormon-bias-finds-cover (accessed January 23, 2007). According to the study, 57 percent of evangelicals have a bias against Mormons, and 50 percent of the evangelicals evaluated a moderate Christian candidate more positively than a conservative Mormon candidate.

51. "Mitt, Stop Being Embarrassed That You're Mormon," Rantings of Stu, October 2, 2007, http://stuthewise.wordpress.com/2007/10/02/mitt-stop-being -embarrassed-that-youre-mormon (accessed November 14, 2007); Craig L. Foster, "Interview with Don Guymon," January 12, 2008; Craig L. Foster, "Telephone Interview with Steven L. Mayfield," December 4, 2007.

52. Damon Linker, "Taking Mormonism Seriously: The Big Test," *New Republic*, January 1, 2007, https://ssl.tnr.com/p/docsub.mhtml?I=20070115&s= linker011507 (accessed June 19, 2007); Thomas Burr, "Will Romney Give That 'I'm-a-Mormon-But-It's-OK' Speech?" *Salt Lake Tribune* http://www.sltrib.com/ portlet/article/html/fragments/print_article.jsp?articleID=6728416 (accessed August 27, 2007).

53. Matt Lewis, "A 'Mormon Speech' May Be Coming Soon," Townhall.com, October 16, 2007, http://www.townhall.com/blog/g/b7c59987-ffa6-41e0-8bbb -7168246ae2d7 (accessed October 17, 2007); Suzanne Struglinski, "Mitt Undecided on a Speech about His Faith," *Deseret Morning News*, November 11, 2007, http:// deseretnews.com/article/content/mobile/0,5223,695226673,00.html (accessed November 12, 2007); Philip Elliott, "Romney Aides Oppose Speech on Religion," *My Way News*, November 11, 2007, http://apnews.myway.com/article/20071111 /D8SR9PHO0.html (accessed November 12, 2007); Glen Johnson, "Romney Faith Speech Decision Highlights Advisers' Impact," *Deseret Morning News*, November 12, 2007, http://deseretnews.com/article/content/mobile/0,5223.695227090,00 .html (accessed November 19, 2007).

54. "Hatch: Romney Should Say He's His Own Man," *Boston Herald*, November 27, 2007, http://www.bostonherald.com/news/national/politics/2008/ view.bg?articleid=1047416 (accessed November 28, 2007); "Hatch to Romney: Discuss Mormonism," *USA Today*, November 27, 2007, http://www.usatoday

.com/news/politics/election2008/2007-11-27-hatch-romney_N.htm (accessed November 29, 2007); Laura Hancock, "Romney Should Give a JFK-Style Speech, Hatch Says at UVSC," *Deseret Morning News*, November 28, 2007, http://deseretnews .com/article/content/mobile/o,5223,695231449,00.html (accessed November 28, 2007); "Romney to Give 'Religion Speech,'" CBS News, December 2, 2007, http:// www.cbsnews.com/stories/2007/12/02/politics/printable3564183.shtml (accessed December 3, 2007); Carole Mikita and Jed Boal, "Political Experts Weigh In on Romney's Planned 'Faith in America' Speech," KSL.com, December 3, 2007, http:// www.ksl.com/index.php?nid=481&sid=2266768 (accessed December 4, 2007).

55. Deborah Bulkeley, "Romney Speech a Hit—on Blogs, Talk Radio," *Deseret Morning News*, December 8, 2007, http://www.deseretnews.com/article/content /mobile/0,5223,695234319,00.html (accessed December 9, 2007); Frank Piganelli and LaVarr Webb, "Romney Left Issue Unresolved," *Deseret Morning News*, December 9, 2007, http://www.deseretnews.com/article/content/mobile/0,5223, 695234087,00.html (accessed December 10, 2007); *Hannity & Colmes*, Fox News, December 6, 2007; Rush Limbaugh, "Mitt Romney's Inspiring Speech," RushLimbaugh.com, December 6, 2007, http://www.rushlimbaugh.com/home/ daily/site_120607/content/01125106.guest.html (accessed December 18, 2007).

56. Michael Levenson, "Pressed, Romney to Speak on His Mormonism," *Boston Globe*, December 3, 2007, http://www.boston.com/news/nation/articles/ 2007/12/03/pressed_romney_to_speak_on_his_mormonism.html (accessed December 4, 2007); Mike Allen and Jonathan Martin, "Romney Speech Is a Huge Gamble," *Politico*, December 3, 2007, http://www.politico.com/news/stories/1207/ 7143.html (accessed December 3, 2007); Lisa Riley Roche, "Mitt's 'JFK speech' Called 'Wild Gamble,'" *Deseret Morning News*, December 4, 2007, http://www .deseretnews.com/article/content/mobile/0,5223,695233014,00.html (accessed December 4, 2007); David Limbaugh, "Mitt Should Can 'The Speech,'" December 4, 2007, http://www.davidlimbaugh.com/mt/archives/2007/12/new_column_mitt .html (accessed December 6, 2007); Tom Baldwin and Tim Reid, "Mitt Romney Gambles on JFK Moment to Stay in the Battle to Be President," *Times*, December 4, 2007, http://www.timesonline.co .uk/tol/news/world/us_and_americas/us_elec-tions/article2994983.ece (accessed December 6, 2007); Jon Meacham, "What Romney Should Say," *Newsweek*, December 5, 2007, http://www.newsweek.com/ id/73863 (accessed December 6, 2007).

57. Maurine Proctor, "Mitt Romney Hits a Home Run," *Meridian Magazine*, December 7, 2007, http://www.meridianmagazine.com/ideas/071207run.html (accessed December 7, 2007).

58. "Excerpts from Romney's Speech," KSL.com, December 6, 2007, http://www.ksl.com/index.php?nid=481&sid=2282205 (accessed December 6, 2007).

59. Amanda Carpenter, "Media Romney Fest Over Faith Speech," Townhall.com, December 6, 2007, http://www.townhall.com/columnists/AmandaCarpenter/2007/12/06/media_romneyfest_over_faith_speech (accessed December 7, 2007); Blake Dvorak, "Dobson: Romney Speech 'Magnificent,'" *Real Clear Politics*, December 6, 2007, http://time-blog.com/real_clear_politics/2007/12/dobson_romney_speech_magnifice.html (accessed December 7, 2007); "Mormon in America," *National Review*, December 6, 2007, http://article.nationalreview.com/?q=NTU3YjBkZWFjM2MyZTYwOWNkZWMzZGE1NWFkYTk (accessed December 7, 2007).

60. Christopher Hitchens, "Holy Nonsense: Mitt Romney's Windy, Worthless Speech," *Slate*, December 6, 2007, http://www.slate.com/id/2179404 (accessed December 6, 2007); Kenneth L. Woodward, "Missed Opportnity: What Mitt Romney Didn't Say Was More Interesting Than What He Did Say," *Newsweek*, December 7, 2007, http://www.newsweek.com/id/74157 (accessed December 7, 2007).

61. Toby Harnden, "Mitt Romney Strives to Win Over Evangelicals," *Telegraph*, June 12, 2007, http://www.telegraph.co.uk/news/main.jhtml?xml=/news/2007/12/06/wuspolls406.xml (accessed December 6, 2007); Collin Hansen, "Romney Dodges Doctrine," *Christianity Today*, December 7, 2007, http://www.christianitytoday.com/ct/2007/decemberweb-only/149-52.0.html (accessed December 7, 2007); Judson Berger, "Mitt Romney Offers Comfort to Religious Conservatives with Faith Speech," FoxNews.com, December 7, 2007, http://www.foxnews.com/story/0,2933,315741,00.html (accessed December 7, 2007); Shirley Ragsdale, "Activists, Pastors in Iowa Question Impact of Romney Speech," *Des Moines Register*, December 7, 2007, http://www.desmoinesregister.com/apps/pbcs.dll/article?AID=/20071207/NEWS/712070374/-1/caucus (accessed December 7, 2007); David Neff, "What Evangelicals Heard in Romney's 'Faith in America' Speech," *Christianity Today*, December 7, 2007, http://www.christianitytoday.com/ct/2007/decemberweb-only/149-42.0.html (accessed December 7, 2007); Thomas Burr, "Hang-Ups over Mormonism Proved Romney's Undoing," *Salt Lake Tribune*, February 10, 2008; Dahleen Glanton and Margaret Ramirez, "Romney a Hard Sell for Evangelicals," *Chicago Tribune*, December 9, 2007, http://www.chicagotribune

.com/news/nationworld/chi-mormons_bddec09,1,6414878.story (accessed December 9, 2007).

62. Carrie A. Moore, "Evangelical Preaches at Salt Lake Tabernacle," *Deseret Morning News*, November 15, 2004, http://www.deseretnews.com/article/content/mobile/0,5223,595105580,00.html (accessed January 2, 2008).

63. Paul Edwards, "Question Mormonism and You're a Bigot?" Townhall.com, December 13, 2007, http://www.townhall.com/columnists/PaulEdwards/2007/12/13/question_mormonism_and_youre_a_bigot (accessed December 17, 2007); Frank Pastore, "Jesus Is Lord? Hewitt, Mormonism, and Bigotry," Townhall.com, June 3, 2007, http://www.townhall.com/Columnists/FrankPastore/2007/06/03/jesus_is_lord__hewitt,_mormonism_and_bigotry (accessed June 4, 2007). Edwards, "Social Conservatives Are 'Mad as Hell,'" Townhall.com, December 25, 2007, http://www.townhall.com/columnists/PaulEdwards/2007/12/25/social_conservatives_are_"mad_as_hell" (accessed December 27, 2007), suggested that it was part of a big plan to "have Romney deliver a major speech about his faith under the guise of being persecuted because of his faith." Even so, there must have been enough of a problem to necessitate Francis J. Beckwith's article, "Is It Permissible for a Christian to Vote for a Mormon?" *Christian Research Journal* 30, no. 5 (2007): 52–53.

64. Andrew Tallman, "What If Mormonism Was the Issue?" Townhall.com, December 20, 2007, http://www.townhall.com/columnists/AndrewTallman/2007/12/20/what_if_mormonism_was_the_issue (accessed January 2, 2008).

65. Rachel Zoll, "Romney Bid Was a Crucible for Mormons," *Mercury News*, February 9, 2008, http://origin.mercurynews.com/religion/ci_8217970 (accessed February 20, 2008); Jan Shipps, "Romney Campaign Was a Mixed Blessing for Mormons," *Salt Lake Tribune*, February 10, 2008, http://www.sltrib.com/opinion/ci_8217523 (accessed February 10, 2008).

66. Suzanne Sataline, "Tabernacle on Trial: Mormons Dismayed by Harsh Spotlight," *Wall Street Journal*, February 8, 2008, http://online.wsj.com/public/article_print/SB12024332372185411.htm (accessed February 8, 2008); Rebecca Walsh, "Republican Party Leaves Mitt in Cold," *Salt Lake Tribune*, February 10, 2008, http://www.sltrib.com/news/ci_8221212 (accessed February 10, 2008); Frank Pignanelli and LaVarr Webb, "Romney's Run Imparts Valuable Lessons," *Deseret Morning News*, February 10, 2008, http://www.deseretnews.com/article/1,5143,695251497,00.html (accessed February 10, 2008).

67. "Church Will Work to Increase Understanding, Apostles Say," LDS Newsroom, February 8, 2008, http://www.newsroom.lds.org/ldsnewsroom/eng/news

-releases-stories/church-will-work-to-increase-understanding-apostles-say (accessed February 11, 2008); Joseph A. Love, statement delivered during LDS Church meeting (January 6, 2008), notes approved by speaker in my possession.

68. "Playing with Fire: Romney Campaign Exposed Anti-Mormonism," *Salt Lake Tribune*, February 12, 2008, http://www.sltrib.com/opinion/ci_8242302 (accessed February 14, 2008).

69. Justin Webb, "Is America Ripe for a Mormon Presidency?" BBC News, December 23, 2006, http://news.bbc.co.uk/1/hi/programmes/from_our_own_correspondent/6203179.stm (accessed March 12, 2008); Scott D. McCoy, "Making Faith a Political Issue Creates a Religious Test," *Deseret Morning News*, December 16, 2007, http://www.deseretnews.com/article/content/mobile/0,5223,695235832,00.html (accessed December 17, 2007).

70. Craig L. Foster, "Interview with Don Guyman." One LDS member of the Utah state central committee had been pro-Huckabee until the Jesus-Satan fiasco. Several committee members were still pro-John McCain. Most committee members, however, were pro-Romney.

71. Emails to FAIR Apologetics List, January 4–5, 2008.

72. "Gnashing Their Teeth: The Latter-day Saints Are Angry with the Republicans," *Economist*, February 21, 2008, http://www.economist.com.hk/world/na/displaystory.cfm?story_id=10740685 (accessed February 22, 2008).

73. Cathleen Falsani, "Are We Ready For a Mormon President?" BeliefNet.com, May 24, 2007, http://www.beliefnet.com/story/219/story_21905.html (accessed May 24, 2007); Peggy Fletcher Stack, "Romney Campaign Took the Pulse of Nation on LDS Faith," *Salt Lake Tribune*, February 8, 2008, http://www.sltrib.com/news/ci_8204331 (accessed February 8, 2008).

74. "Transcript: JFK's Speech on His Religion," NPR, December 5, 2007, http://www.npr.org/templates/story/story.php?storyId=16920600 (accessed June 15, 2008).

Conclusion

On March 4, 2008, John McCain achieved the magic number of 1,191 delegates needed to seize the Republican Party's presidential nomination. Mike Huckabee, McCain's remaining major opponent, conceded that same evening, and the first phase of the Republican race for the presidency of the United States came to an end. McCain's securing the Republican nomination reinforced two factors that are critical for the 2008 election.

The first was the difficult position that the Republican Party has faced regarding the 2008 elections and the party's immediate future. As a result of the continuing war in Iraq, economic downturn, and skyrocketing gasoline prices, the dissatisfaction with George W. Bush's administration and the Republican Party are at an all-time high. As late as May 2008, over "41.4% of Americans consider themselves to be Democrats while only 31.4% [said they were] Republicans." Needless to say, many Republicans were unenthusiastic, not only about their nominee but also the impending elections.[1]

Second, the religious right, despite its internal fragmentation, obviously remains a powerful voting bloc within the Republican Party—a bloc that needs to be taken seriously. Christian conservatives, who make up a significant majority of the religious right, are frustrated with both their party and its nominee. James Dobson, head of Focus on the Family, for example, publicly raised the specter of a large portion of the "sizable evangelical bloc" sitting out the 2008 election because of their dislike of McCain. Many evangelicals already seem to already be looking past 2008 toward 2012. For his part, John McCain seemed to ignore the few evangelical olive branches proffered in his direction.[2]

Furthermore, McCain's positions on some political hot-points frustrated many Christian conservatives. Exacerbating the already uncomfortable association between McCain and potential supporters, McCain spoke out against some evangelical leaders. When the Rev. John Hagee of San Antonio, who had endorsed McCain, referred to "the apostate church" and the "great whore" (terms Catholics claimed were slurs aimed at their church), McCain rejected Hagee's previous endorsement, dismissed Hagee's belated apology, and further alienated some evangelicals.[3]

Adding to the image of Republican intrigue and in-fighting were rumors that Mike Huckabee, whose name was being bruited about as a possible vice-presidential nominee, was behind some of the dissention in the party. Columnist Robert D. Novak announced in mid-May that Huckabee had secretly allied himself with the "fringe position among evangelicals that the pain of an Obama presidency [would be] in keeping with the Bible's prophecy" of a biblical plague falling upon an unworthy nation. In other words, at least some members of the religious right were planning to do exactly what had been threatened: sit out the election or perhaps even vote for Obama. This strategy is based on the knowledge that, while the religious right cannot win the presidency for a Republican candidate, it can certainly lose the election for him. Furthermore, an Obama presidency would then clear the way for "God's candidate," Mike Huckabee, in 2012.[4] Naturally, such a volatile rumor had people lining up on both sides with some emphasizing that Huckabee was always complimentary of McCain and had openly expressed interest in being his running mate. On the other side were Huckabee critics who claimed such Machiavellian actions were typical of his ten-year tenure as Arkansas governor.[5]

Regardless of whether the rumors were true, there was no doubt that Mike Huckabee topped John McCain's short list of possible vice-presidential running mates, in large part because of the support he could bring from the Christian right. Other names thought to be on the list were Florida Governor Charlie Crist, Democratic Senator Joseph Lieberman, Louisiana Governor Bobby Jindal, Minnesota Governor Tim Pawlenty, and Mitt Romney. While each of these men brings positive points as a possible running mate, they also bring possible negatives.

Governor Jindal, for instance, has racked up an impressive legislative and gubernatorial record, spring-boarding him to national fame. According to talk show host and political commentator Austin Hill, however, Jindal's Catholicism might be a stumbling block for evangelicals. "If the recent Republican presidential primary races demonstrated anything, they showed us that, among the religious social conservative movement (a movement mostly comprised of evangelical protestants), theological views and church affiliation trump just about everything else when it comes to selecting a political candidate." Hill's own alma mater, Biola University, published an article in its alumni magazine critical of an "on-again-off-again" movement called "Evangelicals and Catholics Together." The article "featured a theology professor whose objections to this effort of uniting evangelicals and Catholics are based on theological concerns." Hill saw the article as an example of a possible tipping point for Republican evangelicals who "still can't bring themselves to vote for a candidate that doesn't share all or most of their theological views."[6]

If Hill is correct and Jindal's Catholicism makes him ineligible to evangelical voters, then a McCain-Huckabee ticket might mean a possible sweep of the South for the Republicans. While not all of the religious right supported a Huckabee vice-president nomination, enough did that McCain and other Republican leaders had to consider him carefully. Either way, it was obvious that Mike Huckabee had emerged from relative obscurity as a major player "in American politics [for] leading evangelical Christians."[7]

Undercutting the possibility of the projected sweep is the fragmentation and in-fighting of the religious right, characteristics that became crystal clear during the Republican presidential race and its aftermath. Some members were more concerned about social issues like poverty and global warming; others gave top priority to moral issues like abortion and same-sex marriage. While some evangelicals regarded Mike Huckabee to be "God's candidate," others supported John McCain. Some even supported Mitt Romney.

Pat Bagley, "McCain in Utah," *Salt Lake Tribune*, March 31, 2008.

Furthermore, the Romney campaign engendered surprisingly strong emotions, during and even following his failed presidential campaign. When Mitt Romney withdrew his presidential bid on February 7, 2008, he did not drop off the political radar. Instead, he immediately remade himself as one of John McCain's "most active, effective fund-raisers and cheerleaders." He criss-crossed the country, appearing with McCain and even acting as surrogate for him at some events and on multiple television appearances. In fact, some Republican insiders suggested that he may have been the most prolific Republican fund-raiser on behalf of McCain.[8]

Interestingly, Romney as a loyal party soldier also promptly began communicating a more relaxed, genuine persona, a sharp contrast to the stiff and artificial aura he had projected as a candidate. During his campaign, Romney had seemed so concerned the slightest misstatement might hurt him that he never captured the spontaneity and ease that seemed to come naturally to the other candidates. With the pressure of the campaign behind him, a likeable, more human side began to emerge.[9]

As distance softened the edges on the bitter controversies of the early 2008 primary season and as Romney appeared more frequently for McCain, a McCain-Romney ticket seemed more possible, particularly after Romney and some of the other top possible picks spent Memorial Day weekend at McCain's Arizona ranch. Mitt Romney, although modestly commenting that he didn't think it very likely he would be selected, also stated that he would "be honored to be McCain's running mate." While such a political marriage would be welcomed by the party elite and Washington insiders, not to mention most Latter-day Saints, the possibility brought dismay from many from the religious right, particularly among the Huckabee supporters.[10]

In early April 2008, the Government Is Not God-PAC sponsored a "No Mitt VP" campaign aimed at discouraging John McCain from selecting Mitt Romney. The campaign included full-page newspaper advertisements as well as a website where people could sign the petition and leave comments. The advertisement announced: "The unvarnished facts of Mitt Romney's record as governor of Massachusetts make him *utterly unacceptable* as a Vice Presidential choice." The advertisement explained, "The grassroots is nearing a breaking point with Republican Party leadership on many issues, not the least of which is the relentless whitewashing of Mitt Romney as a so-called 'conservative.'"[11]

The backers of the "No Mitt" campaign then threatened to have the Christian conservatives flex their political muscles by boycotting the Republican ticket. "If Governor Romney is on your ticket, many social conservative voters will consider their values repudiated by the Republican Party and either stay away from the polls this November or only vote down the ticket. For the sake of your election, the health of your party, and the future of America you must not allow the obvious electoral consequences of that to occur." Twenty-six people signed the open letter and advertisement.[12]

One of them was Paul Weyrich, a high-profile evangelical leader and former Romney supporter. Apparently, Weyrich had reconsidered his original endorsement of Romney and even apologized to a select group of "Christian right" leaders gathered at the Ritz-Carlton

Hotel in New Orleans in March 2008: "Friends, before all of you and before Almighty God, I want to say I was wrong." He then "essentially confessed that he and the other leaders should have backed Huckabee."[13] At least one source stated that Weyrich's turning against Romney stemmed from his disappointment with Romney's endorsement of John McCain, whom Weyrich strongly opposed. Although Weyrich eventually distanced himself from the anti-Mitt advertisement, his regret at supporting Romney was a significant message from some within the religious right who felt they had made a serious political mistake by supporting the Mormon candidate over the Baptist candidate.[14]

Mike Huckabee said he did not expect McCain to select Romney as his running mate "given their deep philosophical differences,"[15] and denied any involvement with the anti-Mitt Romney advertisement. However, Fox News reporter Molly Henneberg and other members of the media emphasized that many of the signers were Huckabee supporters. Many pundits felt the "No Mitt" campaign was a way to slow Romney's momentum, bring Huckabee back into the public eye, and emphasize the religious right's concerns about Romney's record and positions. Many Latter-day Saints, however, believed there was more to the campaign than simple politics and quickly spread the word that it was another anti-Mormon attack.

William J. Murray, chairman of Government Is Not God-PAC, angrily responded that the ad campaign was not an anti-Mormon attack. He and his PAC had supported Mormon candidates and would do so in the future. He noted that the letter and advertisement had focused on Mitt Romney's problematic positions on social issues like abortion and same-sex marriage. He then complained that people had gone to the website and "used this opportunity to post hateful and bigoted anti-evangelical messages at the site that I cannot reprint here. At one point a volunteer had to work full time to cull out those messages that were too offensive to leave up. We blocked the server at BYU in Utah and the number of offensive messages declined." In describing how offensive some of the messages were, he mentioned that his personal favorite was a message calling them a "bunch of fat, ugly Baptist women."[16]

Murray also added that he "was surprised by the number of anti-evangelical messages and the tone of hatred for evangelicals in general." Furthermore, he was unhappy because "there was an overall dishonesty by the Romney supporters who posted at the 'No Mitt' site. In order to leave a post they had signed a petition saying they did not want Mitt Romney as their VP choice. To be blunt, they lied in order to post pro-Romney or anti-evangelical messages."[17]

While Murray lamented the dishonesty of many Romney supporters who had trashed his website, his accusation was somewhat disingenuous. It is true that those accessing the website had to sign the petition before they could leave their message. The site asked them, however, if they would vote for a McCain/Romney ticket. Thus, some Romney supporters may have genuinely considered that signing the anti-Romney petition was worthwhile since they could then register their desire to vote for a McCain-Romney ticket.[18]

What was disappointing and could not be rationalized were the "hateful and bigoted anti-evangelical" messages, and Mormons who wrote such messages were certainly behaving inappropriately. Nevertheless, Murray's assertion that the twenty-six signers did not have anti-Mormon bias is not completely credible. One of them, Janet Folger, President of "Faith2Action," had published a letter in the e-newspaper, *World Net Daily*, headed, "To Anti-Huck Rock Throwers," mentioned the controversy over Huckabee's "brothers" comment about Jesus and Lucifer, and ended her discussion of Romney with the comment, "The word blasphemy comes to mind. A bit more than a mere 'denominational difference,' don't you think?"[19]

Another example was James Hartline, founder and publisher of *California Christian News*, who wrote an essay headlined: "Breaking News: San Diego Republican Party Hits New Low—Invites Cult Member as Christmas Party Guest of Honor." It included the charge: "Romney's bizarre religious beliefs truly disgrace the birth of Christ. . . . Mormon politics is more about promoting the economic interests of the Mormon Church and its wealthy members rather than any pseudo Biblical beliefs."[20] Not to be outdone, talk show host Gregg Jackson complained that some evangelicals were actually waging a "propaganda blitz trying to mislead evangelicals into doing what would shock most evangelicals in American history: elect a Mormon for president."[21]

While concern over Mitt Romney's stand on issues and his previous record were frequently cited as key reasons for the signatures and ad campaign, bigotry may have played an important, if unacknowledged, part. *American Spectator* published David Tomaselli's op-ed piece, "Slow the Veep Down," in which he admitted, "Whether we like it or not, [Romney's] Mormonism is still a factor to many evangelicals and Christian conservatives."[22]

Mark Charalambous, spokesman for CPF—The Fatherhood Coalition, agreed. In an article discussing McCain's nomination in spite of conservative opposition, he observed that the main argument against a Mitt Romney vice-presidential nomination "is the same one that doomed his presidential candidacy from the start: his religion. Christian conservatives make up a sizeable fraction of the Republican Party. To Christians, a Mormon is as much an apostate as a Muslim."[23]

Not all political pundits, of course, agreed that Romney's faith would demolish his chances to be selected as McCain's running mate. Fred Barnes, for example, insisted, "[Romney] lost the nomination to McCain, but religion wasn't the reason." Talk show host and social commentator Michael Medved agreed: "Romney's Mormon faith always seemed like a bigger problem to some obsessed media commentators than it did to ordinary voters."[24] Medved then analyzed what he saw as a more serious issue: "To me (and many others) Romney's biggest problem as a potential president involved his instincts as a panderer—an eager, palpable, almost panting desire to tell people what they wanted to hear, rather than what they needed to know. His impulses as a people-pleaser led to the reputation for flip-flops." Ironically, Medved saw this trait as an advantage for a vice president. "A Veep isn't supposed to display unshakable convictions on his own: he is, rather, expected to reflect and echo the positions and policies of the top guy." In other words, pandering is a good thing for a vice-presidential nominee and, in Medved's opinion, Mitt Romney would do an excellent job.[25] It was, at best, a back-handed compliment.

Although Medved was far from the first to point out how the perception of flip-flopping damaged Romney's campaign, other factors were also at work. Romney could not shake questions about his motivations in changing position on key social issues. Another fatal perception was the idea that he was not as conservative as he portrayed himself. And it failed to connect with a majority of voters in a way that mobilized support. As I observed his campaign and its demise, these problems seemed to stem from three factors.

First, he did not present himself well and thus came across as smug, artificial, and calculating. The apparent effort to be everything to everyone meant that he was not truly comfortable with himself during much of the campaign. As a result—and this is the second reason for his campaign's failure—he tried to remake himself into a Reagan conservative when he was, in reality, a moderate with a dash of Reagan conservatism. Third, the media obviously had its own discomfort issues with Romney, with the result that the electorate didn't like the public portrayals. Those who were actually able to meet and talk to Romney usually came away with a different perception and, more often than not, became supporters.

In spite of the real and perceived character flaws, Romney's campaign was burdened by a piece of baggage that he would not and could not throw off and which he could not explain in a way that the electorate could accept: his Mormonism. In a presidential campaign where religion played an unprecedented central role for both major political parties, Mitt Romney's Mormonism, which had virtually assured his incredible personal and business success, became his Achilles' heel. It attracted a phenomenal amount of scrutiny and comment, and Romney's strategy of first, refusing to discuss it, and second, of trying to translate it into terms acceptable to evangelicals, simply fell flat.

I see three reasons for this heightened attention. First, despite nearly a century of moving steadily into the mainstream of American life, the LDS Church is not well known nor well understood by a significant number of Americans. Second, Romney's religion was a news magnet because of the mushrooming number of news outlets in the information age. With the ever-increasing access to twenty-four-hour news, networks scramble for enough stories to occupy the air time and keep viewers interested. Romney's religion seemed to be an easy target. LDS Church leaders, processing the situation optimistically, said that ultimately, the increased press as a result of Romney's campaign was good for the Church.[26] Perhaps that is true, but for many rank-and-file members, it was unsettling, even painful.

And that is true because of the third and most obvious reason Romney's religion played such a pivotal role in the campaign—his run at the presidency revealed and unleashed an unsuspected volcano of anti-Mormon bigotry expressed from both ends of the socio/religio/political spectrum. From the "theo-political hothouse of the religious right" to the anti-religious secular progressives on the left, Romney's religion drew outspoken criticism. Many Mormons were "surprised at the level of intensity and sometimes flat out animosity" of the critiques and attacks. Given Mormonism's conservatism on social issues and Romney's effort to run as a conservative Republican, many Mormons expected criticism from the left. It was, however, particularly devastating to conservative Mormons to be so viciously attacked by those within the Republican Party. One Mormon commented despondently, "I never knew so many people hated us." Unfortunately, Latter-day Saints learned that "Mormons are part of the cultural mainstream, but they have not been and are not a part of the religious mainstream."[27]

To be accepted or rejected almost solely on the basis of religion raises unsettling questions about the maturity of American society and politics, particularly since politics, at its very core, represents identity and is the raison-d'être of the individual, group, community, tribe, and nation. In a thought-provoking essay about what Mitt Romney's campaign meant to Latter-day Saints, Nathan B. Oman, a professor of law at William and Mary University, wrote, "So long as a Mormon cannot be elected president because he is Mormon, I am a second-class citizen, part of a clan disqualified from full political participation. In short, the possibility that a Mormon is de facto ineligible for the presidency throws the full citizenship of all Mormons into question."[28]

The ramifications of this issue go beyond Mitt Romney's failed 2008 presidential campaign and the Church of Jesus Christ of Latter-day Saints. If a Mormon cannot be elected president because of his religion, what about other religions considered to be even further from the main currents of American social life? Are American women and men who are members of the Unification Church, or Scientologists, or Muslim, automatically be disqualified as presidential candidates in a country that constitutionally protects all religions? The implications are sobering. If Americans wouldn't support a candidate solely because of his or religion, then, as Kathryn Jean Lopez wrote, "Say your prayers for America."[29]

Notes

1. John Hawkins, "The Republican Party's Real Problem in a Nutshell," Townhall.com, May 9, 2008, http://www.townhall.com/columnists/JohnHawkins/2008/05/09/the_republican_partys_real_problem_in_a_nutshell (accessed May 13, 2008).

2. Phil Brennan, "McCain Rebuffs Dobson: Will Evangelicals Bolt?" Newsmax.com, May 18, 2008, http://www.newsmax.com/insidecover/mccain_dobson_evangelical/2008/05/18/97063.html (accessed May 27, 2008). McCain's rebuff of Dobson may have been yet another example of McCain's infamous temper and long-standing grudges or it may very well have been because Dobson appears not to have the political influence he had commanded during the Reagan administration in the 1980s. According to D. Michael Lindsay, *Faith in the Hall of Power: How Evangelicals Joined the American Elite* (New York: Oxford University Press, 2007), 57–58, of the "more than twenty senior officials in the Bush White House" that Lindsay interviewed, not one mentioned Dobson's name as one of the most influential 'evangelical leaders' they or the White House listened to. Instead, they referred to Dobson's 'lack of political finesse,' 'ineptitude in politics,' and 'inability to focus on the family because he's always focusing on someone else's business.'"

3. "Pastor Hagee Apologizes for Anti-Catholic Remarks," FOXNews.com, May 13, 2008, http://elections.foxnews.com/2008/05/13/pastor-hagee-apologizes-for-anti-catholic-remarks (accessed May 27, 2008); "McCain: To Hell with Hagee,

Rejects Endorsement," Newsmax.com, May 22, 2008, http://www.newsmax.com/insidecover/mccain_reject_hagee/2008/05/22/98246.html (accessed May 27, 2008).

4. Robert D. Novak, "McCain, Huckabee, and the Evangelicals," *Human Events*, May 12, 2008, http://www.humanevents.com/article.php?id=26466 (accessed May 12, 2008).

5. Ibid.

6. Austin Hill, "Governor Jindal, The 'Christian Right,' and The 'Catholic Issue,'" Townhall.com, June 1, 2008, http://www.townhall.com/columnists/AustinHill/2008/06/01/governor_jindal_the_christian_right_and_the_catholic_issue (accessed June 2, 2008).

7. Ibid. See also "Source: Huckabee Tops McCain VP List," Newsmax.com, May 13, 2008, http://www.newsmax.com/insidecover/Huckabee_McCain_VP_list/2008/05/13/95611.html (accessed May 13, 2008); "Huckabee Says He Would Like to Be McCain's No. 2," *Free Republic*, May 18, 2008, http://www.freerepublic.com/focus/f-news/2017748/posts (accessed May 27, 2008). An article titled "Red vs. Blue? New Electoral Map Turns Purple," *Seattle Post-Intelligencer*, June 2, 2008, http://seattlepi.nwsource.com/opinion/365481_purpleonline03.html (accessed June 3, 2008), rpt. from "The Electoral Map: Battlefield America," *Economist*, May 29, 2008, http://www.economist.com/world/na/displaystory.cfm?story_id=11455836 (accessed July 11, 2008), noted that a Huckabee nomination could very well lose the swing state of Nevada because of Mormon antipathy for Huckabee. They "resented the former Arkansas governor's unsubtle digs at their faith during the Republican primary tussle with Mitt Romney."

8. Thomas Burr, "Romney: Former Presidential Hope All About Boosting GOP Hopes," *Salt Lake Tribune*, June 2, 2008, http://www.sltrib.com/ci_9451628 (accessed June 3, 2008).

9. An example of his lighter, funnier side was when he spoke at the annual Radio and Television Correspondents Association awards dinner. He read a David Letterman-style "Top 10" list of why he dropped out of the campaign, in the process poking fun at himself, his wealth, and even Utah and the Mormons. Lisa Riley Roche, "Mitt Mocks Himself, Utah in Surprise Top 10 Routine," *Deseret News*, April 17, 2008, http://deseretnews.com/article/content/mobile/0,5223,695271367,00.html (accessed April 18, 2008). Mitt and Ann Romney also won an award from the Becket Fund, a nonprofit law firm dedicated to defending religious liberty for people of all faiths. The award was for Romney's "Courage in Defense of Religious Liberty." He also gave a speech on "Religion and Freedom" at the same awards din-

ner. "Religion and Freedom," Townhall.com, May 8, 2008, http://www.townhall
.com/columnists/MittRomney/2008/05/08/religion_and_freedom (accessed May 9,
2008).

10. "Mitt Gunning for V.P.?" *Salt Lake Tribune*, April 11, 2008, A7. Among
the Washington insiders and other party leaders pushing for Romney as vice-president were George W. Bush, Jeb Bush, Andrew Card, and Karl Rove.

11. Government Is Not God-PAC, "No Mitt," http://www.govnotgod.org/pdfs
/NoMittPrescottAZ.pdf (accessed July 11, 2008).

12. Ibid.

13. "Paul Weyrich to Evangelical Leaders: We Should Have Backed Huckabee;
Update: Weyrich Disavows Anti-Romney Ad," *Hot Air*, April 8, 2008, http://
hotair.com/archives/2008/04/08/paul-weyrich-tells-evangelical-leaders-we-should
-have-backed-huckabee/ (accessed April 13, 2008).

14. Ibid.; Don Irvine, "Huckabee Denies Involvement in Anti-Mitt Effort,"
Accuracy in Media, April 6, 2008, http://www.aim.org/aim-column/huckabee
-denies-involvement-in-anti-mitt-effort (accessed April 7, 2008).

15. Molly Henneberg, "Anti-Mitt Romney Ad," Fox News Report, Sunday,
April 6, 2008.

16. William J. Murray, "The No Mitt Ad and Mormonism," Government Is
Not God-PAC, April 6, 2008, http://www.govnotgod.org/www2/index.php?option
=com_content&task=view&id=54&Itemid=53 (accessed April 7, 2008).

17. Ibid.

18. Values Voter Coalition, "The Petition," http://www.nomittvp.com/ (accessed June 8, 2008).

19. Janet Folger, "To Anti-Huck Rock Throwers," *World Net Daily*, November 6,
2007, http://www.worldnetdaily.com/index.php?pageId=44388 (accessed June 6, 2008).

20. James Hartline, "Breaking News: San Diego Republican Party Hits New
Low—Invites Cult Member as Christmas Party Guest of Honor," James Hartline
Report, December 3, 2006, http://jameshartlinereport.blogspot.com/2006/12/
breaking-news-san-diego-republican.html (accessed June 6, 2008).

21. Gregg Jackson, "Is This the End of Evangelicalism in America?"
Townhall.com, November 2, 2007, http://www.townhall.com/Columnists/
GreggJackson/2007/11/02/is_this_the_end_of_evangelicalism_in_america (ac-
cessed June 6, 2008). In the article he also commented, "The vast majority of
Christians for most of American history would have been outraged at an evangeli-
cal Christian wearing a sandwich board for a Mormon candidate. As they saw it,

America was a Christian nation to be led by a Christian president, who would be led by the God of the Bible."

22. David Tomaselli, "Slow the Veep Down," *American Spectator*, March 18, 2008, http://www.spectator.org/dsp_article.asp?art_id=12908 (accessed March 18, 2008). Fred Barnes, "The Veepstakes: There's an Obvious Winner," *Weekly Standard* 13, no. 26 (March 17, 2008): http://www.weeklystandard.com/Content/Public/Articles/000/000/014/854gvvhu.asp (accessed March 19, 2008).

23. Mark Charalambous, "Our Long National Nightmare Is Over," *Men's News Daily*, June 8, 2008, http://mensnewsdaily.com/2008/06/08/our-long-national-nightmare-is-over (accessed June 9, 2008).

24. Michael Medved, "Mitt's Weakness for the Top Spot Could Help Him as Veep," Townhall.com, March 12, 2008, http://www.townhall.com/Columnists/MichaelMedved/2008/03/12/mitts_weakness_for_the_top_spot_could_help_him_as_veep (accessed March 12, 2008). Medved explained that Romney performed better among "self-described Evangelical Christians (supposedly consumed by anti-Mormon bigotry) than he did among non-Evangelicals."

25. Ibid.

26. Thomas Burr, "Romney's Run Good for LDS Church," *Salt Lake Tribune*, April 23, 2008, http://www.sltrib.com/portlet/article=9023231 (accessed April 23, 2008). Elder M. Russell Ballard of the Quorum of the Twelve commented good-naturedly, "I'd much rather have people talking about us than ignoring us."

27. Nathan B. Oman, "Mormonism's Al Smith Moment?" *San Francisco Chronicle*, January 2, 2008, http://www.sfgate.com/cgi-bin/article.cgi?f=/c/a/2008/01/02/EDO7U7M03.DTL (accessed January 2, 2008); Rachel Zoll, "Romney Bid Was a Crucible for Mormons," *Seattle Times*, February 9, 2008, http://seattletimes.nwsource.com/html/nationworld/2004174040_apsurvivingmitt09.html (accessed February 20, 2008); Howard Berkes, "Mormons Confront Faith's Negative Reputation," National Public Radio, February 12, 2008, http://www.npr.org/templates/story/story.php?storyID=18905399 (accessed February 12, 2008).

28. Nathan B. Oman, "Latter-day Saints Have a Big Stake in Romney's Campaign," *Salt Lake Tribune*, January 5, 2008, http://www.sltrib.com/opinion/ci_7890853 (accessed January 7, 2008).

29. Kathryn Jean Lopez, "A Mormon Can Be President," *National Review Online*, November 27, 2007, http://article.nationalreview.com/?q=NmFhZjcxNDRhY2RjZTkxYzhmNjAzODI1MTlhMWFmNjg (accessed June 8, 2008).

Appendix A

"Faith in America"

An address given by Mitt Romney at the George H. W. Bush Presidential Library in College Station, Texas, on December 6, 2007.

Thank you, Mr. President, for your kind introduction. It is an honor to be here today. This is an inspiring place because of you and the First Lady and because of the film exhibited across the way in the Presidential library. For those who have not seen it, it shows the President as a young pilot, shot down during the Second World War, being rescued from his life-raft by the crew of an American submarine. It is a moving reminder that when America has faced challenge and peril, Americans rise to the occasion, willing to risk their very lives to defend freedom and preserve our nation. We are in your debt. Thank you, Mr. President.

Mr. President, your generation rose to the occasion, first to defeat Fascism and then to vanquish the Soviet Union. You left us, your children, a free and strong America. It is why we call yours the greatest generation. It is now my generation's turn. How we respond to today's challenges will define our generation. And it will determine what kind of America we will leave our children, and theirs.

America faces a new generation of challenges. Radical violent Islam seeks to destroy us. An emerging China endeavors to surpass our economic leadership. And we are troubled at home by government overspending, overuse of foreign oil, and the breakdown of the family.

Over the last year, we have embarked on a national debate on how best to preserve American leadership. Today, I wish to address a topic which I believe is fundamental to America's greatness: our religious liberty. I will also offer perspectives on how my own faith would inform my Presidency, if I were elected.

There are some who may feel that religion is not a matter to be seriously considered in the context of the weighty threats that face us. If so, they are at odds with the nation's founders, for they, when our nation faced its greatest peril, sought the blessings of the Creator. And further, they discovered the essential connection between the survival of a free land and the protection of religious freedom. In John Adams' words: "We have no government armed with power capable of contending with human passions unbridled by morality and religion. . . . Our constitution was made for a moral and religious people."

Freedom requires religion just as religion requires freedom. Freedom opens the windows of the soul so that man can discover his most profound beliefs and commune with God. Freedom and religion endure together, or perish alone.

Given our grand tradition of religious tolerance and liberty, some wonder whether there are any questions regarding an aspiring candidate's religion that are appropriate. I believe there are. And I will answer them today.

Almost 50 years ago another candidate from Massachusetts explained that he was an American running for president, not a Catholic running for president. Like him, I am an American running for president. I do not define my candidacy by my religion. A person should not be elected because of his faith nor should he be rejected because of his faith.

Let me assure you that no authorities of my church, or of any other church for that matter, will ever exert influence on presidential decisions. Their authority is theirs, within the province of church affairs, and it ends where the affairs of the nation begin.

As governor, I tried to do the right as best I knew it, serving the law and answering to the Constitution. I did not confuse the particular teachings of my church with the obligations of the office and of the Constitution—and of course, I would not do so as President. I will put no doctrine of any church above the plain duties of the office and the sovereign authority of the law.

As a young man, Lincoln described what he called America's "political religion"—the commitment to defend the rule of law and the Constitution. When I place my hand on the Bible and take the oath of office, that oath becomes my highest promise to God. If I am fortunate to become your president, I will serve no one religion, no one group, no one cause, and no one interest. A President must serve only the common cause of the people of the United States.

There are some for whom these commitments are not enough. They would prefer it if I would simply distance myself from my religion, say that it is more a tradition than my personal conviction, or disavow one or another of its precepts. That I will not do. I believe in my Mormon faith and I endeavor to live by it. My faith is the faith of my fathers—I will be true to them and to my beliefs.

Some believe that such a confession of my faith will sink my candidacy. If they are right, so be it. But I think they underestimate the American people. Americans do not respect believers of convenience.

Americans tire of those who would jettison their beliefs, even to gain the world.

There is one fundamental question about which I often am asked. What do I believe about Jesus Christ? I believe that Jesus Christ is the Son of God and the Savior of mankind. My church's beliefs about Christ may not all be the same as those of other faiths. Each religion has its own unique doctrines and history. These are not bases for criticism but rather a test of our tolerance. Religious tolerance would be a shallow principle indeed if it were reserved only for faiths with which we agree.

There are some who would have a presidential candidate describe and explain his church's distinctive doctrines. To do so would enable the very religious test the founders prohibited in the Constitution. No candidate should become the spokesman for his faith. For if he becomes President he will need the prayers of the people of all faiths.

I believe that every faith I have encountered draws its adherents closer to God. And in every faith I have come to know, there are features I wish were in my own: I love the profound ceremony of the Catholic Mass, the approachability of God in the prayers of the evangelicals, the tenderness of spirit among the Pentecostals, the confident independence of the Lutherans, the ancient traditions of the Jews, unchanged through the ages, and the commitment to frequent prayer of the Muslims. As I travel across the country and see our towns and cities, I am always moved by the many houses of worship with their steeples, all pointing to heaven, reminding us of the source of life's blessings.

It is important to recognize that while differences in theology exist between the churches in America, we share a common creed of moral convictions. And where the affairs of our nation are concerned, it's usually a sound rule to focus on the latter—on the great moral principles that urge us all on a common course. Whether it was the cause of abolition, or civil rights, or the right to life itself, no movement of conscience can succeed in America that cannot speak to the convictions of religious people.

We separate church and state affairs in this country, and for good reason. No religion should dictate to the state nor should the state interfere with the free practice of religion. But in recent years, the notion of the separation of church and state has been taken by some well beyond its original meaning. They seek to remove from the public domain any acknowledgment of God. Religion is seen as merely a private affair with no place in public life. It is as if they are intent on establishing a new religion in America—the religion of secularism. They are wrong.

The founders proscribed the establishment of a state religion, but they did not countenance the elimination of religion from the public square. We are a nation "Under God" and in God, we do indeed trust.

We should acknowledge the Creator as did the Founders—in ceremony and word. He should remain on our currency, in our pledge, in the teaching of our history, and during the holiday season, nativity scenes and menorahs should be welcome in our public places. Our greatness would not long endure without judges who respect the foundation of faith upon which our constitution rests. I will take care to separate the affairs of government from any religion, but I will not separate us from "the God who gave us liberty."

Nor would I separate us from our religious heritage. Perhaps the most important question to ask a person of faith who seeks a political office, is this: Does he share these American values—the equality of human kind, the obligation to serve one another, and a steadfast commitment to liberty?

They are not unique to any one denomination. They belong to the great moral inheritance we hold in common. They are the firm ground on which Americans of different faiths meet and stand as a nation, united.

We believe that every single human being is a child of God—we are all part of the human family. The conviction of the inherent and inalienable worth of every life is still the most revolutionary political proposition ever advanced. John Adams put it that we are "thrown into the world all equal and alike."

The consequence of our common humanity is our responsibility to one another, to our fellow Americans foremost, but also to every child of God. It is an obligation which is fulfilled by Americans every day, here and across the globe, without regard to creed or race or nationality.

Americans acknowledge that liberty is a gift of God, not an indulgence of government. No people in the history of the world have sacrificed as much for liberty. The lives of hundreds of thousands of America's sons and daughters were laid down during the last century to preserve freedom, for us and for freedom-loving people throughout the world. America took nothing from that Century's terrible wars—no land from Germany or Japan or Korea, no treasure, no oath of fealty. America's resolve in the defense of liberty has been tested time and again. It has not been found wanting, nor must it ever be. America must never falter in holding high the banner of freedom.

These American values, this great moral heritage, is shared and lived in my religion as it is in yours. I was taught in my home to honor God and love my neighbor. I saw my father march with Martin Luther King. I saw my parents provide compassionate care to others, in personal ways to people nearby, and in just as consequential ways in leading national volunteer movements. I am moved by the Lord's words: "For I was an hungered, and ye gave me meat: I was thirsty, and ye gave me drink: I was a stranger, and ye took me in: naked, and ye clothed me."

My faith is grounded on these truths. You can witness them in Ann and my marriage and in our family. We are a long way from perfect, and we have surely stumbled along the way, but our aspirations, our values, are the self-same as those from the other faiths that stand upon this common foundation. And these convictions will indeed inform my presidency.

Today's generations of Americans have always known religious liberty. Perhaps we forget the long and arduous path our nation's forbearers took to achieve it. They came here from England to seek freedom of religion. But upon finding it for themselves, they at first denied it to others. Because of their diverse beliefs, Ann Hutchinson was exiled from Massachusetts Bay, a banished Roger Williams founded Rhode Island, and two centuries later, Brigham Young set out for the West. Americans were unable to accommodate their commitment to their own faith with an appreciation for the convictions of others to different faiths. In this, they were very much like those of the European nations they had left.

It was in Philadelphia that our founding fathers defined a revolutionary vision of liberty, grounded on self-evident truths about the equality of all, and the inalienable rights with which each is endowed by his Creator.

We cherish these sacred rights and secure them in our Constitutional order. Foremost do we protect religious liberty, not as a matter of policy but as a matter of right. There will be no established church, and we are guaranteed the free exercise of our religion.

I'm not sure that we fully appreciate the profound implications of our tradition of religious liberty. I have visited many of the magnificent cathedrals in Europe. They are so inspired, so grand, so empty. Raised up over generations, long ago, so many of the cathedrals now stand as the postcard backdrop to societies just too busy or too "enlightened" to venture inside and kneel in prayer. The establishment of state religions in Europe did no favor to Europe's churches. And though you will find many people of strong faith there, the churches themselves seem to be withering away.

Infinitely worse is the other extreme, the creed of conversion by conquest: violent Jihad, murder as martyrdom, killing Christians,

Jews, and Muslims with equal indifference. These radical Islamists do their preaching not by reason or example but in the coercion of minds and the shedding of blood. We face no greater danger today than theocratic tyranny and the boundless suffering these states and groups could inflict if given the chance.

The diversity of our cultural expression and the vibrancy of our religious dialogue has [sic] kept America in the forefront of civilized nations even as others regard religious freedom as something to be destroyed.

In such a world, we can be deeply thankful that we live in a land where reason and religion are friends and allies in the cause of liberty, joined against the evils and dangers of the day. And you can be certain of this: Any believer in religious freedom, any person who has knelt in prayer to the Almighty, has a friend and ally in me. And so it is for hundreds of millions of our countrymen: we do not insist on a single strain of religion—rather, we welcome our nation's symphony of faith.

Recall the early days of the First Continental Congress in Philadelphia, during the fall of 1774. With Boston occupied by British troops, there were rumors of imminent hostilities and fears of an impending war. In this time of peril, someone suggested that they pray. But there were objections. "They were too divided in religious sentiments," what with Episcopalians and Quakers, Anabaptists and Congregationalists, Presbyterians and Catholics.

Then Sam Adams rose and said he would "hear a prayer from anyone of piety and good character, as long as they were a patriot."

And so together they prayed, and together they fought, and together, by the grace of God, they founded this great nation.

In that spirit, let us give thanks to the divine "author of liberty." And together, let us pray that this land may always be blessed "with freedom's holy light."

God bless the United States of America.

Appendix B
Ten Mormon Candidates

The following nine men and one woman were, as *Deseret News* book critic Dennis Lythgoe so eloquently stated, "Mormons, ex-Mormons, or about-to-be-Mormons" who ran for the country's highest office.* Their ideologies spanned the entire political spectrum, thus demonstrating incredible diversity within the Mormon religious tradition.

Joseph Smith Jr. The first president of the Church of Jesus Christ of Latter-day Saints and not only the first Mormon but also the first clergyman to run for president, he waged a vigorous but short-lived campaign in 1844. He ran as an independent on a highly detailed and progressive third-party platform. Smith's candidacy was cut short when he was killed by a mob on June 27, 1844. He thus also became the first presidential candidate to be assassinated in the middle of a presidential campaign.

Parley P. Christensen. Although not a baptized member of the LDS Church, Christensen grew up in a Mormon family and spent most of his youth and early adulthood in Utah. He was thus certainly influenced by Mormon culture. He was a Utah resident when he ran for president in 1920 on the left-wing Farmer-Labor Party ticket.

Ezra Taft Benson. While never a formal candidate, between 1966 and 1967 Benson, an outspoken conservative, was part of a third-party effort to mount a presidential campaign. This effort was spearheaded by "The 1976 Committee" with Benson at the top of the

---

* This quote is from an endorsement located on the back cover of Newell G. Bringhurst and Craig L. Foster, *The Mormon Quest for the Presidency* (Independence, Mo.: John Whitmer Books, 2008).

ticket and South Carolina Senator Strom Thurmond for vice-president. Their efforts were abandoned in deference to former Alabama governor George Wallace's own third-party candidacy. Wallace actively recruited Benson to be his running mate, and Benson manifested considerable interest. However, on advice of the Church president, Spencer W. Kimball, he eventually declined the offer. Benson later served as president of the LDS Church (1984–94).

George W. Romney. In 1967, Romney, governor of Michigan and former automobile executive, began a campaign for president on the Republican ticket. Considered an early front-runner, Romney's folksy style of campaigning and off-the-cuff comments to the media caught up to him when he claimed to have been "brainwashed" by military officials when he visited Vietnam. Between Romney's changing position on Vietnam and an image of being too pious, he was out of the race before the first primary vote was cast.

Eldredge Cleaver. Cleaver was not yet a Mormon when he ran for president on the Peace and Freedom Party ticket in 1968 but joined the LDS Church in 1983. Cleaver's religious and political odyssey took him from an angry, militant Black Panther leader in the 1960s to a conservative Mormon Republican in the 1980s.

Morris "Mo" Udall. While born and raised in a prominent Arizona Mormon family and a member of record all his life, he withdrew from active engagement in his youth and had strong disagreements on some doctrinal and policy positions. Nevertheless, his Mormon background was used against him during his run for president in 1976 where he put up a strong challenge to his fellow Democratic candidate, Jimmy Carter. Before and after his failed presidential campaign, Udall was a highly effective U.S. Representative from Arizona.

Sonia Johnson. By the time she ran on the left-wing Citizens Party's 1984 ticket, she had already been excommunicated by the LDS Church because of her controversial leadership of Mormons for the ERA. The Equal Rights Amendment fell short of ratification, in part, at least, because of strong opposition from the LDS Church. Johnson billed herself as the first woman to run in a general election since Victoria Woodhull in 1872—over a century earlier.

James Gordon "Bo" Gritz. A much-decorated Vietnam War veteran and outspoken conservative, Gritz ran for president on the right-wing Populist Party ticket in 1992. Gritz had converted to Mormonism in the mid-1980s and successfully used his Mormon connections with their more right-wing elements during his campaign. Gritz eventually became disgruntled with the LDS Church and, a few years after the 1992 election, asked to have his name removed from the Church's records.

Orrin G. Hatch. Born into an old Utah family, he was raised in Pennsylvania and returned to Utah as an adult. An effective, powerful member of the U.S. Senate representing Utah, he joined the 2000 Republican residential race late in a quixotic quest for the presidency. He bowed out of the race after coming in last in the Iowa caucus and returned to his seat in the Senate.

W. Mitt Romney. Running for president in the 2008 campaign on the Republican ticket, he garnered more votes and delegates than any previous candidate of Mormon background but failed to achieve the party's nomination.

Source: Newell G. Bringhurst and Craig L. Foster, *The Mormon Quest for the Presidency* (Independence, Mo.: John Whitmer Books, 2008).

Index

Campolo, Tony, 190

Campose, Paul, 188

Carpentar, Joel, 9

Carson, Stephen W., 5, 12

Carter, Jimmy, 11, 187

Catholics. *See* Roman Catholicism.

Catholic League for Religious and Civil Rights, 88

Chamberlin, Craig, 151–52

Charalambous, Mark, 218

Chervisnky, Gerry, 87

Christian Broadcast Network, 16

Christian Coalition, 15, 17, 18, 27

Christian Right/Religious Right, 1, 2, 11, 17, 31, 100, 159, 178, 194, 211, 212, 215, 218, 220
    fear of legitimizing Mormonism, 155
    stereotype of, 10

Christianity and Christians, vii; xiii, 1, 3, 4, 5, 6, 12, 14, 17, 26, 28, 30, 34, 36, 50, 60, 104, 120, 121, 125, 131, 134, 151, 152, 154, 157, 159, 173, 178, 180, 181, 185, 186, 192, 194

Church of Christ, 32, 44, 100

Church of Jesus Christ of Latter-day Saints (Mormons), x, 27, 30, 32, 69, 92, 93, 119
    accusations of sheep stealing, poaching, 156–58
    accused of causing olympic scandal, 177
    fear of legitimization of, from reilgious right, 155
    fear of political power of, 137, 161–63
    Mormon question, xiii, 121, 122, 160, 176, 191
    public relations efforts of, 122, 123
    racial issues of, 133–35

    social characteristics of, 28–29
    support of Romney's campaign, 97
    temple garments, 121, 125, 126, 154, 160
    viewed as a cult by critics, 27, 40, 152, 153, 162, 173, 174, 176, 177, 182, 192, 193, 217

Cleveland, Grover, 65

Clinton, Bill, 17, 87, 163, 164

Clinton, Hillary Rodham, 39, 98, 126

Cobabe, George, 52

Congregationalists, 2, 3

Conservative Political Action Conference, 105

Constitution of the United States, divinely inspired, 50, 51, 52, 57, 61, 62, 70, 71

Cooley, Everett, 66

Council of Fifty, 59, 60, 61, 62

Couric, Katie, 35

Crist, Charlie, 105

Cumming, Alfred, 67

Cumming, Elizabeth, 67

Danites, 127

Darrow, Clarence, 6, 7, 8

Davidson, Lynn, 129

Dawson, Katon, 174

Decker, Ed, 161, 162

Democratic party, 31, 32, 66, 87, 195

DeMoss, Mark, 151

Denton, Sally, 137

Deseret alphabet, 65

Deseret national flag, 65

Exploring Mormon Thought
The Series

Vol. 1: The Attributes of God
Vol. 2: The Problems of Theism and the Love of God
(Coming Soon!!) Vol. 3: Of God and Gods
by Blake T. Ostler

In Volume 2 of the three-volume series, *Exploring Mormon Thought: The Problems of Theism and the Love of God*, Blake Ostler explores issues related to soteriology, or the theory of salvation. He argues that God's love for us and his commitment to respect our dignity as persons entails that God must leave us free to choose whether to have a saving relationship with him. Ostler explores the "logic of love" and argues that the LDS doctrine of a "war in heaven" embodies this commitment. He explores the nature of personal prayer and the contributions of LDS beliefs to a robust prayer dialogue. Offering a view consistent with LDS commitments, this approach makes sense out of asking God to assist others, to alter the natural environment, and to grow in a more intense relationship with him.

Praise for the *Exploring Mormon Thought* series:

"These books are the most important works on Mormon theology ever written. There is nothing currently available that is even close to the rigor and sophistication of these volumes. B. H. Roberts and John A. Widtsoe may have had interesting insights in the early part of the twentieth century, but they had neither the temperament nor the training to give a rigorous defense of their views in dialogue with a wider stream of Christian theology. Sterling McMurrin and Truman Madsen had the capacity to engage Mormon theology at this level, but neither one did."

—Richard Sherlock, *FARMS Review*

Vol. 1, 526 pages, Hardcover, ISBN 978-1-58958-003-9
Vol. 2, 503 pages, Hardcover, ISBN 978-1-58958-095-4
Vol. 3, 483 pages, Hardcover, ISBN 978-1-58958-107-4

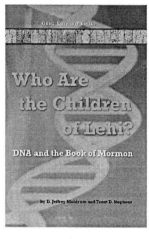

WHO ARE THE CHILDREN OF LEHI? DNA and the Book of Mormon

by D. Jeffrey Meldrum and Trent D. Stephens

How does the Book of Mormon, keystone of the LDS faith, stand up to data about DNA sequencing that puts the ancestors of modern Native Americans in northeast Asia instead of Palestine?

In *Who Are the Children of Lehi?* Meldrum and Stephens examine the merits and the fallacies of DNA-based interpretations that challenge the Book of Mormon's historicity. They provide clear guides to the science, summarize the studies, illuminate technical points with easy-to-grasp examples, and spell out the data's implications.

The results? There is no straight-line conclusion between DNA evidence and "Lamanites." The Book of Mormon's validity lies beyond the purview of scientific empiricism—as it always has. And finally, inspiringly, they affirm Lehi's kinship as one of covenant, not genes.

About the authors

D. Jeffrey Meldrum, Ph.D., is an associate professor of anatomy and anthropology at Idaho State University and an affiliate curator of vertebrate paleontology at the Idaho Museum of Natural History. His degrees are from Brigham Young University and the State University of New York at Stony Brook with postdoctoral experience at Duke University. Before coming to ISU in 1994, he was an assistant professor in the Evolutionary Morphology Group at Northwestern University Medical School and a repeat invited speaker at the Chicago Center for Religion and Science. At ISU, he teaches human anatomy, organic evolution, and primate studies. He is presently investigating the dynamics of the hominoid foot and the emergence of human bipedalism. Paleontological field experience has taken him to Argentina, Colombia, and the Intermountain West.

Trent D. Stephens, Ph.D., is professor of anatomy and embryology at Idaho State University. His degrees are from Brigham Young University and the University of Pennsylvania. He taught anatomy for four years in the University of Washington's Medical School and has been teaching anatomy and embryology at Idaho State University since 1981 where he was honored as its Distinguished Teacher (1992), as the Sigma Xi Jerome Bigalow Award recipient for combining teaching and research (1992), and as an Outstanding Researcher (2000). Trent's research investigates the developmental origins of vertebrate form and the mechanism of the drug thalidomide in causing birth defects. He has published more than eighty scientific papers and books, including several leading textbooks for anatomy and physiology. Trent and Kathleen have five children and ten grandchildren.

Hardcover, 140 pages, ISBN: 978-1-58958-048-0

The Complete Set, For the First Time Ever

THE BRIGHAM YOUNG UNIVERSITY BOOK OF MORMON SYMPOSIUM SERIES

A series of lectures delivered at BYU by a wide and exciting array of the finest gospel scholars in the Church. Get valuable insights from foremost authorities including General authorities, BYU Professors and Church Educational System instructors. No gospel library will be complete without this valuable resource. Anyone interested in knowing what the top gospel scholars in the Church are saying about such important subjects as historiography, geography, and faith in Christ will be sure to enjoy this handsome box set. This is the perfect gift for any student of the Book of Mormon.

Nine-volume paperback box set, ISBN: 978-1-58958-087-9

DISCOURSES IN MORMON THEOLOGY:
Philosophical and Theological Possibilities

A mere two hundred years old, Mormonism is still in its infancy compared to other theological disciplines (Judaism, Catholicism, Buddhism, etc.). This volume will introduce its reader to the rich blend of theological viewpoints that exist within Mormonism. The essays break new ground in Mormon studies by exploring the vast expanse of philosophical territory left largely untouched by traditional approaches to Mormon theology. It presents philosophical and theological essays by many of the finest minds associated with Mormonism in an organized and easy-to-understand manner and provides the reader with a window into the fascinating diversity amongst Mormon philosophers. Open-minded students of pure religion will appreciate this volume's thoughtful inquiries.

These essays were delivered at a recent conference of the Society for Mormon Philosophy and Theology.

Paperback, 301 pages, ISBN: 978-1-58958-104-3

By the author of *Joseph Smith: Rough Stone Rolling*

ON THE ROAD WITH JOSEPH SMITH:
An Author's Diary
by Richard Lyman Bushman

After living with Joseph Smith for seven years, biographer Richard Lyman Bushman went "on the road" for a year. After delivering the final proofs of his landmark study, *Joseph Smith: Rough Stone Rolling* to Knopf in July 2005, Bushman criss-crossed the country from coast to coast, delivering numerous addresses on Joseph Smith at scholarly conferences, academic symposia, and firesides. This startlingly candid memoir concludes eleven months later with an article written for *Common-Place* in August 2006.

Bushman confesses to hope and humility, an unexpected numbness when he expected moments of triumph, and genuine apprehension as he awaits reviews. He frets at the polarization that dismissed the book as either too hard on Joseph Smith or too easy. He yields to a very human compulsion to check sales figures on amazon.com, but partway through the process stepped back with the recognition, "The book seems to be cutting its own path now, just as [I] hoped."

For readers coming to grips with the ongoing puzzle of the Prophet and the troublesome dimensions of their own faith, Richard Bushman, a temple sealer and stake patriarch but also a prize-winning scholar, openly but not insistently presents himself as a believer. "I believe enough to take Joseph Smith seriously," he says. He draws comfort both from what he calls his "mantra" ("Today I will be a follower of Jesus Christ") and also from ongoing engagement with the intellectual challenges of explaining Joseph Smith.

"The diary is possibly unparalleled—an author of a recent book candidly dissecting his experiences with both Mormon and non-Mormon audiences . . . certainly deserves wider distribution—in part because it shows a talented historian laying open his vulnerabilities, and also because it shows how much any historian lays on the line when he writes about Joseph Smith."
—Dennis Lythgoe, *Deseret News*

"By turns humorous and poignant, this behind-the-scenes look at Richard Bushman's public and private ruminations about Joseph Smith reveals a great deal—not only about the inner life of one of our greatest scholars, but about Mormonism at the dawn of the 21st century."
—Jana Riess, co-author of *Mormonism for Dummies*

Paperback, 140 pages, ISBN 978-1-58958-102-9

Brand New Series!

Analytical & Contextual Commentary
on the Book of Mormon

VOLUME ONE

First Nephi

Brant A. Gardner

GREG KOFFORD BOOKS

SECOND WITNESS: ANALYTICAL AND CONTEXTUAL COMMENTATRY ON THE BOOK OF MORMON
by Brant Gardner

Stop looking for the Book of Mormon in Mesoamerica and start looking for Mesoamerica in the Book of Mormon! *Second Witness*, a new six-volume series from Greg Kofford Books, takes a detailed, verse-by-verse look at the Book of Mormon. It marshals the best of modern scholarship and new insights into a consistent picture of the Book of Mormon as a historical document. Taking a faithful but scholarly approach to the text and reading it through the insights of linguistics, anthropology, and ethnohistory, the commentary approaches the text from a variety of perspectives: how it was created, how it relates to history and culture, and what religious insights it provides.

The commentary accepts the best modern scholarship, which focuses on a particular region of Mesoamerica as the most plausible location for the Book of Mormon's setting. For the first time, that location—its peoples, cultures, and historical trends—are used as the backdrop for reading the text. The historical background is not presented as proof, but rather as an explanatory context.

The commentary does not forget Mormon's purpose in writing. It discusses the doctrinal and theological aspects of the text and highlights the way in which Mormon created it to meet his goal of "convincing . . . the Jew and Gentile that Jesus is the Christ, the Eternal God."

About the author

Brant Gardner received an M.A. in anthropology from the State University of New York, Albany, emphasizing Mesoamerican ethnohistory. His research into the Mesoamerican setting of the Book of Mormon has led to publications in the *FARMS Review of Books* and the online *Meridian* magazine. He has made several presentations to the annual Foundation for Apologetic Information and Research conference and has also presented at the Book of Mormon Archaeological Forum, Sunstone, and other academic symposia.

Vol. 1, 1 Nephi,   ISBN 1-58958-041-9, 442 pages.
Vol. 2, 2 Nephi–Jacob,   ISBN 1-58958-042-7, 600 pages.
Vol. 3, Enos–Mosiah,   ISBN 1-58958-043-5, 508 pages.
Vol. 4, Alma,   ISBN 1-58958-044-3, 790 pages.
Vol. 5, Helaman–3 Nephi, ISBN 1-58958-045-1, 622 pages.
Vol. 6, 4 Nephi–Moroni, ISBN 1-58958-046-X, 496 pages.
Six-volume set,   ISBN 1-58958-047-8

Greg Kofford Books is joining hands with the BYU Religious Studies
Center to bring you another high-quality title

APOCRYPHAL WRITINGS
AND THE LATTER-DAY SAINTS

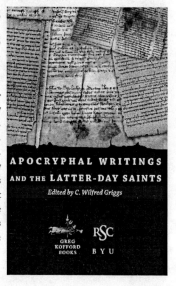

This sought-after volume of essays takes an in-
depth look at the apocrypha and how Latter-day
Saints should approach it in their gospel study.
With notable LDS authors such as Stephen E.
Robinson, Joseph F. McConkie, and Robert L.
Millet, this volume is an essential addition to any
well-rounded Mormon studies library. Essays
include: "Whose Apocrypha? Viewing Ancient
Apocrypha from the Vantage of Events in the
Present Dispensation," "Lying for God: The Uses
of Apocrypha," and "The Nag Hammadi Library:
A Mormon Perspective."

Edited by C. Wilfred Griggs
Religious Studies Center—Brigham Young University

333 pages

Limited, Signed and Numbered Leather Edition, ISBN 978-1-58958-088-6

Paper, ISBN 978-1-58958-089-3

Winner of the Mormon History Association's Best
Biography Award

Hugh Nibley: A Consecrated Life

The Authorized
Biography by
Boyd Jay Petersen

As one of the LDS Church's most widely recognized scholars, Hugh Nibley is both an icon and an enigma. Through complete access to Nibley's correspondence, journals, notes, and papers, Petersen has painted a portrait that reveals the man behind the legend.

Starting with a foreword written by Zina Nibley Petersen and finishing with appendices that include some of the best of Nibley's personal correspondence, the biography reveals aspects of the tapestry of the life of one who has truly consecrated his life to the service of the Lord.

"Hugh Nibley is generally touted as one of Mormonism's greatest minds and perhaps its most prolific scholarly apologist. Just as hefty as some of Nibley's largest tomes, this authorized biography is delightfully accessible and full of the scholar's delicious wordplay and wit, not to mention some astonishing war stories and insights into Nibley's phenomenal acquisition of languages. Introduced by a personable foreword from the author's wife (who is Nibley's daughter), the book is written with enthusiasm, respect and insight. . . . On the whole, Petersen is a careful scholar who provides helpful historical context. . . . This project is far from hagiography. It fills an important gap in LDS history and will appeal to a wide Mormon audience."

—*Publishers Weekly*

"Well written and thoroughly researched, Petersen's biography is a must-have for anyone struggling to reconcile faith and reason."

—Greg Taggart, Association for Mormon Letters

Hardcover, 447 pages, ISBN 978-1-58958-019-0
Signed, Numbered, and Limited Leather, ISBN 978-1-58958-020-6

"This book is a 'must have' document for the serious student of this contentious issue."

—Richard Tolman, professor of biology
Utah Valley State College

MORMONISM AND
EVOLUTION: The
Authoritative LDS
Statements
William E. Evenson and
Duane E. Jeffrey, eds.

The Church of Jesus Christ of Latter-day Saints (the Mormon Church) has generally been viewed by the public as anti-evolutionary in its doctrine and teachings. But official statements on the subject by the Church's highest governing quorum and/or president have been considerably more open and diverse than is popularly believed.

This book compiles in full all known authoritative statements (either authored or formally approved for publication) by the Church's highest leaders on the topics of evolution and the

MORMONISM
AND EVOLUTION:
THE AUTHORITATIVE
LDS STATEMENTS

William E. Evenson & Duane E. Jeffery

origin of human beings. The editors provide historical context for these statements that allows the reader to see what stimulated the issuing of each particular document and how they stand in relation to one another.

About the editors

William Evenson is a physics professor at Utah Valley State College. Previously, his thirty-four year tenure at Brigham Young University included service as dean of the College of Physical and Mathematical Sciences.

Duane E. Jeffery is a professor of integrative biology at Brigham Young University.

Paperback, 120 pages, ISBN 978-1-58958-093-0

Released in the U.S. for the first time!

THE HISTORY OF THE MORMONS IN ARGENTINA
by Néstor Curbelo

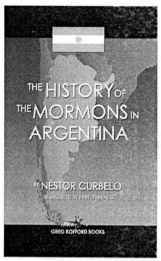

Originally published in Spanish, Curbelo's *The History of the Mormons in Argentina* is a groundbreaking book detailing the growth of the Church in this Latin American country.

Through numerous interviews and access to other primary resources, Curbelo has constructed a timeline, and then documents the story of the Church's growth. Starting with a brief discussion of Parley P. Pratt's assignment to preside over the Pacific and South American regions, continuing on with the translation of the scriptures into Spanish, the opening of the first missions in South America, and the building of temples, the book provides a survey history of the Church in Argentina. This book will be of interest not only to history buffs but also to thousands of past, present, and future missionaries.

Translated by Erin Jennings

300 pages

Limited, Signed and Numbered Leather Edition, ISBN 978-1-58958-051-0

Spanish Language, Paperback, ISBN 978-1-58958-059-6
English Language, Paperback, ISBN 978-1-58958-052-7

Collected and bound for the first time ever!

THE WASP

A newspaper published in Nauvoo from April 16, 1842, through April 26, 1843, *The Wasp* provides a crucial window into firsthand accounts of the happenings and concerns of the Saints in Nauvoo. It was initially edited by William Smith, younger brother of Joseph Smith. William was succeeded by John Taylor as editor and Taylor and Wilford Woodruff as printers and publishers. Some of the main stories covered in the newspaper are the August 1842 elections where local candidates endorsed by the Mormons easily won against their opponents, the fall from grace of John C. Bennett, the attempt by the state of Missouri to extradite Joseph Smith as an accessory in the attempted murder of Lilburn W. Boggs, and the Illinois legislature's effort to repeal the Nauvoo charter.

With a foreword by Peter Crawley putting the newspaper in historical context, this first-ever reproduction of the entire run of the *The Wasp* is essential to anyone interested in the Nauvoo period of Mormonism.

216 pages, Oversized 11" X 17"

Limited Edition, 3/4 Leather with hand-marbled boards, 120 numbered copies, ISBN 978-1-58958-049-7

Hardcover, ISBN 978-1-58958-050-3

LDS Biographical Encyclopedia

by Andrew Jenson

In the Preface to the first volume Jenson writes, "On the rolls of the Church of Jesus Christ of Latter-day Saints are found the names of a host of men and women of worth—heroes and heroines of a higher type—who have been and are willing to sacrifice fortune and life for the sake of their religion. It is for the purpose of perpetuating the memory of these, and to place on record deeds worthy of imitation, that [this set] makes its appearance."

With over 5,000 biographical entries of "heroes and heroines" complete with more than 2,000 photographs, the LDS Biographical Encyclopedia is an essential reference for the study of early Church history. Nearly anyone with pioneer heritage will find exciting and interesting history about ancestors in these volumes

Andrew Jenson was an assistant historian for the Church of Jesus Christ of Latter-day Saints from 1897 to 1941.

4 Volumes, 832 pages each.

Limited, Signed and Numbered Leather Edition, ISBN 978-1-58958-026-8

Hardcover, ISBN 978-1-58958-031-2

EXCAVATING
MORMON PASTS:
The New Historiography
of the Last Half Century
Edited by
Newell C. Bringhurst and
Lavina Fielding Anderson

Includes Mormon History Association Award Winning Essay by Roger Launius.

Excavating Mormon Pasts assembles sixteen knowledgeable scholars from both LDS and the Community of Christ traditions who have long participated skillfully in this dialogue. It presents their insightful and sometimes incisive surveys of where the New Mormon History has come from and which fields remain unexplored. It is both a vital reference work and a stimulating picture of the New Mormon History in the early twenty-first century.

"[*Excavating Mormon Pasts* is] a valuable tool in the ongoing quest for clarity, for truth, for certainty. It is one of several volumes I've seen in the past few years that qualify for a 'must have' rating."

—Jeffrey Needle, Association for Mormon Letters

Hardcover, 442 pages, ISBN 978-1-58958-091-6

Winner of the John Whitmer Historical Association's
Smith-Pettit Best Book Award !

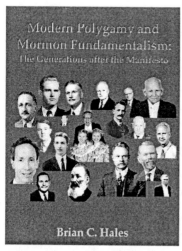

MODERN POLYGAMY AND MORMON FUNDAMENTALISM:
The Generations after the
Manifesto
by Brian C. Hales

Under the subject of alternative lifestyles, the issue of polygamous relationships falls squarely in the middle of the debate. Polygamous marriages are a common practice in many other countries, but the United States has vehemently opposed such unions and will no doubt find itself disputing its position on them again in the near future. As with the same-sex marriage issue, a firestorm of controversy surrounds the question since the right to participate in a polygamous union is very much tied to the right to live out one's preferences, religious or not. Detailed accounts of sexual abuse and child brides are frequently leaked from the various polygamous societies, notwithstanding their extreme efforts to remain under the radar of law enforcement and the press. A by-product of these mysterious societies is that public interest is vitalized by their continuous efforts to gain independence from traditionalist culture.

This fascinating study seeks to trace the historical tapestry that is early Mormon polygamy, details the official discontinuation of the practice by the Church, and, for the first time, describes the many zeal-driven organizations that arose in the wake of that decision. Among the polygamous groups discussed are the LeBaronites, whose "blood atonement" killings sent fear throughout Mormon communities in the late seventies and the eighties; the FLDS Church, which made news recently over its construction of a compound and temple in Texas (Warren Jeffs, the leader of that church, is now standing trial on two felony counts after his being profiled on America's Most Wanted resulted in his capture); and the Allred and Kingston groups, two major factions with substantial membership statistics both in and out of the United States. All these fascinating histories, along with those of the smaller independent groups, are examined and explained in a way that all can appreciate.

"This book is the most thorough and comprehensive study written on the subgject to date, providing readers with a clear, candid, and broad sweeping overview of the history, teachings, and practices of modern fundamentalist groups."
—Alexander L. Baugh, associate professor of Church history and doctrine,
Brigham Young University

Hardcover, 530 pages, ISBN 978-1-58958-035-0
Paperback, ISBN 978-1-58958-109-8
Limited, signed, and numbered leather edition, ISBN 978-1-58958-110-4

Second Edition Revised and Enlarged

MORMON POLYGAMOUS FAMILIES:
Life in the Principle
by Jessie L. Embry

Mormons and non-Mormons all have their views about how polygamy was practiced in the Church of Jesus Christ of Latter-day Saints during the late nineteenth and early twentieth centuries. Embry has examined the participants themselves in order to understand how men and women living a nineteenth-century Victorian lifestyle adapted to polygamy. Based on records and oral histories with husbands, wives, and children who lived in Mormon polygamous households, this study explores the diverse experiences of individual families and stereotypes about polygamy.

The interviews are in some cases the only sources of primary information on how plural families were organized. In addition, children from monogamous families who grew up during the same period were interviewed to form a comparison group. When carefully examined, most of the stereotypes about polygamous marriages do not hold true. In this work it becomes clear that Mormon polygamous families were not much different from Mormon monogamous families and other non-Mormon families of the same era. Embry offers a new perspective on the Mormon practice of polygamy that enables readers to gain better understanding of Mormonism historically.

About the author

Jessie L. Embry is the associate director of the Charles Redd Center for Western Studies and an associate research professor at Brigahm Young University. She is the author of eight books and over 100 articles on oral history, western American history, and ethnic Mormon history. She has just published a book, *Mormons and Polygamy*, as part of a series to answer questions about Mormonism.

Paperback, 274 pages, ISBN 978-1-58958-098-5

"Provide[s] important insight into the nature of British anti-Mormonism in [the] mid-nineteenth century."

—James B. Allen, Emeritus Professor of History, Brigham Young University

PENNY TRACTS AND POLEMICS:

A Critical Analysis of Anti-Mormon Pamphleteering in Great Britain, 1837–1860

by Craig L. Foster

By 1860, Mormonism had enjoyed a presence in Great Britain for over twenty years. Mormon missionaries experienced unprecedented success in conversions and many new converts had left Britain's shores for a new life and a new religion in the far western mountains of the American continent.

With the success of the Mormons came tales of duplicity, priestcraft, sexual seduction, and uninhibited depravity among the new religious adherents. Thousands of pamphlets were sold or given to the British populace as a way of discouraging people from joining the Mormon Church. Foster places the creation of these English anti-Mormon pamphlets in their historical context. He discusses the authors, the impact of the publications and the Mormon response. With illustrations and detailed bibliography.

About the author

Craig L. Foster earned a B.A. and M.A. in history and an MLIS from Brigham Young University. He works as a research specialist at the Family History Library in Salt Lake City. He resides in Layton with his wife, Suzanne, and their three children, but prefers to be at the family cabin in southern Utah, hiding from the world. When he is not dreaming of another way to get back to the British Isles, Foster is actively involved in several scholarly and heritage organizations. He has published in a number of scholarly journals including *BYU Studies, Dialogue: A Journal of Mormon Thought, Journal of Mormon History,* and *Utah Historical Quarterly.*

Hardcover, 260 pages, ISBN 978-1-58958-005-3
Signed, Numbered Limited Leather, ISBN 978-1-58958-004-6

Now Available!

A HOUSE FOR THE MOST HIGH: The Story of the Original Nauvoo Temple
by Matthew McBride

This awe-inspiring book is a tribute to the perseverance of the human spirit. *A House for the Most High* is a groundbreaking work from beginning to end with its faithful and comprehensive documentation of the Nauvoo Temple's conception. The behind-the-scenes stories of those determined Saints involved in the great struggle to raise the sacred edifice bring a new appreciation to all readers. McBride's painstaking research now gives us access to valuable first-hand accounts that are drawn straight from the newspaper articles, private diaries, journals, and letters of the steadfast participants. The opening of this volume gives the reader an extraordinary window into the early temple-building labors of the besieged Church of Jesus Christ of Latter-day Saints, the development of what would become temple-related doctrines in the decade prior to the Nauvoo era, and the 1839 advent of the Saints in Illinois. The main body of this fascinating history covers the significant years, starting from 1840, when this temple was first considered, to the temple's early destruction by a devastating natural disaster. A well-thought-out conclusion completes the epic by telling of the repurchase of the temple lot by the Church in 1937, the lot's excavation in 1962, and the grand announcement in 1999 that the temple would indeed be rebuilt. Also included are an astonishing appendix containing rare and fascinating eyewitness descriptions of the temple and a bibliography of all major source materials. Mormons and non-Mormons alike will discover, within the pages of this book, a true sense of wonder and gratitude for a determined people whose sole desire was to build a sacred and holy temple for the worship of their God.

Hardcover, 448 pages, ISBN 978-1-58958-016-9

Limited, Signed, and Numbered Leather Edition, ISBN 978-1-58958-021-3

Award-winning author!

PEOPLE AND POWER OF NAUVOO:
Themes from the Nauvoo Experience
by Milton V. Backman Jr.

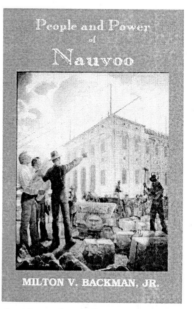

Between May 1839 and September 1846, Latter-day Saints gained spiritual strength that enabled them to eventually become a mighty people in the midst of the Rockies. Before gathering near the crescent bend of the Mississippi, Latter-day Saints had experienced a refiner's fire. That purification continued as these converts directed their attention from worldly gain to spiritual pursuits in Nauvoo. Drawing on numerous journals and other primary sources, Professor Backman sketches for us the founding, growth, and development of Nauvoo. Discussed are the sacrifices made to construct its temple, the second built by Joseph's people but the first in which the highest LDS ordinances were introduced.

About the author
Dr. Milton V. Backman, Jr. is an emeritus professor of Church History and Doctrine from Brigham Young University where he taught for thirty-one years. After retiring in 1991, he served several missions in Nauvoo, helped organize the BYU Semester Program in that historic community, and taught LDS Church history and early American history in that program for eight semesters.

Paperback, 170 pages, ISBN 978-1-58958-017-6

Signed, Numbered Limited Leather, ISBN 978-1-58958-006-0

THE INCOMPARABLE JESUS
by Grant H. Palmer

Distilled from his personal experiences in teaching Jesus to the hard-to-reach, this professional educator has produced a tender testament to the incomparable Jesus. It describes a Savior who walked with him through the halls of the county jail where he served as chaplain, succoring those in need.

In this slim volume, Palmer sensitively shares his understanding of what it means to know Jesus by doing his works. He lists the qualities of divine character attested to by the Apostles Peter and Paul, and also those that Jesus revealed about himself in his masterful Sermon on the Mount, particularly in the beatitudes.

With reverence Palmer shares personal spiritual experiences that were life-changing assurances of Jesus's love for him—a love poured out unstintingly in equally life-changing blessings on prisoners whose crimes had not stopped short of sexual abuse and murder. Reading this book offers a deeper understanding of the Savior's mercy, a stronger sense of his love, and a deeper commitment to follow him.

About the author

Grant Palmer closed his thirty-four-year career teaching for the LDS Church Educational System with the final thirteen years as a chaplain and LDS Institute director at the Salt Lake County Jail.

Paperback, 157 pages, ISBN 978-1-58958-092-3